Age and the Acquisition of
as a Foreign Language

SECOND LANGUAGE ACQUISITION
Series Editor: Professor David Singleton, *Trinity College, Dublin, Ireland*

This new series will bring together titles dealing with a variety of aspects of language acquisition and processing in situations where a language or languages other than the native language is involved. Second language will thus be interpreted in its broadest possible sense. The volumes included in the series will all in their different ways offer, on the one hand, exposition and discussion of empirical findings and, on the other, some degree of theoretical reflection. In this latter connection, no particular theoretical stance will be privileged in the series; nor will any relevant perspective – sociolinguistic, psycholinguistic, neurolinguistic, etc. – be deemed out of place. The intended readership of the series will be final-year undergraduates working on second language acquisition projects, postgraduate students involved in second language acquisition research, and researchers and teachers in general whose interests include a second language acquisition component.

Other Books in the Series
Effects of Second Language on the First
    Vivian Cook (ed.)
Learning to Request in a Second Language: A Study of Child Interlanguage Pragmatics
    Machiko Achiba
Portraits of the L2 User
    Vivian Cook (ed.)

Other Books of Interest
Audible Difference: ESL and Social Identity in Schools
    Jennifer Miller
Context and Culture in Language Teaching and Learning
    Michael Byram and Peter Grundy (eds)
Cross-linguistic Influence in Third Language Acquisition
    J. Cenoz, B. Hufeisen and U. Jessner (eds)
Developing Intercultural Competence in Practice
    Michael Byram, Adam Nichols and David Stevens (eds)
English in Europe: The Acquisition of a Third Language
    Jasone Cenoz and Ulrike Jessner (eds)
How Different Are We? Spoken Discourse in Intercultural Communication
    Helen Fitzgerald
Language and Society in a Changing Italy
    Arturo Tosi
Languages in America: A Pluralist View
    Susan J. Dicker
Language Learners as Ethnographers
    Celia Roberts, Michael Byram, Ana Barro, Shirley Jordan and Brian Street
Motivating Language Learners
    Gary N. Chambers
Multilingualism in Spain
    M. Teresa Turell (ed.)

Please contact us for the latest book information:
Multilingual Matters, Frankfurt Lodge, Clevedon Hall,
Victoria Road, Clevedon, BS21 7HH, England
http://www.multilingual-matters.com

SECOND LANGUAGE ACQUISITION 4
Series Editor: David Singleton, *Trinity College, Dublin, Ireland*

Age and the Acquisition of English as a Foreign Language

Edited by
María del Pilar García Mayo
and María Luisa García Lecumberri

MULTILINGUAL MATTERS LTD
Clevedon • Buffalo • Toronto • Sydney

To: Vicente and Irene – M.P.G.M.
Mar and Belén – M.L.G.L.

Library of Congress Cataloging in Publication Data
Age and the Acquisition of English as a Foreign Language/Edited by María del Pilar
García Mayo and María Luisa García Lecumberri.
Second Language Acquisition: 4
Includes bibliographical references.
1. Language acquisition–Age factors. 2. Language and languages–Study and teaching.
3. English language–Study and teaching–Foreign speakers. 4. Bilingualism in
children. I. García Mayo, María del Pilar. II. García Lecumberri, M. Luisa (Maria
Luisa). III. Series.
P118.65 .A37 2003
418–dc21   2002015944

British Library Cataloguing in Publication Data
A catalogue entry for this book is available from the British Library.

ISBN 1-85359-639-6 (hbk)
ISBN 1-85359-638-8 (pbk)

Multilingual Matters Ltd
UK: Frankfurt Lodge, Clevedon Hall, Victoria Road, Clevedon BS21 7HH.
USA: UTP, 2250 Military Road, Tonawanda, NY 14150, USA.
Canada: UTP, 5201 Dufferin Street, North York, Ontario M3H 5T8, Canada.
Australia: Footprint Books, PO Box 418, Church Point, NSW 2103, Australia.

Typeset by Archetype-IT Ltd (http://www.archetype-it.com).
Printed and bound in Great Britain by the Cromwell Press Ltd.

Contents

Introduction

MARÍA DEL PILAR GARCÍA MAYO and MARÍA LUISA GARCÍA LECUMBERRI

The issue of how the age at which a person is first exposed to a language that is not his/her first influences the learning experience has been one of the topics most frequently considered in second language acquisition (SLA) research. Several books (Birdsong, 1999; Harley, 1986; Singleton, 1989; Singleton & Lengyel, 1995) and numerous articles to be mentioned here deal with the topic from various theoretical perspectives.

The reasons for the interest in the so-called 'age issue' relate not only to theoretical matters (Is there a difference between how children and adults learn a second language? Is there still room for an innate faculty to continue its work in adulthood?) but also to practical questions that have to do with when it would be more appropriate to begin instruction in a second/ foreign language, which are obviously of great interest for language planners.

However, looking at the literature, one realises that most of the studies on the age issue have been carried out in second language (L2) situations in which the learner has access to the L2 not only in the classroom but in the world in which s/he is daily immersed. This is, obviously, very different from foreign language (FL) settings in which the learner has access to the input provided in the classroom and little else (Cook, 1999).

In July 2000, some of the contributors to this volume converged in San Sebastián (Spain) to participate in a University of the Basque Country Summer Course entitled 'El factor edad en la adquisición de lenguas extranjeras' (The age factor in foreign language acquisition). One of the purposes of the course was to familiarise high-school teachers, researchers and the general public with recent research on the age issue and to present the results from two longitudinal projects carried out in the Basque Autonomous Community and Catalonia on the topic.

The present volume is one of the outcomes of that meeting. We believe it sets itself apart from other books focusing on the age factor because (1) it

vii

deals with the acquisition of a foreign (rather than a second) language, and (2) it discusses issues surrounding the learning of English as a third language in two bilingual communities: the Basque Country and Catalonia. The purpose of the volume is twofold: on the one hand, the three chapters included in the Theoretical Issues section provide an overview of the most current research on the issue of age in FL learning. On the other, the six chapters in the Fieldwork in Bilingual Communities section present research on the age factor carried out in two English as a foreign language (EFL) instructional settings in Spain.

Within the first section, David Singleton (Chapter 1: Critical Period or General Age Factor(s)?) considers the question that, in the author's own words 'continues to divide the field of SLA research, namely, whether age effects constitute a manifestation of a pre-programmed critical period specifically related to language' or whether they are the result of a general decline related to aging and to other factors such as motivation, exposure and instruction. The concept of the critical period is analysed from different perspectives and as related to both native-language and FL acquisition. After examining a wide amount of evidence the author concludes that age must be seen to involve a number of issues, amongst them and notably the knowledge of previous languages, which may be more significant than neurological questions.

Jonathan Leather (Chapter 2: Phonological Acquisition in Multilingualism) addresses the acquisition of FL phonology, reviewing an extensive amount of up-to-date research. Before exploring the relationship between age and FL acquisition, the author deals with fundamental questions such as the connection between perception and production and goes on to explore theoretical issues related to the study of phonological acquisiton. He appraises the frameworks which researchers have adopted from the 1950s structuralists to current models such as Optimality Theory, Autosegmental Phonology or Phenomenological Phonology. The effect on FL acquisition of learners' characteristics such as age is considered in addition to other factors such as motivation, aptitude and native language influence as well as phonological questions such as sound markedness and universals. In the last section, Leather reflects on the methods of phonological acquisition research, advocating longitudinal studies that may be more successful in isolating the differet factors involved, and highlighting the value of FL research for linguistic theory and for the understanding of native languages.

Chapter 3 by Stefka Marinova-Todd (Know Your Grammar: What the Knowledge of Syntax and Morphology in an L2 Reveals about the Existence of a Critical Period for SLA) focuses on the knowledge of syntax and morphology as one of the more reliable and valid measures of L2 proficiency. The author presents a critical review of the literature on the acquisition of L2 morphosyntax which, in most cases, shows that older learners achieve lower levels of success in the L2 than younger learners. However, recent evidence of adult learners with near-native performance in the L2 challenges the claim made by the Critical Period Hypothesis (CPH) and the study of those individual cases, Marinova-Todd argues, should be of extreme importance to SLA research. The implications for FL programme designers seems to be that it is not the age of the students only but the availability of and access to high-quality FL instruction and other factors such as motivation.

In the second part, Fieldwork in Bilingual Communities, the book presents research on the age factor carried out in two English as a foreign language (EFL) instructional settings in Spain. As we have already mentioned, this research has been carried out with bilingual subjects who were learning English as a third language (L3) in two bilingual communities: the Basque Country and Catalonia. The six chapters included in this section report on research which, as a whole, provides evidence for the claim that the early introduction of an FL in a formal instructional setting does not contribute to better results as regards to proficiency in that language.

In her contribution (Chapter 4: The Influence of Age on the Acquisition of English: General Proficiency, Attitudes and Code Mixing) Jasone Cenoz sets the scene for hers and the following three papers (García Mayo, García Lecumberri and Gallardo, and Lasagabaster and Doiz) explaining the general characteristics and results of a research project being carried out at the Department of English, University of the Basque Country by members of the Research in English Applied Linguistics (REAL) group. This project addresses the influence of age and other factors on the acquisition of English as an FL in Basque bilingual schools. Cenoz explores the effect of the introduction of English as a foreign language at three different ages on general proficiency in English, attitudes towards learning English and code-mixing. She finds that younger learners show better attitudes and motivation towards language learning. However, older learners progress more quickly in FL acquisition, which may be due to cognitive maturity and different input types at different ages.

Chapter 5 by María del Pilar García Mayo (Age, Length of Exposure and Grammaticality Judgements in the Acquisition of English as a Foreign Language) deals with the issue of grammaticality judgements (GJs) by bilingual (Basque/Spanish) learners of different age groups in an EFL setting. The author reports on a study whose main aims were: (1) to establish comparisons between GJs provided by (a) EFL learners of different age groups at the time of first exposure to English but with the same amount of exposure to the language, and (b) the same group of learners at time 1 (396 hours) and time 2 (564 hours) of exposure to English; and (2) to determine whether 'higher' cognitive development is related to 'higher' metalinguistic awareness. The author concludes that there is evidence in favour of the hypothesis that the longer the exposure to the language, the more native-like performance becomes. However, an earlier start does not produce significantly better results in a situation of FL acquisition. These findings are commented on in the light of the issue of the early introduction of English as a third language in institutional settings.

Chapter 6 (English FL Sounds in School Learners of Different Ages) by M. Luisa García Lecumberri and Francisco Gallardo concentrates on the acquisition of L3 phonetics and phonology by bilingual children in a formal instruction setting. They consider theoretical and methodological issues related to FL pronunciation acquisition research and highlight factors which are believed to be relevant for phonological acquisition, such as age, transfer and exposure and explore connections amongst them. Later the authors present data on the acquisition of English as an L3 elicited in order to estimate overall production, perception of vowels and consonants, estimated intelligibility and degree of foreign accent. The results indicate that most of these measures favour older starters. Some inter-group differences were seen as related to strategies employed depending on cognitive maturation, rather than on instruction starting age. The authors conclude that, as expected, early age does not prove to be an advantage in the medium term and in a formal instructional setting as far as various indicators of phonetic development are concerned.

In the next chapter (Chapter 7: Maturational Constraints on Foreign Language Written Production) David Lasagabaster and Aintzane Doiz analyse the impact of the age factor on the written production in English as an FL. As in other studies within the project being carried out within the group, these authors study bilingual students belonging to three age groups who have the same time of exposure to the FL, but who have started instruction at different ages. They apply three different analyses to their data: (1) a communicative holistic analysis, (2) a quantitative analysis and (3) an error analysis. They observe that older students prove to be significantly better than the younger ones in the holistic and quantitative measures. The authors suggest that this is related to the cognitive stage and amount of writing experience, which are connected to age and length of educational exposure. Error analysis revealed that each age group made different types of errors, which are seen as stemming from the varying degrees of competence and complexity of structures used, which, in turn, are related to age.

Carmen Muñoz (Chapter 8: Variation in Oral Skills Development and Age of Onset) describes a research project that is being carried out in Catalonia. This project analyses the effect of starting age in Catalan–

Spanish bilingual EFL school learners. Students progress is monitored at two different points during their instruction period (after 200 and 416 hours). Muñoz focuses on the development of oral communicative skills, the relationship between length of instruction and language development and the use of native languages in the FL as related to instruction onset age. As was found in the other chapters, the results show that the older learners have an advantage at both analysis times for communicative oral and aural interactive tests whereas for listening comprehension there were no significant differences. The author discusses the results appealing to such factors as cognitive maturity, general language aptitude, learners' age and FL instruction onset age and draws implications for language planning and curriculum design.

Mia Victori and Elsa Tragant consider language learning strategies and age (Chapter 9: Learner Strategies: A Cross-sectional and Longitudinal Study of Primary and High-school EFL Learners). The authors analyse Catalan–Spanish bilingual learners of English to investigate differences in reported strategy use as a factor of linguistic competence and of age amongst subjects from four different age groups (10, 14, 17 year-olds and adults). Additionally, a subsample of learners are followed up to monitor changes over time in strategy use. Results indicate that, despite considerable individual variation, older students display overall a larger number of strategies and more cognitively demanding ones. The longitudinal analysis shows that as they become older and FL proficiency increases so does the variety of strategies used.

The book is addressed to both professionals and graduate students interested in FL acquisition. We hope it will contribute to revise some spurious beliefs about age and language learning, and to clarify the essential differences between FL instructional settings and other language acquisition contexts. We also hope it will be of use to both language planners in general and specifically to those in multilingual communities where an FL is introduced at school.

We would like to express our gratitude for the financial support provided by the different research grants from the Spanish Ministry of Education and Culture (DGICYT PS95–0025, DGES PB97–0611 and BFF–2000–0101) and the Basque Government (PI–1998–96) without which the work presented in some of these chapters would not have been possible.

References

Birdsong, D. (ed.) (1999) *Second Language Acquisition: The Critical Period Hypothesis.* Mahwah, NJ: Lawrence Erlbaum.

Cook, V. (1999) Using SLA research in language teaching. *International Journal of Applied Linguistics* 9 (2), 267–84.

Harley, B. (1986) *Age and Second Language Acquisition*. Clevedon: Multilingual Matters.

Singleton, D. (1989) *Language Acquisition: The Age Factor*. Clevedon: Multilingual Matters.

Singleton, D. and Lengyel, Z. (eds) (1995) *The Age Factor in Second Language Acquisition*. Clevedon: Multilingual Matters.

Part 1

Theoretical Issues

Chapter 1

Critical Period or General Age Factor(s)?

DAVID SINGLETON

Introduction

The question of whether there is an age factor in language development is perennially a topic which attracts wide interest and generates fierce debate. The reasons why it continues to be so energetically discussed are both theoretical and practical in nature. On the theoretical front there is an interaction between the notion of maturational constraints on language acquisition and the idea that language development is underpinned by special bioprogramming; and on the practical level the claim that younger L2 beginners have an advantage over older beginners is constantly invoked and disputed when decisions are being taken about the optimal starting point for L2 instruction in schools.

In fact, few L2 researchers now question the proposition that those learners whose exposure to the L2 begins early in life (and whose exposure to the language is substantial) for most part eventually attain higher levels of proficiency than those whose exposure begins in adolescence or adulthood. The question that continues to divide the field, however, is whether age effects in L2 acquisition constitute a manifestation of a pre-programmed critical period specifically related to language or whether they reflect other, more general, factors which may militate against the learning of new skills and which happen to be concomitants of increasing age. The present chapter addresses this question first by looking at some early work on the age factor, second by looking at the notion of the critical period and some relevant evidence in respect of L1 acquisition, third by examining the L2 evidence for three different interpretations of the Critical Period Hypothesis bearing on L2 acquisition, and finally by exploring some explanations of age effects which do not rely on the idea of a critical period for language.

Anecdote and Assumptions in the Genesis of the Critical Period Hypothesis

Whereas in recent times the issue of maturation and language acquisition has been addressed with a high degree of empirical rigour, in the past discussion of this matter (especially in an L2 context) was largely based on anecdote and assumption. For example, Tomb (1925) referred simply to the 'common experience' of hearing English children in Bengal (in the days of the British Raj) fluently conversing in English, Bengali, Santali and Hindustani with various members of the household, while their elders had scarcely enough Hindustani to give instructions to the servants. Stengel (1939), for his part, proposed a highly sophisticated Freudian analysis of the age factor in L2 learning but, again, his ideas about children's language learning were based simply on impressionistic observation.

Science appeared to enter the picture in the 1950s, when the neurologist Penfield took an interest in the discussion. Penfield cited evidence (Penfield & Roberts, 1959: 240) suggesting that children are normally able to re-learn language when injury or disease damages speech areas in the dominant language hemisphere (usually the left), whereas speech recovery in adults is much more problematic, and that whereas in young children the speech mechanism is often successfully transferred from the injured dominant hemisphere to the healthy minor hemisphere, such transfers do not seem to occur in the case of adults. He used such evidence as a basis for asserting that 'for the purposes of learning languages, the human brain becomes progressively stiff and rigid after the age of nine' (Penfield & Roberts, 1959: 236). He went on to advocate that children should be introduced to L2s early in life, asserting that 'when languages are taken up for the first time in the second decade of life, it is difficult . . . to achieve a good result' (p. 255). However, despite the fact that Penfield made much in his writings of the 'unphysiological' nature of language learning beyond the childhood years, thus implying that his advocacy of early L2 instruction was firmly rooted in his neurological expertise, in fact, as Dechert (1995) demonstrates, his views in relation to L2 learning owed more to his personal experience (successful, he claimed) of immersing his own children in FLs at an early age than to his work as a scientist.

Penfield's notion about the 'unphysiological' nature of later language learning was very much echoed in the work of Lenneberg, the person who is generally acknowledged as the 'father' of the Critical Period Hypothesis relative to language acquisition. Lenneberg saw the human capacity for language acquisition as constrained by a critical period beginning at age two and ending around puberty, this period coinciding with the lateralization process – the specialisation of the dominant hemisphere of the brain for language functions. He adduced a wide range of evidence pointing to changes in the brain that were occurring during this period. However, his claim that lateralisation ends at puberty has been significantly undermined by later studies which reinterpret the data in question as indicating that the process is already complete in early childhood (see, e.g., Kinsbourne & Hiscock, 1977; Krashen, 1973). Moreover, that part of Lenneberg's argument which referred to L2 learning, namely his suggestion that after puberty the learning of L2s required 'labored effort' and foreign accents could not be 'overcome easily' (Lenneberg, 1967: 176) was of dubious status in scientific terms. While his arguments in relation to the maturation of the brain development were supported with a range of neurological evidence (some of which has, as has been noted, since been reinterpreted), no evidence was offered in respect of his claims regarding post-pubertal L2 learning, which relied instead simply on an implicit appeal to popular assumptions.

The Concept of Critical Period

Before we proceed further in our discussion of the Critical Period Hypothesis (henceforth CPH), it may be worth reminding ourselves how the concept of critical period is usually understood in the biological sciences. The example that is usually cited in this connection is that provided by Lorenz (1958), who noted that new-born goslings became irreversibly attached to the first moving object they perceived after hatching. Usually, the first moving object in question is the gosling's mother. However, any other moving object will trigger the relevant reaction if it comes into the gosling's line of vision in the post-hatching period. The period during which the attachment of this kind may be effected is limited in duration, and beyond that period the gosling will no longer fix its following behaviour in the way described. Indeed, when this particular period ends, goslings will retreat from rather than follow moving objects.

Critical periods in biology can, on this basis, be characterised as follows.

(1) They relate to very specific activities or behaviours.
(2) Their duration is limited within well-defined and predictable termini.
(3) Beyond the confines of the period in question the relevant behaviour is not acquired.

If language acquisition in human beings is rigidly constrained by the limits of a critical period of this kind, the implication is that L1 development begins only at the onset of this period and that unless it gets under way during the period in question it will not happen at all. A further implication may be that even if L1 development begins within the critical period it does not *continue* beyond the end of that period.

The CPH in respect of L1 acquisition is not, one has to say, particularly well supported by the available evidence. With regard to the starting point of the critical period, Lenneberg (1967: 155) claims that whereas 'children deafened before completion of the second year do not have any facilitation [in relation to oral skills] in comparison with the congenitally deaf', those who lose their hearing after having been exposed – even for a short time – to the experience of [oral] language subsequent to this point 'can be trained much more easily in all the [oral] language arts' (p. 155). He interprets this as indicating that the critical period is to be seen as beginning around the age of two years. However, his own synthesis of the language acquisition timetable undermines his interpretation; thus, his summary of development between 4 and 20 months is 'from babbling to words' (p. 180). Also, research relative to the acquisition of phonology suggests that there is no sharp break in the developmental progression from prespeech to speech (see, e.g., Stark, 1986: 171), and research into conceptual and lexical development indicates that comprehension of linguistically mediated communicative functions is established early in the second half of the child's first year (see, e.g., Griffiths, 1986). Lenneberg's own evidence is somewhat vague and anecdotal in nature and bears interpretations other than the one he proposes (see, e.g., Singleton, 1989: 44).

In relation to the notion that unless L1 development begins during the critical period it will not happen at all, two kinds of evidence have been cited in this connection: evidence from 'wolf-children' – children who have grown up in isolation from normal human society and who have then been rescued – and evidence from the late acquisition of sign language. Some wolf-children have been brought into contact with language only around the age of puberty, the point at which some researchers, including Lenneberg, claim the critical period for language acquisition ends. Two much discussed cases of this kind are those of Victor (see e.g., Lane, 1976), and Genie (see, e.g., Curtiss, 1977; Rymer, 1993). The problem with such instances is that the evidence is extremely difficult to interpret, especially since there is often a deficiency of information about the child – the precise amount of exposure to language he/she experienced, the extent of the trauma induced by his/her experience, etc. The typical pattern is that some post-rescue progress in language development is observed – but of a limited and abnormal kind. Some researchers see this as 'first language acquisition after the critical age of puberty' (De Villiers & De Villiers, 1978: 219), while others consider that it indicates 'specific constraints and limitations on the nature of language acquisition outside of . . . the critical maturational period' (Curtiss, 1977: 234). Interestingly, Lenneberg himself is sceptical about evidence from this kind of source, his comment being that all one can conclude from such cases is that 'life in dark closets, wolves' dens, forests or sadistic parents' backyards is not conducive to good health and normal development' (Lenneberg, 1967: 142).

It has been suggested that the clearest evidence for a critical period in respect of L1 development comes from studies of deaf subjects who are deprived of language input in their early years and who then acquire sign language as their L1 at a later stage. Long (1990: 258f.) cites a number of studies indicating that the later acquisition of sign language as L1 is characterised by deficits of various kinds. Thus Woodward (1973) found that some American Sign Language (ASL) rules were acquired more often by individuals exposed to sign before age 6, and Mayberry *et al.* (1983) note similar long-term advantages for individuals who began acquiring ASL in childhood over adult beginners have been reported for the processing of ASL. Likewise, the study of 'Chelsea', a deaf adult who began acquiring ASL as a first language in her early thirties reveals good lexical and semantic abilities after six years of exposure but impaired morphology and syntax (Curtiss, 1988), and a large-scale project reported in Newport (1984) and Newport & Supalla (1987) shows that late/adult learners first exposed to ASL after age 12 fell far short of native standards in their signing (cf. also Neville *et al.*, 1997). Two observations come to mind in relation to such research. First, the studies in question do not appear to indicate that language completely fails to develop after a given maturational point, which is what one might expect in the case of a critical period for language. Second, with regard to the abnormalities and deficits recorded in late beginners, it is now clear (see, e.g., Peterson & Siegal, 1995) that deprivation of language input during the phase in a child's life when cognitive development is at its most intense has quite general psychological/cognitive effects, and it may be these general effects that are reflected in later language development (see, e.g., Lundy, 1999) rather than effects relating specifically to a critical period for language.

Finally on the subject of an upper age limit to L1 development, a strong version of the CPH would predict that even if such development starts within the critical period, the process does not continue beyond the end of this period. In a three-year observational study of 54 Down's syndrome subjects Lenneberg *et al.* (1964) were able to record progress in language development only in children younger than 14. This is taken by Lenneberg (1967: 155) to indicate that 'progress in language learning comes to a standstill after maturity'. Alternative interpretations of these data (see Singleton, 1989: 58f.) are (1) that what Lenneberg and his colleagues were observing was a general developmental cut-off point (widely reported in the literature on mental retardation); (2) that what was involved was not a complete arrestation but a temporary plateau (which is again referred to in the literature on mental retardation); and / or (3) that the halt in progress was due to the absence of the right kind of stimulation. In any case, with regard to normal L1 development, there are ample indications that this continues well past puberty. For example, in a study of L1 morphology in Dutch between ages 7 and 17, Smedts (1988) found that his 7-year-old subjects displayed a mastery of, on average, only 14% of a range of Dutch morphology, that his 13-year-olds knew just 51% of the rules tested, and that even his 17-year-olds demonstrated a command of no more than 66% of these rules. In fact, at least some aspects of L1 development extend well into adulthood. Thus, for instance, Carroll (1971: 124) concludes from his review of a number of lexical studies that L1 vocabulary tends to increase significantly up to at least the age of 40 or 50, while Diller (1971: 29) reports research which suggests that there is no point before death at which L1 vocabulary acquisition can be predicted to cease (cf. also, e.g., Singleton, 1989: 54–8).

With regard to L2 acquisition, the way in which the CPH is interpreted varies according to researchers' theoretical predispositions. Three commonly advanced views – which are not incompatible but which are advocated to different extents by different schools of thought – are the following:

(1) after a certain maturational point the L2 learner is no longer capable of attaining native-like levels of proficiency;
(2) after a certain maturational point successful L2 learning requires markedly more effort than before this point; and
(3) after a certain maturational point L2 learning is no longer subserved by the same mechanisms that subserve child language acquisition.

Since, however, the notion of a critical period inherently carries with it a claim regarding a marked qualitative change in learning capacity at a particular stage of maturation, all interpretations of the CPH predict that at the maturational stage in question a sharp decline in L2 learning potential will be observable (which is of its nature different from the more gradual age-related declines in the organism's general learning capacity). The sections that follow will address these issues with reference to relevant research findings.

A Critical Period for the Attainment of Native-like Proficiency in an L2?

A number of researchers in recent years have affirmed that there is a maturational limit (usually set around puberty) beyond which it is simply impossible to acquire an L2 (or certain aspects thereof) to native levels. For example, Scovel (1988) claims that those who begin to be exposed to an L2 after age 12 cannot ever 'pass themselves off as native speakers phonologically' (p. 185) (a position which, it must be added, he has more recently qualified – Scovel, 2000). Long (1990: 274) reads the evidence on accent in precisely the same way as Scovel (1988), but also claims that the *sine qua non* for the acquisition of L2 morphology and syntax to native levels is exposure to the L2 before age 15.

Such claims have been undermined by a range of studies which have focused on older beginners attaining very high levels of L2 proficiency. For instance, Birdsong (1992) found that 15 out of his 20 Anglophone adult subjects who began acquiring French as adults in France fell within the range of native-speaker performance on a grammaticality-judgement task; Ioup *et al.*'s (1994) study of two subjects who learned Arabic as adults in an Arabic-speaking environment established that both were attaining levels of performance close to native norms across a range of areas; and Bongaerts *et al.* (1995) demonstrated that Dutch learners of English who began learning English in a formal instructional setting after age 12 were able to attain English pronunciation ratings within the same range as those attained by native-speaker controls. More recently still, Bongaerts and his colleagues have expanded upon their earlier study (see, e.g., Bongaerts 1999). A further investigation has been conducted in respect of the learning of English as an L2 by Dutch subjects (Bongaerts *et al.*, 1997), and there have also been studies of the learning of French as an L2 by Dutch subjects (Palmen *et al.*, 1997); and the late learning of Dutch as an L2 (Bongaerts *et al.*, 2000). These studies essentially replicate the findings of Bongaerts *et al.*'s (1995) study in showing that some learners whose experience of an L2 begins after age 12 can, nevertheless, acquire an L2 accent which is per-ceived as native by native speakers.

A further study worth mentioning in this connection is Moyer's (1999) investigation of the L2 phonological attainment of 24 Anglophone gradu-ates in German, none of whom had had any exposure to German before age 11. In general, the ratings for these subjects' German accents did not overlap with those obtained by native speaker controls. However, one of the subjects *was* mistaken by the raters for a native speaker. This individual had begun learning German at age 22 and was largely self-taught. What distinguished him from his peers was a particularly deep fascination with the German language and culture and a particularly strong desire to sound German.

It is true, as Hyltenstam and Abrahamsson (2000: 155) claim, that there is no case on record of a post-pubertal L2 beginner who has been demon-strated to behave in every last linguistic detail like a native speaker. However, it is also true, as Hyltestam and Abrahamson recognise, that the more closely we study very early L2 beginners the more we realise that, at the level of subtle detail, they too differ from monoglot native speakers (see also later). It may be, therefore, that the maturational issue is less important in this connection than the very fact of the possession of knowledge of another language (cf., e.g. , Cook, 1995; Grosjean, 1992). Accordingly, the appropriate comparison in the investigation of age effects in L2 acquisition is not between post-pubertal L2 beginners and monoglot native speakers but between post-pubertal L2 beginners and those who begin to acquire an L2 in childhood.

A Critical Period for the Effortless Acquisition of an L2?

Reference was made earlier to Lenneberg's claim that post-pubertal L2 learning required 'labored effort'. To place this claim in a slightly fuller context, what Lenneberg wrote on this matter was as follows:

> automatic acquisition from mere exposure to a given language seems to disappear [after puberty], and foreign languages have to be taught and learned through a conscious and labored effort. (Lenneberg, 1967: 176)

In their (2000) discussion of the components of the CPH, Hyltenstam and Abrahamsson include this claim as an essential dimension of the hypothesis, re-wording it thus:

> Younger learners acquire second languages automatically from mere exposure, while older learners have to make conscious and labored efforts. (Hyltenstam & Abrahamsson, 2000: 152)

A number of researchers who do not necessarily accept the notion of a critical period for language in Lenneberg's sense have, nevertheless, lent support to the idea of post-pubertal L2 learning being more conscious and effortful. For example, Krashen, whose approach to the age factor in language learning has tended to be cognitive-developmentally rather than neurologically based, nevertheless concurs with Lenneberg's basic claim, relating the change in question to the onset of Piagetian formal operations:

> the person who has reached the stage of formal operations may have not only the ability but also need to construct a conscious theory . . . of the language he is learning. (Krashen, 1975: 220)

This, according to Krashen, might cause the adult to adopt a rule-by-rule approach to language learning, which might be limiting.

Furthermore, Bongaerts, whose work appears to challenge the CPH (see earlier), comments that the results he and his colleagues obtained may be partly explicable in terms of the very intensive training received by his subjects – thus appearing to give credence to the proposition that post-pubertal L2 learning is not an automatic affair:

> in the course of their studies at the university, the highly successful learners in our experiments had all received intensive perceptual training that focused their attention on subtle phonetic contrasts between the speech sounds of the target language and those of their L1 . . . In addition, the very advanced learners had all received intensive training in the production of L2 speech sounds aimed at developing the finely tuned motor control required for accurate pronunciation. (Bongaerts, 1999: 154–5)

Two comments suggest themselves with regard to the foregoing. First, there is some evidence that 'input enhancement' of the kind described by Bongaerts is not an absolute prerequisite for successful late L2 learning. One of Ioup's highly successful adult learners of Arabic was untutored. It is true that there was a certain amount of self-generated input enhancement in her experience, since she consciously worked on certain areas of linguistic form, but her performance was native-like even in areas of which she was unaware:

> She was not consciously aware of the structural regularities pertaining to the subtle aspects of syntax and morphophonology. Yet the data show that she has mastered the majority of rule governed constructs in these domains. (Ioup, 1995: 118)

Second, even if it were to be the case that post-pubertal L2 learning were more effortful than pre-pubertal L2 learning, surely this would not be solely attributable to the ending of a critical period for language. Krashen mentions in this connection the possible role of the onset of a particular stage posited by Piaget in general cognitive development – formal operations. However, one does not have to be a Piagetian to recognise that the conscious, deliberate dimension of learning in *all* domains increases as cognitive development advances.

A Critical Period for Access to Particular Language-acquiring/Processing Mechanisms?

A third perspective on the critical period is the idea that children and adults may have fundamentally different mechanisms at their disposal. Thus, some adherents of the Universal Grammar (UG) school of thought claim that post-pubertal L2 language learning has no access to UG principles and parameters. Cook and Newson summarize the kinds of arguments that have been put by such researchers in the following terms.

General arguments in favour of no access are: the knowledge of the L2 is not complete (Schachter, 1988; Bley-Vroman, 1989); some L2s are more difficult to learn than others (Schachter, 1988); the L2 gets fossilized (Schachter, 1988); and L2 learners vary in ways that L1 learners do not. The proponents of no access have therefore sought to find explanations for how it is possible to learn an L2 without UG; the typical solution is seen as general problem solving combined with the knowledge of the L1 (Bley-Vroman, 1989). (Cook & Newson, 1996: 295)

The empirical basis for this perspective was, let it be said, never conclusive (cf., e.g., Flynn, 1987; Martohardjono & Flynn, 1995; see also Hawkins, 2001: 353–9), and, as Braidi (1999: 67) points out, recent changes in Chomskyan theory now render evaluation of earlier studies extremely difficult, although she also notes that 'L2 learners do not seem to exhibit grammars that are not sanctioned by UG'. It might be added that much recent research indicates that post-pubertal L2 learners deal in the same way as L1 acquirers with features purportedly having a UG basis (see, e.g., Bruhn de Garavito, 1999; Dekydtspotter *et al.*, 1998).

With regard to non-UG-oriented research in this connection, a study conducted by Liu *et al.* (1992) examines how age of first encounter with the L2 affects the processing of L2 sentences (in terms of the use of word order and animacy as cues to interpretation) by Chinese learners of English. Their results suggest that whereas those who began to acquire English after age 20 transferred Chinese processing strategies into English, those who began before age 13 deployed the same strategies as monolingual English speakers. This is an interesting result, but it can be explained without recourse to the notion that at a particular maturational point language acquisition mechanisms undergo a qualitative shift – namely, in terms of the increasing extent to which the L1 influences L2 processing as a function of years of experience of the L1 and the degree to which it is entrenched. We shall return to this question later.

Another non-UG-focused study bearing on what underlies L2 learning at different ages is Harley and Hart's (1997) investigation of the role of language aptitude in two groups of Anglophone secondary school students who had entered French immersion programmes in grade 1 and grade 7 respectively. It emerged that the early beginners' L2 outcomes 'were much more likely to be associated with a memory measure than with a measure of language ability' (Harley & Hart, 1997: 395), whereas the reverse was true of the later beginners. De Keyser's (2000) study yields not dissimilar results: the adult beginners in his study who scored within the range of the child beginners had high levels of verbal analytical ability, an ability which played no role in the performance of the child beginners. De

Keyser interprets his results as suggesting that maturational constraints apply only to implicit language-learning mechanisms. Harley and Hart, for their part, point to the possible influence of different instructional styles associated with primary versus secondary-level education. A further possibility is that both sets of results are related to general cognitive changes which impact on language learning but not *only* on language learning.

A particularly exciting research approach which has become available in recent times is that involving brain-imaging, and some of such research has addressed the question of whether early acquisition of an L2 results in different representations in the brain from late acquisition. For instance, Kim *et al.* (1997) used magnetic resonance imaging to investigate the spatial representation of L1 and L2 in the cerebral cortex of early and late bilinguals during a sentence-generation task. The results revealed little or no age-related separation of activity in Wernicke's area but differences did emerge in respect of activity in Broca's area. Among the late bilinguals two distinct but adjacent centres of activation were revealed for L1 and L2, whereas in the early bilinguals a single area of activation for both languages emerged. This looks like evidence of different kinds of brain organisation in early and late bilinguals.

However, there are reasons to treat such evidence with caution. Marinova-Todd *et al.* (2000) note that in Kim *et al.*'s study there is no control of the proficiency level of the later beginners. Accordingly there is the possibility 'that the adult learners assessed . . . were poorly selected and do not represent highly proficient adult bilinguals' (Marinova-Todd *et al.*, 2000: 17–18). If this were so, then the neurological differences observed might simply reflect different proficiency levels. This kind of interpretation becomes all the more plausible in the light of the recognition by the neurosciences that the direction of causation may be the reverse of the one usually assumed – that is, that brain differences are as likely to reflect different kinds of learning experience as to determine these experiences (see, e.g., Bialystok & Hakuta, 1999; Gazzaniga, 1992; Robertson, 1999).

All in all, the case for fundamental differences between children and adults in respect of the language-acquiring/processing mechanisms that are available to them is not by any means proven. There are, of course, differences between child and adult cognitive systems and child and adult brains, but these differences have yet to be shown to be specifically related to language and/or to have a specific bearing on language-learning capacity. As Marinova-Todd *et al.* note in relation to neurological differences, for example, children and adults may 'localize their learning differently without showing different levels of learning' (Marinova-Todd *et al.*, 2000: 17).

A Sharp Decline in L2 Learning Potential at the end of Childhood?

There is, as was indicated at the very beginning of this chapter, no real quarrel among SLA researchers over the proposition that individuals who begin to acquire an L2 early in life generally do better in the long run that those who begin as adults. The balance of evidence broadly favours the eventual attainment-focused line taken by Krashen *et al.* (1979): namely, that, with regard to long-term outcomes in situations of 'naturalistic' exposure, generally speaking, the earlier exposure to the target language begins the better (see, e.g., Hyltenstam, 1992; Johnson & Newport, 1989; Oyama,1976, 1978; Patkowski, 1980), although in the initial stages of learning older beginners tend to outperform their juniors – at least in some respects . Strong empirical support for the Krashen *et al.* position comes from studies carried out by Snow and Hoefnagel-Höhle (e.g., 1978a, 1978b) which investigated the development in Dutch of 69 English-speaking residents in The Netherlands; these studies provide clear evidence of more rapid learning on the part of adult and adolescent subjects in the early stages and of younger beginners catching up on and beginning to outstrip their elders after a year or so.

As far as instructed L2 learning is concerned, the consistent finding which has emerged from research focused on primary-level L2 programmes in schools where the general medium of instruction is the L1 (see, e.g., Burstall *et al.*, 1974; Oller & Nagato, 1974; Stankowski-Gratton, 1980) is that pupils who are given early exposure to an L2 and are then integrated into classes containing pupils without such experience do not maintain a clear advantage for more than a relatively short period over pupils who begin to learn the language only at secondary level. The apparent discrepancy between such evidence from school-based studies and evidence from naturalistic studies can, however, probably be related to the blurring effect resulting from mixing beginners and non-beginners in the same classes (see, e.g., Singleton, 1992; Stern, 1976) and can, in any case, be accounted for in terms of gross differences in exposure time between naturalistic and instructed learners. I (1989, 1992) have suggested that the initial advantage of older learners, which in the naturalistic learning situation appears to last about a year, may, under the régime of vastly sparser exposure of the formal learning situation, last for several years. This would readily account for the effect within the normal secondary-school cycle of pupils without primary-level L2 instruction 'catching up' with pupils who have received such instruction. On this view, the eventual benefits of early L2 learning in a formal (L1-medium) instructional environment might be expected to show up only in rather longer-term studies than have to date been attempted. It is interesting to note in this connection that, whereas evaluations of L2 programmes in L1-medium primary schools tend to yield rather disappointing results even where there is no comparative element (see, e.g., Audin *et al.*, 1999), the results of studies of L2 *immersion* programmes, where amounts of L2 exposure are much greater, 'favor . . . early programs over delayed and, in most cases, late programs' (Holobow *et al.*, 1991: 180).

Accordingly, both naturalistic evidence and formal instructional evidence can be interpreted as being consistent with what may be termed the 'younger = better in the long run' view. However, such an inference needs to be qualified in at least three ways. First, it is clear that the available empirical evidence cannot be taken to license the simplistic 'younger = better in all circumstances over any timescale' perspective which seems to underlie some of the 'classic' treatments of age and L2 learning (e.g. Lenneberg, 1967; Penfield & Roberts, 1959; Stengel, 1939; Tomb, 1925 – see earlier comments).

Second, even the 'younger = better in the long run' view is valid only in terms of a general tendency. Both research and the observations of those who are in daily contact with L2 learners suggest that an early start in a second language is neither a strictly necessary nor a universally sufficient condition for the attainment of native-like proficiency. Even Penfield was prepared to recognize that under some circumstances an individual adult beginner *may* become a 'master' of his/her target L2 (Penfield & Roberts, 1959: 24) – an assertion very much confirmed by the work such as that of Bongaerts and of Ioup (see earlier comments) – and the literature on early bilingualism strongly indicates that the age at which one first encounters a second language is only one of the determinants of the ultimate level of proficiency attained in that language (see, e.g., Romaine, 1989: 232–44). On this latter point a number of recent studies have shown that even very young L2 beginners diverge at the level of fine linguistic detail from native speakers. Thus, for example, Hyltenstam and Abrahamsson (2000: 161) cite research by Ekberg (1998) into bilingual teenagers in Sweden who were exposed to Swedish outside the home as small children but whose output in Swedish differs in a number of lexico-grammatical respects from their native-speaker peers. At the phonological level too, it appears from Flege's work (e.g. 1999) that subjects who begin to be exposed to an L2 in an L2 environment as very young children are, nevertheless, quite likely to end up speaking the L2 with a non-native accent.

Third, there is a strong question-mark over the issue of the existence or non-existence of a cut-off point such as would normally be associated with a critical period. This matter is addressed by Bialystok and Hakuta (Bialystok, 1997; Bialystok & Hakuta, 1994), whose re-analysis of Johnson and Newport's data suggests 'that the tendency for proficiency to decline with age projects well into adulthood and does not mark some defined change in learning potential at around puberty' (Bialystok, 1997: 122). More recently, Bialystok and Hakuta (1999) have analysed census data on age of arrival and reported English proficiency for Chinese-speakers and Spanish-speakers who had resided in New York State for at least 10 years; what emerges is, on the one hand, a steady linear decline of reported English proficiency as age of arrival increases but, on the other, no indication of a dramatically sharper rate of decline at any point between infancy and senescence. Recent data on the relationship between L2 accent and age of arrival obtained by Flege and his colleagues (see, e.g., Flege, 1999) show a similarly continuous decline.

In sum, it appears that any decline in L2-learning capacity that occurs at the end of childhood is not of the same magnitude from individual to individual across the human species; this kind of variation is not what one would expect if the underlying cause of the decline were a critical period for language, which, as Bialystok (1997: 118) says, ought to reveal itself in an unambiguous linkage between L2 proficiency levels and age of first exposure which is 'consistent across studies'. It also appears that any decline in L2-learning capacity with age is not in the nature of a sharp cut-off but something rather more continuous and linear, which, again, is not in keeping with the usual understanding of the notion of critical period.

Non-CPH Explanations for Age Effects

If the age effects observable in L2 learning are not to be explained in terms of a critical period for language acquisition, how are they to be explained? Four alternative kinds of factors have been proposed in the recent literature. These are: motivational factors, cross-linguistic factors, educational factors and general cognitive factors

It has long been a feature of discussion of age-related differences in L2 learning outcomes that different levels or types of motivation types have been evoked as possibly underlying such differences (see, e.g., Schumann, 1978). Marinova-Todd *et al.* (2000) have pointed to the fact that some of the recently studied older beginners who achieve native-like proficiency are characterized by very high levels of motivation. They refer to Ioup's subjects (Ioup *et al.*, 1994) but other instances also spring to mind – e.g. the exceptional case mentioned by Moyer (1999) (see earlier comments).

A particular dimension of the motivation issue relates to the question of language dominance. Older arrivals in an L2 environment often make choices which bring them into frequent contact with fellow native speakers of their L1 and which accordingly restrict their contact with the L2; such choices may have to do with the avoidance of isolation and/or the desire to maintain a particular linguistico-cultural identity. Fewer choices are available to younger arrivals – because of compulsory schooling. In any case, their linguistico-cultural identity is not as fully formed as that of their elders, and so the motivation to maintain it is likely to be weaker. According to Jia and Aaronson (1999) the consequence of these contrasting circumstances is that, whereas immigrants arriving after age 10 tend to maintain their L1, immigrants arriving before age 10 seem to switch their dominant language from the home language to the language of the host country. One possible implication of this phenomenon is that some studies purportedly focusing on L2 proficiency may, in fact, be reporting on a language which has effectively become an L1 for the subjects in question (cf. Bialystok, 1997: 123).

This last point brings us to explanations of age effects which refer to cross-linguistic factors, since it clearly raises issues concerning the impact of different amounts and patterns of L2 input and use. Much of the recent work by Flege and his colleagues has demonstrated the importance of environmental factors for L2 pronunciation, with time spent in a country where the target language is in use (Riney & Flege, 1998) and time spent in the company of native-speakers (Flege *et al.*, 1997) emerging as major determinants of quality of L2 accent. Like Jia and Aaronson (1999) Flege sees a trade-off between L2 and L1 proficiency. His line is that 'bilinguals are unable to fully separate the L1 and the L2 phonetic system' so that 'the phonic elements of the L1 subsystem necessarily influence phonic elements in the L2 system, and vice versa' (Flete, 1999: 106). On this view, young children may acquire a good L2 accent at the expense of their L1 accent or may develop an authentic accent in their L1 at the cost of a non-native accent in their L2. Flege's suggestion is that, as L1 phonology continues to be refined, its influence on L2 phonology acquisition continuously increases accordingly.

Concerning the educational dimension, Bialystok (1997: 123) points out that immigrants who arrive as children enter the education system at a point where explicit language instruction is on offer to all pupils, whereas immigrants arriving in early adulthood are unlikely to receive language training of this kind. Similarly, Bialystok and Hakuta (1999) suggest that the presence or absence of literacy skills in the L2 may have a bearing on L2 proficiency and note that immigrants who arrive young are likely to have literacy skills in good measure – because of experience at school – while those who arrive later have fewer opportunities to develop such skills.

Finally, in relation to cognitive factors in a broad sense, Bialystok and Hakuta (1999) point to a deterioration over the lifespan in such areas as capacity to perform tasks under time pressure, risk-taking, establishing long-term memory codes, and ability to recall details. They comment (p.

172): 'if age-related changes in ultimate language proficiency are to be attributable to these cognitive changes . . . then the decline in ultimate proficiency . . . should . . . be gradual and constant'. The evidence, as we have seen, suggests that this is precisely how it is.

Conclusion

In the light of the foregoing, it is difficult not to infer that talking about *an* age factor may be misconceived, and that we should rather be thinking in terms of a range of age factors. This was, in fact, my own reading of the evidence more than a decade ago (Singleton, 1989: 266), when my conclusion – which I have not discarded – was that 'the various age-related phenomena . . . probably result from the interaction of a multiplicity of causes'. Such a perspective can certainly encompass the notion that decreasing cerebral plasticity and/or other changes in the brain may play a role but the notion that L2 age effects are exclusively a matter of neurologically predetermination, that they are associated with absolute, well-defined maturational limits and that they are particular to language looks less and less plausible. In other words, the idea of a critical period for language development may well have had its day.

References

Audin, L., Ligozat, M.-A. and Luc, C. (1999) *Enseignement des langues vivantes au CM2.* Paris: Institut National de Recherche Pédagogique.
Bialystok, E. (1997) The structure of age: In search of barriers to second language acquisition. *Second Language Research* 13, 116–37.
Bialystok, E. and Hakuta, K. (1994) *In Other Words: The Science and Psychology of Second Language Acquisition.* New York: Basic Books.
Bialystok, E. and Hakuta, K. (1999) Confounded age: Linguistic and cognitive factors in age differences for second language acquisition. In D. Birdsong (ed.) *Second Language Acquisition and the Critical Period Hypothesis* (pp. 162–81). Mahwah, NJ: Erlbaum.
Birdsong, D. (1992) Ultimate attainment in second language acquisition. *Language* 68, 706–55.
Bley-Vroman, R.W. (1989) What is the logical problem of foreign language learning? In S.M. Gass and J. Schachter (eds) *Linguistic Perspectives on Second Language Acquisition* (pp. 41–68). Cambridge: Cambridge University Press.
Bongaerts, T. (1999) Ultimate attainment in L2 pronunciation: The case of very advanced late L2 learners. In D. Birdsong (ed.) *Second Language Acquisition and the Critical Period Hypothesis* (pp. 33–159). Mahwah, NJ: Lawrence Erlbaum.
Bongaerts, T., Mennen, S. and Van der Slik, F. (2000) Authenticity of pronunciation in naturalistic second language acquisition: The case of very advanced late learners of Dutch as a second language. *Studia Linguistica* 54 (2), 298–308.
Bongaerts, T., Planken, B. and Schils, E. (1995) Can late starters attain a native accent in a foreign language: A test of the Critical Period Hypothesis. In D. Singleton and Z. Lengyel (eds) *The Age Factor in Second Language Acquisition* (pp. 30–50). Clevedon: Multilingual Matters.

Bongaerts, T., van Summeren, C., Planken, B. and Schils, E. (1997) Age and ultimate attainment in the pronunciation of a foreign language. *Studies in Second Language Acquisition* 19, 447–65.

Braidi, S.M. (1999) *The Acquisition of Second Language Syntax.* London: Edward Arnold.

Bruhn de Garavito, J.L.S. (1999) Adult SLA of *se* constructions in Spanish: Evidence against pattern learning. *Proceedings of the Boston University Conference on Language Development* 23, 112–19.

Burstall, C., Jamieson, M., Cohen, S. and Hargreaves, M. (1974) *Primary French in the Balance.* Windsor: NFER.

Carroll, J. (1971) Development of native language skills beyond the early years. In C. Reed (ed.) *The Learning of Language* (pp. 97–156). New York: Appleton-Century-Crofts.

Cook, V. (1995) Multicompetence and effects of age. In D. Singleton and Z. Lengyel (eds) *The Age Factor in Second Language Acquisition* (pp. 51–66). Clevedon: Multilingual Matters.

Cook, V. and Newson, M. (1996) *Chomsky's Universal Grammar: An Introduction* (2nd edn). Oxford: Blackwell.

Curtiss, S. (1977) *Genie: A Psycholinguistic Study of a Modern- day 'Wild Child'.* New York: Academic Press.

Curtiss, S. (1988) Abnormal language acquisition and the modularity of language. In F.J. Newmeyer (ed.) *Linguistics: The Cambridge Survey: Vol. 2. Linguistic Theory: Extensions and Implications* (pp. 90–116). Cambridge: Cambridge University Press.

Dechert, H. (1995) Some critical remarks concerning Penfield's theory of second language acquisition. In D. Singleton and Z. Lengyel (eds) *The Age Factor in Second Language Acquisition* (pp. 67–94). Clevedon: Multilingual Matters.

De Keyser, R.M. (2000) The robustness of critical period effects in second language acquisition. *Studies in Second Language Acquisition* 22, 499–533.

Dekydtspotter, L., Sprouse, R.A. and Thyre, R. (1998) Evidence of full UG access in L2 acquisition from the interpretive interface: Quantification at a distance in English–French interlanguage. *Proceedings of the Boston University Conference on Language Development* 22, 141–52.

De Villiers J. and De Villiers, P. (1978) *Language Acquisition.* Cambridge, MA: Harvard University Press.

Diller, K. (1971) *Generative Grammar, Structural Linguistics and Language Teaching.* Rowley, MA: Newbury House.

Ekberg, L. (1998) Regeltillämpning kontra lexikonkunskap in svenskan hos invandrarbarn i Malmö. In J. Møller, P. Quist, A. Holmen and J Jørgensen (eds) *Nordiske Sprog som andet Sprog. Københavnerstudier i Tosprogethed* 30 (pp. 247–63). Copenhagen: Institut for humanistike fag, Danmarks Lærerhøjskole.

Flege, J. (1999) Age of learning and second language speech. In D. Birdsong (ed.) *Second Language Acquisition and the Critical Period Hypothesis* (pp. 101–31). Mahwah, NJ: Erlbaum.

Flege, J., Frieda, E. & Nozawa, T. (1997) Amount of native language (L1) use affects the pronunciation of an L2. *Journal of Phonetics* 25, 169–86.

Flynn, S. (1987) *A Parameter-setting Model of L2 Acquisition: Experimental Studies in Anaphora.* Dordrecht: Reidel.

Gazzaniga, M.S. (1992) *Nature's Mind: The Biological Roots of Thinking, Emotions, Sexuality, Language, and Intelligence.* New York: Basic Books.

Griffiths, P. (1986) Early vocabulary. In P. Fletcher and M. Garman (eds) *Language Acquisition: Studies in First Language Development* (2nd edn). (pp. 279–306). Cambridge: Cambridge University Press.

Grosjean, F. (1992) *Life with Two Languages*. Cambridge, MA: Harvard University Press.

Harley, B. and Hart, D. (1997) Language aptitude and second language proficiency in classroom learners of different starting ages. *Studies in Second Language Acquisition* 19, 379–400.

Hawkins, R. (2001) *Second Language Syntax: A Generative Introduction*. Oxford: Blackwell.

Holobow, N., Genesee, F. and Lambert, W. (1991) The effectiveness of a foreign language immersion program for children from different ethnic and social class backgrounds: Report 2. *Applied Psycholinguistics* 12, 179–98.

Hyltenstam, K. (1992) Non-native features of near-native speakers: On the ultimate attainment of childhood L2 learners. In R. Harris (ed.) *Cognitive Processing in Bilinguals* (pp. 351–368). Amsterdam: Elsevier.

Hyltenstam, K. and Abrahamsson, N. (2000) Who can become native-like in a second language? All, some or none? On the maturational contraints controversy in second language acquisition. *Studia Linguistica* 54 (2), 150–66.

Ioup, G. (1995) Evaluating the need for input enhancement in post-critical period language acquisition. In D. Singleton and Z. Lengyel (eds) *The Age Factor in Second Language Acquisition* (pp.95–123). Clevedon: Multilingual Matters.

Ioup, G., Boustagui, E., Tigi, M. and Moselle, M. (1994) Reexamining the critical period hypothesis: A case of successful adult SLA in a naturalistic environment. *Studies in Second Language Acquisition* 16, 73–98.

Jia, G. and Aaronson, D. (1999) Age differences in second language acquisition: The Dominant Language Switch and Maintenance Hypothesis. *Proceedings of the Boston University Conference on Language Development* 23, 301–12.

Johnson, J. and Newport, E. (1989) Critical period effects in second language learning: The influence of maturational state on the acquisition of ESL. *Cognitive Psychology* 21, 60–99.

Kim, K.H.S., Relkin, N.R., Kyoung-Min, L. and Hirsch, J. (1997) Distinct cortical areas associated with native and second languages. *Nature* 388, 171–74.

Kinsbourne, M. and Hiscock, M (1977) Does cerebral dominance develop? In S. Segalowitz and F. Gruber (eds) *Language Development and Neurological Theory* (pp. 171–91). New York: Academic Press.

Krashen, S. (1973) Lateralization, language learning and the critical period: Some new evidence. *Language Learning* 23, 63–74.

Krashen, S. (1975) The critical period for language acquisition and its possible bases. In D. Aaronson and R. Rieber (eds) *Developmental Psycholinguistics and Communication Disorders* (pp. 211–24). New York: New York Academy of Sciences.

Krashen, S., Long, M. and Scarcella, R. (1979) Age, rate and eventual attainment in second language acquisition. *TESOL Quarterly* 13, 573–82.

Lane, H. (1976) *The Wild Boy of Aveyron*. Cambridge, MA: Harvard University Press.

Lenneberg, E. (1967) *Biological Foundations of Language*. New York: Wiley.

Lenneberg, E.H., Nichols, I. and Rosenberger, E. (1964) Primitive stages of language development in mongolism. *Disorders of Communication* 42, 119–37.

Liu, H., Bates, E. and Li, P. (1992) Sentence interpretation in bilingual speakers of English and Chinese. *Applied Psycholinguistics* 12, 451–84.

Long, M. (1990) Maturational constraints on language development. *Studies in Second Language Acquisition* 12, 251–85.

Lorenz, K.Z. (1958) The evolution of behavior. *Scientific American* 119 (6), 67–78.

Lundy, J.E.B. (1999) Theory of mind development in deaf children. *Perspectives in Education and Deafness* 18 (1), 1–5.

Marinova-Todd, S.H., Marshall, D.B. and Snow, C.E. (2000) Three misconceptions about age and L2 learning. *TESOL Quarterly* 34, 9–34.

Martohardjono, G. and Flynn, S. (1995) Is there an age factor for Universal Grammar? In D. Singleton and Z. Lengyel (eds) *The Age Factor in Second Language Acquisition* (pp. 135–53). Clevedon: Multilingual Matters.

Mayberry, R., Fischer, S. and Hatfield, N. (1983) Sentence repetition in American Sign Language. In J. Kyle and B. Woll (eds) *Language in Sign: International Perspectives on Sign Language* (pp. 83–97). London: Croom Helm.

Moyer, A. (1999) Ultimate attainment in L2 phonology: The critical factors of age, motivation and instruction. *Studies in Second Language Acquisition* 21, 81–108.

Neville, H., Coffey, S.A., Lawson, D.S., Fischer, A. Emmorey, K. and Bellugi, U. (1997) Neural systems mediating American Sign Language: Effects of sensory experiences and age of acquisition. *Brain and Language* 57, 285–308.

Newport, E. (1984) Constraints on learning: Studies in the acquisition of American Sign Language. *Papers and Reports on Child Language Development* 23, 1–22.

Newport, E. and Supalla, T. (1987) Critical period effects in the acquisition of a primary language. Unpublished manuscript.

Oller, J. and Nagato, N. (1974) The long-term effect of FLES: An experiment. *Modern Language Journal* 58, 15–19.

Oyama, S. (1976) A sensitive period for the acquisition of a non-native phonological system. *Journal of Psycholinguistic Research* 5, 261–84.

Oyama, S. (1978) The sensitive period and comprehension of speech. *Working Papers on Bilingualism* 16, 1–17.

Palmen, M.-J., Bongaerts, T. and Schils, E. (1997) L'authenticité de la prononciation dans l'acquisition d'une langue étrangère au-delà de la période critique: Des apprenants néerlandais parvenus à un niveau très avancé en français. *Acquisition et Interaction en Langue Etrangère* 9, 173–91.

Patkowski, M. (1980) The sensitive period for the acquisition of syntax in a second language. *Language Learning* 30, 449–72.

Penfield, W. and Roberts, L. (1959) *Speech and Brain Mechanisms*. Princeton, NJ: Princeton University Press.

Peterson, C.C. and Siegal, M. (1995) Deafness, conversation, and theory of mind. *Journal of Child Psychology and Psychiatry* 36, 459–74.

Robertson, I.H. (1999) *Mind Sculpture*. London: Bantam.

Rymer, R. (1993) *Genie: An Abused Child's Flight from Silence*. New York: HarperCollins.

Riney T. and Flege, J. (1998) Changes over time in global foreign accent and liquid identifiability and accuracy. *Studies in Second Language Acquisition* 20, 213–43.

Romaine, S. (1989) *Bilingualism*. Oxford: Blackwell.

Schachter, J. (1988) Second language acquisition and its relationship to Universal Grammar. *Applied Linguistics* 9, 219–35.

Schumann, J. (1978) *The Pidginization Process: A Model for Second Language Acquisition*. Rowley, MA: Newbury House.

Scovel, T. (1988) *A Time to Speak: A Psycholinguistic Inquiry into the Critical Period for Human Language*. Rowley, MA: Newbury House.

Scovel, T. (2000) A critical review of the Critical Period Hypothesis. *Annual Review of Applied Linguistics* 20, 213–23.
Singleton, D. (1989) *Language Acquisition: The Age Factor.* Clevedon: Multilingual Matters. (Second edition currently in preparation.)
Singleton, D. (1992) Second language instruction: The when and the how. *AILA Review* 9, 46–54.
Smedts, W. (1988) De beheersing van de nederlandse woordvorming tussen 7 en 17. In F. van Besien (ed.) *First Language Acquisition (ABLA Papers* No. 12) (pp. 103–27). Antwerp: Association Belge de Linguistique Appliquée/Universitaire Instelling Antwerpen.
Snow, C. and Hoefnagel-Höhle, M. (1978a) Age differences in second language acquisition. In E. Hatch (ed.) *Second Language Acquisition: A Book of Readings* (pp. 333–44). Rowley, MA: Newbury Press.
Snow, C. and Hoefnagel-Höhle, M. (1978b) The critical period for language acquisition: evidence from second language learning. *Child Development* 49, 1114–28.
Stankowski Gratton, R. (1980) Una ricerca sperimentale sull'insegnamento del tedesco dalla prima classe elementare. *Rassegna Italiana di Linguistica Applicata* 12 (3), 119–41.
Stark, R. (1986) Prespeech segmental feature development. In P. Fletcher and M. Garman (eds) *Language Acquisition: Studies in First Language Development* (2nd edn) (pp. 149–73). Cambridge: Cambridge University Press.
Stengel, E. (1939) On learning a new language. *International Journal of Psychoanalysis* 20, 471–9.
Stern, H. (1976) Optimal age: Myth or reality? *Canadian Modern Language Review*, 32, 283–94.
Tomb, J. (1925) On the intuitive capacity of children to understand spoken languages. *British Journal of Psychology* 16, 53–4.
Woodward, J.C. (1973) Some characteristics of pidgin sign English. *Sign Language Studies* 3, 39–59.

Chapter 2

Phonological Acquisition in Multilingualism

JONATHAN LEATHER

L_1, L_2 . . . L_n: Ontogenesis of Multilingual Speech

While only a minority of the world's children acquire language in an environment that is 'monolingual' (Edwards, 1994; Romaine, 1996), most studies in language acquisition have reflected the essentially monolingual view of society and socialisation that informs western science (Leather & Van Dam, to appear; Nayar, 1994; Phillipson & Skutnabb-Kangas, 1996). Researchers have thus tended to assume – however tacitly – a large measure of isomorphy between linguistic, political and cultural communities: such categorical distinctions are reflected in the terms 'L1', 'L2' and so on. The object of research has been either the 'mother-tongue' (L1) or a language learned later – often in adulthood. In the western world inhabited by most authors of published research the 'L1' and the 'L2' are not difficult to keep distinct because of their codification as 'standards' (and we may note that the linguist's notions of *code-switching* and *code-mixing* presuppose the codes are distinct). By contrast, in the many societies where language blends are abundant and mother-tongues lack the norms that explicitly define western standard languages, it is often far from clear how to identify what 'language' is being spoken at any particular moment. Leather (to appear) gives illustrative data from a Dominican kwéyòl-speaking child, arguing that the standard approaches to modelling phonological acquisition fall short because (1) they address single languages as closed systems and (2) they exclude from consideration non-phonetic factors – lexical and pragmatic, for instance – which may be relevant to the acquisition process. Moreover, the very notion of a determinate target system against which transitional forms can be evaluated, while central to many acquisition studies, is problematic: as Charles Ferguson put it: 'The phonology of a language variety . . . is a *composite* of individual phonologies in

23

which the shared structure inevitably has indeterminacies, fuzzy boundaries, and both dialectal and idiosyncratic variation' (Ferguson, 1979: 198).

As Kachru (1996) has pointed out, under the hegemony of the monolingual world view the patterns and complexities of multilinguals' language behaviour are marginalised. The multiple language development of the many whose lives belie the 'monolingual' model tend to be considered as the *final* challenge to any theory of language acquisition. Yet the very complexity of 'multilingual' development can also be seen as an invitation to theoretical reappraisal and as the default case which we should address *first* (Leather, to appear).

Following the monolingual perspective it may be thought that speakers with two or more languages develop and maintain a separate phonological system for each language. Yet although there has been comparatively little longitudinal research on multilingual phonological acquisition, there is evidence that in the process of multiple acquisition the several languages may interact, so that the acquisition of each is qualitatively different from that of the monolingual speaker (Holm & Dodd, 1999). Laeufer (1997) reviews studies dating from the 1940s which address the question of whether bilinguals develop separate systems for their languages or have a single, all-encompassing, merged system. (Even with separate systems a bilingual may 'economise' in production routines by making some processing common to both of the languages [Watson, 1991]). Laeufer shows from a variety of recent acoustic–phonetic studies that a third possibility is a 'super-subordinate' system, in which bilinguals have native-like values for one language and values which are very similar for the other language as well. Such a typology could obviously also be applied to speakers of more than two languages.

Systematicity being one of the cornerstones of Western linguistic theory (with *system* most often equated to *mental representation or mechanism*) we are naturally inclined to project it upon acquirers' performance data. Yet we should be careful not to rule out *non*-systematic explanations for the data: what at a particular moment in an individual's phonological development appears systematic need not be a reflection of an underlying coherence or *system* in their phonological resources: it may simply be that a certain constellation of difficulties at that stage of that individual's development makes some sounds easier to produce than others (see Schnitzer, 1990; Schnitzer & Krasinski, 1994). Schnitzer and Krasinski (1996), for instance, found no evidence of any particular 'stage' on the way to their child informant achieving target phonetic values but could discern only the development of a segmental repertoire.

With the theme of the present volume in mind, therefore, we will not attempt to distinguish categorically between L1, L2, L3, and so on, but use

L1 to denote the language acquired earliest, and L2 as a generic term to refer to any language acquired subsequently. Consistent with the L1/L2 distinction is the notional difference between (naturalistic) *acquisition* and *learning* (which can involve explicit study and/or instruction): we will not attempt a consistent and sharp distinction. In the same vein we will use *native* and *non-native* as convenient terms with a ready meaning in western applied linguistics, while fully acknowledging that the social and political validity of the terms are easy – and important – to question.

Modelling Acquisition

Speech perception, speech production and their interaction

In the broadest terms, we may conceive of phonological competence as 'a system of knowledge that includes both representations and processes' (Archibald, 1995: xxi). Acquiring phonological competence in another language after the establishment of the mother-tongue can be seen as involving 'reattunement of perceptual phonetic processes and the perceptual reorganization of phonological categories' (Strange, 1992), together with reprogramming at the level of motor commands until 'the production of an L2 sound eventually corresponds to the properties present in its phonetic category representation' (Flege, 1995: 239). How acquirers progress in either case towards competence, and how along the way their perceptual and productive phonological learning interrelate, remain the central questions for investigation.

The core problem in speech perception is to explain how the listener maps acoustically varying productions onto constant phonetic categories. Much research on the perceptual categorisation of speech sounds has gone into exploring the boundaries 'between' phonetic categories (see e.g. the detailed survey by Repp, [1984]). It is not only the language of their environment that infants perceive in terms of phonetic category boundaries but unknown languages as well. In adults, by contrast, these perceptual category boundaries are sharp for known but not for unknown languages: confronted with speech in an unknown language, adult listeners tend to map it into the segment categories of their L1 (for references on cross-language categorical perception see, e.g., Leather and James [1991] and Strange [1995: *passim*]).

An alternative paradigm in speech perception research concentrates not on the boundaries between phonetic categories but their internal organisation and the hypothetical ideal exemplar on the basis of which listeners differentiate between 'good' and less good exemplars of the categories (see the review in Kuhl, [1992]). Kuhl's (1993) suggestion is that a phonetic *prototype* assimilates non-prototypical members of the same category, as if it were shrinking the acoustic–phonetic space towards it. For L2 learners there is a Native-Language Magnet (NLM) effect: prototypes of the L1 constrain adult learners' abilities to perceive contrasts in the L2 by the 'pulls' they exert. Thus, in experiments with 6-month-old infants in Sweden and the USA (Kuhl, 1992), American infants in Sweden evidenced a significantly greater 'perceptual magnet' effect than Swedish infants for stimuli with acoustic structures close to an English vowel prototype, while the Swedish infants in the USA reversed this perceptual pattern. A comparable magnet effect could be seen in Nakai's (1997) experiments with native perception of the vowels of Greek and Japanese.

A competent listener is able to find phonetic constancies in the widely varying, idiosyncratic productions of the many different speakers they hear. Learners have to develop talker-independent phonetic representations that will enable them to do this (see, e.g., Leather, 1987) and strategies for (re)calibrating perceptual category dimensions to the norms of each individual talker they encounter (see, e.g., Gussenhoven & Rietveld, 1998; Leather, 1983). Thus, in a study of the acquisition of Chinese lexical tone by non-tonal English and Dutch speakers, Leather (1997) found that learners who were 'trained' on the tone exemplars of one speaker, when exposed to 'new' speakers, apparently restructured their tone space in an attempt to maintain systematicity. One talker's instantiations of a phonetic contrast do not provide any data on inter-speaker variation. Five example speakers were also too few to 'train' Japanese learners of English distinguish between the /l/ and /r/ of new speakers in the experiment by Logan *et al.* (1991).

Speech perception and production are often mutually facilitative (Leather & James, 1996; Rochet, 1995). For instance, Yamada *et al.* (1996) and Bradlow *et al.* (1996) found that training Japanese subjects to perceive English /r/ and /l/ also improved their accuracy in producing these sounds, though they received no production training. Also, the Japanese subjects of Matthews (1997) who received training only in the production of new (English) contrasts improved significantly in their ability to discriminate the particular segments concerned. Yet while it is clear from research – as well as common observation – that while speech perception and speech production are interrelated, it is hardly helpful to view production as simply a mirror image of perception. The experimental learners in a study by Leather (1997) followed computer-managed training with visual feedback to produce the standard Chinese lexical tones. Although they did not in their production training hear any exemplars of the tones, they were later mostly successful in perceiving tone contrasts. Conversely, another group of learners who were trained to perceive the tonal contrasts were subsequently able to produce them with an accuracy largely commensurate with their perceptual abilities. At the individual level, however, the evolving patterns of perceptual and productive abilities suggested an interrelation between perception and production that was neither simple nor direct.

Other studies reviewed by Leather and James (1996: 284) also, when taken together, provide no clear evidence of any constant interrelation between perception and production but suggest a need for analyses that are developmentally differentiated. A general developmental sequence has been proposed by Broselow and Park (1995) with their Split Parameter Setting Hypothesis: learners move through developmental stages in which perception and production are 'split', based on the different 'parameter settings' of L1 and L2. To begin with, the L1 setting governs both perception and production. Next, the L2 setting governs perception while L1 continues to govern production. Finally, L2 settings are achieved for both perception and production.

What Gerald Neufeld terms the *phonological asymmetry* between perception and production may also be related to learners' practical communicative goals: learners who are more successful in perceptually detecting segmental errors than in avoiding producing them may, in effect, be 'deprioritizing linguistic levels during production that do not contribute directly to meaning' (Neufeld, 1988, 1997). Moreover, at the sociolinguistic level of overall 'accent', perception and production may be less interdependent, in that a learner's ability to perceive distinctive phonetic detail in the speech of others may not correlate well with the accuracy of their own phonetic production. Flege (1988) found that the ability of non-natives to judge degree of foreign-accentedness was not simply inversely correlated with their own foreign-accentedness.

While speech perception research has naturally focused on the acoustic–auditory modality, some studies in recent years have drawn attention to the role played by the visual modality. Hardison (1999) argues that the use of visual cues to speech crucially depends on the listener's perception of their information value. Sekiyama and Tohkura (1993) suggest that a listener does not attempt to integrate visual with auditory cues in a phonetic percept so long as the auditory information appears sufficient. Markham (1997: 136) similarly claims that the learner attends to visual information only when auditory information is degraded or absent. It seems likely that strategies for the integration of speech information from the various modalities are learned during the acquisition of the primary language, so that there may be language-specific biases in the choice and use of visual cues to speech. An indication of how these might be explored is given by MacEachern (2000), who claims a high degree of visual distinctiveness for the English lexicon, attributable to the segment inventory and the phonotactics of the language (MacEachern, 2000). Sekiyama and Tohkura (1993) suggest that Japanese listeners make comparatively little use of visual information. Auditory–visual integration strategies learned for the perception of L1 are then unlikely to serve the L2 listener equally well.

Attitudes, motivation and the sociocultural context

Language acquisition is intimately bound up with language socialisation – socialisation *to* language as well as socialisation *through* language (see, e.g., Ochs & Schieffelin, 1983). Phonological acquisition is patently a social as well as a linguistic undertaking, since accent is a defining factor in social identity (Scherer & Giles, 1979). It is also at the social level that language attitudes and most learning motivations are determined; how much the individual acquirer cares about minimising their foreign accent will depend on social convention and personal predispositions. Smit and Dalton-Puffer (1997) found that high intrinsic motivation towards good pronunciation in the foreign language correlated with low anxiety and a high level of 'self-efficacy' (i.e. confident self-awareness), while extrinsic motivation was relatively independent of these other factors. An acquirer who wants to integrate in the target language community is more likely to attain native like or near-native pronunciation; a positive attitude does seems to be a prerequisite for high attainment. Acquirers' attitude will, in part, depend on the attitudes of native listeners towards them as non-natives, which are, in part, culturally determined (Cunningham-Anderson, 1997; Eisenstein, 1983) and often include stereotypical judgements. Koster and Koet (1993) found that Dutch listeners who were teachers judged the English accents of Dutch speakers more harshly than native English listeners. The Dutch judges attached significantly more importance than the natives to the speakers' vowels – perhaps because they paid closer attention to obvious *markers* (in the sociolinguistic sense) of a speaker's non-nativeness.

The native judges in the study by Munro and Derwing (1999) achieved high agreement (significant at the 5% level) in their ratings of non-native speakers' comprehensibility and accentedness. Yet their findings suggest that while strength of foreign accent is inversely correlated with intelligibility and comprehensibility, a strong foreign accent may not be the direct cause of reduced intelligibility or comprehensibility.

While many well-motivated learners hope that minimising their foreign accent in L2 maximises their personal acceptability to native speakers, there is no conclusive evidence that this is the case. Moreover, global foreign accent subsumes various un-native like forms that, to varying degrees, intersect with the sociolinguistic speech markers and stigmatized forms of the native speakers of the L2. The native listener evidently assesses foreign accent on the basis of a range of – but not necessarily all – phonetic and phonological factors (Magen, 1998), as well as grammatical accuracy (see, e.g., Varonis & Gass, 1982) and culturally acquired expectations (Cunningham-Anderson, 1997).

Age

The critical period hypothesis

Repeated claims have been made for a 'critical period' for speech, usually located around puberty, after which the capacity to acquire native like speech is hypothetically impaired (Lamendella, 1977; Lenneberg, 1967; Patkowski, 1990; Penfield & Roberts, 1959; Scovel, 1969, 1988). In 'strong' versions of the critical period hypothesis (CPH), the hypothetical impairment of acquisition ability is attributed to organic changes (e.g. hemispheric specialisation or neurofunctional reorganisation) which are a normal part of maturation. The CPH receives common-sense support from the popular and undifferentiated belief that children are better able to learn new languages than adults; and there is indeed no shortage of evidence that the age at which an L2 is learned can be a factor in foreign accent (Piske *et al.*, 2001). However, while the CPH has generated considerable discussion, a body of research findings, and a fair measure of scientific support (see Singleton & Lengyel, 1995), the evidence for an irreversible neurobiological change that impedes post-primary language acquisition is inconclusive. There are some indications that primary and post-primary language activity are neurologically different (Hernandez & Bates, 1999), but this does not prove impaired potential (see also Flege *et al.*, 1997b).

Interaction with L1 development

There is *prima facie* evidence against the CPH. Learners who begin in early childhood may evidence a foreign accent in their eventual L2 (Flege & Liu, 2001; Flege *et al.*, 1995, 1997b; Piske & MacKay, 1999); while there is at the same time evidence that adults can – even if not many do – achieve native-sounding pronunciation of a language learned *after* any putative critical period (see Bongaerts, 1999; Bongaerts *et al.*1995, 1997; Ioup *et al.*, 1994). In research on the CPH it proves extremely difficult to disentangle the many factors that seem to contribute to determining ultimate attainment in L2 pronunciation, and the distinction is not consistently made between the neurobiological *potential* for acquisition (as understood in the CPH) and the opportunity or motivation to exploit such potential. As Singleton (1989: 266: 2001) puts it: 'The various age-related phenomena isolated by language acquisition research probably result from the interaction of a multiplicity of causes'.

One such interacting cause is the state of acquisition of the L1. In Flege's Speech Learning Model (SLM) L1 and L2 are seen as interacting through the phonetic categories established for position-sensitive allophones of vowels and consonants. The ability to learn speech remains intact through-out life but as the phonetic categories of L1 develop through childhood and into adolescence, they are progressively more likely to perceptually assimi-late the speech sounds of L2, thus impeding the formation of new, L2-specific categories (Flege, 1997; Flege & Liu, 2001; Flege *et al.*, 1995). Foreign accents, then, are not the result of lost or reduced speech learning abilities but a function of previous phonetic development. They may also reflect a greater proportion of use of L1 in comparison to L2. Among the Quichua–Spanish bilinguals examined by Guion *et al.* (2000) there was a correlation between the amount of L1 use and the strength of foreign accent in L2. Piske *et al.* (2001) also found that the amount of continued L1 use predicted foreign accent.

Onset versus immersion

School-age learners may have little opportunity for extensive exposure to L2, while adult migrants in the L2 society may have full exposure but receive little or no specific or systematic instruction. Because of probable differences in the availability and nature of (L2) input (Flege & Liu, 2001) it is important to distinguish between age of *onset* (i.e. when L2 is begun) and age of *immersion* in the L2 environment. While exposure to L2 might be thought an advantage for the immigrant, the duration of immersion in the L2 environment appears to be a poor predictor of foreign accent (Fathman, 1975; Johnson & Newport, 1989; Moyer, 1999). Data on migrants have mostly shown that it is the age of arrival in the new language environment, and not biological age or experience of immersion, which best correlates with strength of foreign accent (Flege, 1995). Flege *et al.* (1997a) examined the English of native speakers of German, Korean, Mandarin and Spanish who as adults had arrived and were residing in the USA, finding that adults *can* make progress in learning to produce vowels of L2, although – for reasons yet to be understood – some of these immigrants did markedly better than others. Yeni-Komshian *et al.* (1997) found that the older their Korean-speaking subjects were when they arrived to settle in the USA, the less accurately (in the judgement of native listeners) they pronounced English. However, Moyer's (1999) study underlines the importance of con-sidering age in relation to other influences, since age of exposure – whether through instruction or immersion – only proved a significant factor when taken in conjunction with personal motivation and the amount and type of instruction received.

Speech and socialisation

Attempts to explain the common observation that children are more 'successful' than adults in their L2 phonological acquisition tend to underestimate the role of socialisation in language acquisition (and *vice versa*): this is manifestly different as between, say, young children and middle-aged adults. As accent is a primary marker of social allegiance and distinction (e.g. Labov, 1972; Scherer & Giles, 1979); so a learner's phonetic development in the L2 can be seen as bound up, in principle, with the construction (or in the case of migrants possibly a *re*construction) of sociocultural identity. Lave and Wenger's (1991) notion of 'communities of practice' applies to our more or less continuous learning of new ways of speaking (in the broadest sense) as throughout life we engage in various different collective endeavours. In such learning what we acquire is not so much – or not only – new rules or codes, but new ways of acting and new kinds of participation. Phonological acquisition can thus be seen as a process of negotiating community membership.

According to Krashen (1985) an 'affective filter' from puberty onwards constrains the acquirer's attention to the L2 'input' upon which they must operate (though Krashen does not specify in any testable form the nature and operation of such a 'filter'). A learner with strong motivation to integrate in the L2 community would thus process the environmental language somewhat differently than a tourist who only wishes to 'get by'. McLaughlin (1985) has argued that the 'best' age for non-primary language acquisition, in terms of both rate of progress and final attainment, may be early adolescence. Though the evidence for this is not conclusive, it may be no coincidence that early adolescence is the age when, in anthropological terms, individuals are most actively defining their affiliations and social group memberships. This is achieved in part through speech forms: the phonology that older children acquire tends to be that of their peer-group rather than that of their parents (Baron-Cohen & Staunton, 1994). In later life perhaps only migration, with the pressure to construct a new social and cultural identity, entails a comparable degree of social self-definition. It is not only linguistic markers of affiliation that engage the language acquirer or learner with the social patterning of a community. Johnson *et al.* (1999) found that listeners' subjective, stereotypical expectations of a speaker play a role in speech perception at the phonetic level – and such expectations, too, may differ between L1 and L2.

Acquisition and learning strategies

The L2 learner has more – and different – learning experience than the L1 acquirer. Wingfield and Byrnes (1981) point out that young children know little about their own memory or about learning strategies; but taught a simple rehearsal strategy they can easily improve their scores on short-term memory tests. With age, learner's approaches to a task often become more sophisticated and more efficient. Their attentional resources may be differently deployed, whether in terms of simple alertness, 'set' (expectations concerning the information to be processed) or which elements of the stimulus to focus most closely on (Tomlin & Villa, 1994). Their cognitive styles may differ in such respects as degree of field dependence (Elliott, 1995). The prior acquisition of L1 provides the acquirer of L2 with, at the very least, experiential knowledge about how languages and language acquisition work; so for L2 the learner can draw upon – and for better or worse will apply – cognitive and processing strategies and tactics already developed.

The older L2 learner is also an older L1 acquirer. Singleton (1989) reviews clear evidence that all aspects of normal L1 development continue into adulthood – and some aspects at least continue through middle age. At the phonological level, the sharpening of phoneme perceptual categories continues well into the second decade of life (Hazan & Barrett, 2000). It is to be expected that the influence of L1 on L2 learning will differ correspondingly. For instance, for L2 as for L1 (Hazan & Barrett, 2000), adult learners may make use of more flexible perceptual strategies than children in their processing of speech stimuli that embody only limited acoustic cue information.

Also, older L2 learners may make greater use of metalinguistic knowledge and judgement: Pertz and Bever (1975) found that teenagers were better than children at conscious phonological judgements. Yet since the nature of metalinguistic knowledge seems to be related to a person's individual language background (Liouw & Poon, 1998), it seems likely that its application in L2 learning will reflect conceptions of L1.

Individual differences in 'aptitude', memory and experience

Research studies often show large individual differences in data on the acquisition of L2 speech (see e.g., Markham, 2000) – for instance in subjects' ability to perceive non-native phonetic contrasts and in the progress they make under training (Strange, 1992). While it is important to try and tease out the interacting influences of stimulus and task variables in individual subjects (Jenkins, 1979; Strange, 1992), there is often no way of knowing how far individual differences in performance may be due to individual linguistic histories and how far to other factors in acquirers' lives. It is therefore not easy to imagine how the popular notion of a 'good ear' for languages could be operationalised in research on L2 speech. There is some evidence that a complex variable corresponding to what is commonly termed *language aptitude,* and constituted by various cognitive abilities and strategies, can predict some of the attainments of L2 learners in the acquisition of syntax and lexis (Harley & Hart, 1997; Skehan, 1989); but the prediction does not extend to phonology. There is also little evidence that individual learners' progress and ultimate attainments are significantly constrained by neurobiological differences in awareness of, and control over the changing configurations of the articulators, or by differences in auditory sensitivities (Leather & James, 1991).

Theoretical frameworks

Phonological processes, representations and rules

The frameworks within which data on phonological acquisition have been analysed owe much to the models of theoretical linguistics. Earlier L2 research conformed largely to the 'structuralist' paradigm (see, e.g., Lado, 1957), with comparisons of L1 and L2 that were based on phonemics (e.g. Haugen, 1956; Weinreich, 1953). In later work analyses were based on distinctive features (e.g. Nemser, 1971, Weinreich, 1957) or feature hierarchies (Ritchie, 1968). Then, while theoretical views on the nature of phonological representations changed considerably in the decades following the publication of Chomsky and Halle's (1968) classic generative model, most acquisition research continued – until recently – to see the task of the learner of a language in terms of acquiring a set of rules based on the surface patterns of that language. Such a model, however, cannot convincingly account for the learner's formulation of rules that are not motivated by surface patterning or for the effects of universal constraints like markedness (Broselow *et al.*, 1998: 262).

The universal speech constraints to which all speaker–hearers are subject are addressed by Natural Phonology (NP), which sees the phonology of any language as 'the residue of a universal set of processes reflecting all the language-innocent phonetic limitations of the infant' (Donegan & Stampe, 1979: 127; Dressler, 1984). According to NP, in the acquisition of a primary language these processes are variously applied, some remaining operative while others are suppressed or remain only latent. In the acquisition of any subsequent language the learner must identify a new set of constraints upon the universal processes, and assign to certain of those processes correspondingly different roles in the L2 than in L1.

NP has the considerable advantage, as Major (1987) has pointed out, of accounting for diachronic, synchronic and child language phenomena in a single framework which applies to L2 acquisition as well. NP permits predictions on how acquirers will attempt to overcome their difficulties with certain sounds of L2 by reducing articulatory effort or reinforcing perceptual distinctions. They may, for example, in the acquisition of the L2 address the L1 'fortitions' that impose limits on the *'set of sounds that can be perceived by the learner as intended-by-the-speaker'* (Donegan, 1985: 26). Dziubalska-Kołaczyk (1987), for instance, was able with NP to give a better account of the nasalization effects of L1 Polish speakers in L2 English than a generative rule-typological analysis of the same phenomenon (Rubach, 1984).

One problem with NP, as Kershhofer-Puhalo (1997) points out, is that even if the implicational hierarchies of NP can predict that within a given sound class a process will be applied, they cannot predict *which* process a learner will choose on any particular occasion, since the implicational relations do not hold *between* processes (Donegan, 1978). Another problem with the NP hypothesis on language acquisition is that the natural processes postulated are often totally absent in small children or – like phonological palatalisation in Polish – appear only irregularly (Zborowska, 1997). The 'weak hypothesis' that is now more widely accepted is based on a self-organisation model and assumes an *interplay* between genetic programming and the selection and evaluation of postnatal information according to preferences for parallelism, frequency and regularity (Dressler, 1996; Karpf, 1991). The acquirer's sound system at any stage will then be the result of previous information processing experiences, so that detailed explanations need, in principle, to be sought in individual learners' 'full history' of exposure to a language. According to the Naturalness Differential Hypothesis (Schmid, 1997), the learners' L2 tends to retain L1 properties that are the outcome of a natural process, whereas elements of L1 that are 'marked' may well be abandoned. Examining the sound substitutions made by Spanish-speaking learners of Italian, Schmid was able to explain their foreign accent as the result of an interaction between L1-based representations and universal preferences implied by NP. This interaction could be seen both in the learners' phoneme inventory for L2, and in allophonic processes at the postlexical level.

Research in the NP framework has pointed up a need to distinguish between *rules* and *processes*. The goal of the adult L2 acquirer is to suppress the L1 processes that cause interference, while applying other processes that are present in L2 but absent from L1. If acquirers cannot master the processes required by L2 'naturally', they will be forced to learn them as *rules* – which they consequently would not apply in all and only the suitable contexts (Dziubalska-Kołaczyk, 1987; Zborowska, 1997).

Lexical Phonology (for an overview see Kaisse & Shaw, 1985) makes an essential distinction between rules that are fed by the morphology to derive a lexical representation, and *postlexical* rules that then apply – over larger domains as well as words. The lexical rules are comparable to quite traditional morphophonemic rules, while the postlexical rules rather resemble the processes of Natural Phonology or the allophonic processes of (pre-generative) phonemics. There is some evidence that postlexical rules are susceptible to transfer from L1 to L2, while the lexical rules are not (Broselow, 1987; Rubach, 1984; Young-Scholten, 1997a).

Early generative theory (e.g. Chomsky & Halle, 1968) conceived of a phonological representation as a linear organisation of segments, each of which consists in an unstructured aggregate of distinctive features. One of the motivations for revising the theory (see Dinnsen, 1997: 78) is that if the segment and the feature are inseparable, no phonological rule can operate on one without affecting the other. In more recent designs, therefore, features are specified independently of segments – hence the term *non-segmental phonology* – and organised into bundles that implement structure. Moreover, not all features are present – or, if present, specified – in all representations. Underspecification Theory (UT) acknowledges that some feature specifications are automatically determined during speech production processes by the redundancies inherent in the phonological system, and only specified in underlying representations those features which contrast segments (Steriade, 1987) – and possibly then only those that are marked (Archangeli, 1988). McAllister *et al.* (2000) propose, with data on duration, that an L2 contrastive category will be difficult to acquire if it is based on a phonetic feature not exploited in the L1. Weinberger (1997) is able with UT to explain the 'differential substitutions' made by L2 learners: for English /θ/ and /ð/. French speakers substituted /s/ and /z/, but Russian speakers substituted /t/ and /d/ – even though French and Russian both have /t, d, s, z/.

Archibald (1998) argues that abstract hierarchical representations are needed at various linguistic levels to account for learners' speech. Studies of L2 sound substitutions by Hancin-Bhatt and Bhatt (1992), Weinberger (1997) and Archibald (1997) assume a universal and hierarchical organisation of features. The theoretical models usually referred to under the rubric of *feature geometry* (see, e.g., Clements, 1985; Clements & Hume, 1995) follow autosegmental theory in representing features on a level independent of segments but propose hierarchical ordering among the various features so as to account for phonological processes in which a feature's scope is extended over more than one segment (as in assimilation) or reduced (as in neutralisation). Matthews (1997) investigates the implications of feature-geometric modelling for phonological acquisition. They argue that a child acquiring a primary language proceeds from a universal base, adding structure to a feature hierarchy in response to contrasts s/he detects in her/his input (Matthews, 1997: 227). When subsequently learning an L2, the range of possible new segmental representations she will be able to construct will be constrained by the feature geometry acquired during the acquisition of L1. Because this feature geometry imposes constraints on the acoustic–phonetic perceptual system, the learner will only be sensitive to those non-native contrasts that are distinguished along dimensions corresponding to features in the geometry; and non-native contrasts that would require new structure to be added to the feature geometry are perceived as instances of an existing category. This can be seen in the responses of Japanese learners to the English /l/ and /r/, which are distinguished by the presence or absence of the feature [lateral] under [approximant] in the feature geometry. Lacking this dependent feature in their L1, Japanese listeners will categorise both /l/ and /r/ as approximants, treating differences between them as within-category variation (Matthews, 1997).

The criteria by which the learner explores the compatibility of sound structures in L2 with those of L1 are not necessarily based on the units provided by phonological description (Leather & James, 1996: 287). For example, the feature [+/– voiced] cannot account for the phonetic detail of distinctions between /p, t, k/ and /b, d, g/ in the L2 French of German-speaking learners (Kohler, 1981). In Hancin-Bhatt's Feature Competition Model, the values of features are not binary but continuous, with features that are more widely distributed throughout a phoneme inventory having greater prominence. During the perception of an L2, features 'compete to be noticed' and 'those of higher prominence bias the perception of L2 segments, forcing specific L2–L1 pattern associations' (Hancin-Bhatt, 1994: 254).

Optimality theory and connectionism

As Natural Phonology postulates a universal set of natural processes, Optimality Theory (see Barlow & Gierut, 1999; Prince & Smolensky, 1993) claims there is a set of constraints shared by all speaker–hearers. These constraints are not all inviolable; some, which are violable, can serve to capture patterns which do not occur throughout the language, even if they are widespread. Optimality Theory (OT) sees the speaker as acting on their knowledge of the relative importance of the various constraints to achieve an *optimal* output – that is, one that violates only constraints that *may* be violated and is consistent with their rankings. These rankings hypothetically differ among individual child acquirers and from one language to another.

Hancin-Bhatt and Bhatt (1997) showed OT could give an explicit account of the interactions between transfer and developmental effects in L2 speech: the OT framework provided both an explanation of why Spanish- and Japanese-speaking learners had difficulty producing complex onsets and codas of English, and an account of how they resolved it. In another study, Broselow *et al.* (1998) explain why native speakers of Mandarin tend in their English productions to devoice final voiced obstruents and to prefer bisyllabic forms – neither tendency being obviously motivated by the phonology of L1 or L2. They point out in terms of OT that these tendencies result from universal markedness constraints that are 'masked' in the L1 grammar by other constraints that are more highly ranked

Recent theoretical work often shows the influence of _connectionism_, seeking solutions in the interplay of operations distributed between a number of simple components rather than in a single processor that must perform numerous complex consecutive operations (Goldsmith, 1993: 7). Mohanan, for instance, proposes principles with the status of neither rules nor constraints but _fields of attraction_ – consistent with a view of language as a 'self-organizing dynamical system' (Mohanan, 1993: 106, 111): comparisons may be made between such fields of attraction and the 'magnetic' forces exerted by phonetic prototypes in Kuhl's NLM. To model the speech development of a hypothetical Hindi speaker learning English, Hancin-Bhatt and Bhatt (1992) adopt a connectionist device assigning different 'weights' to the connections between nodes in a feature hierarchy. The connectionist conception of a phonology as a set of sub-systems working at different levels as an interconnected whole encourages a view in which L1 and L2 constitute a single phonological space within which the sound structures of both languages are defined and may developmentally interact (Flege, 1997; James, 1986; Leather & James, 1996). It thus promotes the notion that phonology 'emerges' from the interplay of speech perception and speech production (Plaut & Kello, 1999).

Other theoretical models

Contemporary concern in phonology with nonsegmental issues such as tone, intonation and word stress has given rise to a number of recent proposals that offer more differentiated analyses of L2 learning data (James, 1989). One such framework, Autosegmental Phonology (ASP), claims that speech cannot plausibly be represented only as a sequence of discrete segments, since articulatory activities (glottal, velar, labial, etc.) and the acoustic correlates of the perceptual cues to phonetic contrasts are not organised in simple and simultaneous left-to-right fashion. On these grounds ASP would, for example, represent segmental and tonal features on separate and autonomous _tiers_.

The phonetic realism of ASP is furthered in another approach that is explicitly based on articulation. While the primes proposed for phonological modelling have, in recent decades, mostly been abstract units of structure or organisation (such as the _phoneme_ or the _foot_) or parameters grounded in perception (such as the _distinctive feature_ or the _sonority scale_), Articulatory Phonology (AP) makes articulatory movements or 'gestures' central to phonological representation. In the proposals of Browman and Goldstein (1986, 1992), *gestures* are 'abstract characterisations of articulatory events' (which, in effect, classify articulatory movements), and a *gestural score* specifies the movements, in sequence, for an utterance. Also, AP does not presuppose an unrealistically linear relation between linguistic units and the process of speech production but shares with the laboratory approach of Ohala (Ohala, 1986; Ohala & Jaeger, 1986) a foundation in phonetically grounded representation. In addressing the L2 learner's interlingual processing AP thus has an advantage over other phonological models that do not provide phonetic representations of any kind. While AP does not yet seem to have had applications in L2 speech research or training, it is a possible advantage of AP that it bases phonological representations directly on articulation, for it is often far from clear how the 'outputs' of other phonologies should be interpreted in articulatory terms.

The pervasive influence of the computing paradigm in linguistic and communication theory is underlined by Fraser (1997a, b) in proposals for a Phenomenological Phonology (PP). As Fraser points out, all the standard approaches in phonology make the fundamental assumption that phonological ability is underlain by a system that is essentially computational (in that it involves processes which operate according to the formal properties of representations, rather than according to context or possible meanings. Phenomenological Phonology (PP) is motivated by the argument that the computational analogy does not work as an account of what human beings do with language (Fraser, 1997a), since phonology is 'something that is done by a whole person, not something that happens in a module of a computational system' (Fraser, 1997b: 89). The phonological representations of PP are not the *basis* of mental processes (as in standard phonology) but their *product*, and so more felicitously referred to as *descriptions*. What language users do, in the PP view, is not to transform representations into other representations, but to create *descriptions* on the basis of categories developed from experience and knowledge. PP suggests we may see the learner's *descriptions* as a product (like any other description) of the interaction between 'a phonetic Something', a context and 'a Subjective viewpoint' (Fraser, 1997a: 93). The particular interest of PP for the study of language learning is that, while not denying the value of rules in analysing language, PP would discourage us from hypothesising rules or processes that attempt simply to derive a learner's pronunciation at any developmental stage from the pronunciation of native speakers (or linguists).

Levels of structure

Many of the recent developments in phonological theory look beyond the segment – to the syllable, the mora, the word and aspects of prosody.

There is some evidence from speech recognition research that the syllable could be the primary unit of lexical access (e.g. Dupoux & Mehler, 1990; Mehler & Christophe, 1992); and some L2 studies have seen the syllable as more central to the learner's processing than either the segment or the distinctive feature (Benson, 1988; Brière, 1968; Carlisle, 1999; Eckman & Iverson, 1994; Greenberg, 1983; Hodne, 1985; Kløve, 1992; Major, 1996a; Sato, 1984; Selinker, 1972; Tarone, 1972, 1980; Trammell, 1999; Weinberger, 1987). Accounts of the ways in which learners commonly assimilate words in L2 to the syllable structure of L1 follow, according to Archibald (1998), two major approaches: the *structural*, as illustrated by Broselow (1988), and the *typological*, as in the work of Eckman (1991). Broselow and Finer (1991) have argued that the way learners deal with syllables in the L2 can be understood in relation to Minimal Sonority Distances (Selkirk, 1984), while Eckman and Iverson (1994) argue that the same data can be explained in terms of typological markedness and the Sonority Dispersion Principle (Clements, 1990). However Teixeira-Rebello's (1997) analysis of the production of initial /s/ clusters in English by Portuguese-speaking learners yields only equivocal outcomes: the data do not fulfil universal-based predictions of difficulties in respect of cluster length, sonority hierarchy and strength relations.

Renewed interest in the syllable has called forth new discussion of the notion of ambisyllabicity and the criteria for syllabification (Trammell, 1999). Related to the syllable because it captures cross-linguistically the differential behaviour of certain syllable types is the mora (Archibald, 1998: 194). From a study of Cantonese speakers learning Norwegian, Kløve (1992) suggests that a moraic analysis offers better insight into the developing syllable template than, for instance, C and V analysis. Again, Broselow and Park (1995), observing that Korean learners of English add an extra vowel to some English words but not others, invoke the theory of the mora to explain this.

Sonority

The most important principle known to govern constraints on syllable structure, *sonority*, also appears to correlate with the patterning of acquisition. Phonetically, sonority has traditionally been understood as a property of a segment that could be best (though not perfectly) determined by instrumental means, through measurements of acoustic intensity (Ladefoged, 1975). Structurally, sonority is most often defined (e.g. Selkirk, 1984) in terms of the probability of co-occurrence in syllable structure of a hierarchy of segment types (e.g. from most to least sonorous: vowels, glides, liquids, nasals, fricatives, plosives). In studies of the acquisition of German syllable structure by Spanish speakers Tropf (1983, 1987) found that the degree of sonority of segments correlated well with the order of their acquisition. Archibald (1997, 1998) has proposed a model of hierarchical segment structure which (following Rice, 1992) treats sonority as a phonological construct derived from the complexity of segmental representation, and from which phonetic consequences can be drawn: the more structure a segment has under a *sonorant voice* node in a feature geometry, the greater its sonority. It remains to be seen how well this 'derived' sonority might correlate with order and / or difficulty of acquisition. Dziubalska-Kołaczyk (1997) analysing how informants with 13 different L1s segmented German, proposed that it is universal phonotactic preferences – which are of a much more general nature than syllable structure constraints – that define sonority distances between segments.

Prosody

Prosody is now comparatively well represented in research on L2 phonological acquisition (e.g. Archibald, 1992a, 1992b, 1994, 1997; Broselow *et al.*, 1987; Grosser, 1989; Harley *et al.*, 1995; Husby, 1997; Kaltenbacher, 1997; Mairs, 1989; Markham & Nagano-Madsen, 1996). There is good evidence of the importance of prosody in L2 speech (e.g. Gibson, 1997; Holden & Hogan, 1993). But it is also important, as Beckman and Edwards (1992: 360) point out, to understand prosody as more than just a cover term for a subset of the phonetic parameters of F0, duration and intensity that constitute some kind of autonomous structural level. 'Segmental' and 'suprasegmental' phenomena are mutually produced in that, for instance, higher-level phonological structures interact with segments to determine the timing patterns of articulatory gestures (Fant, 1987). It may, therefore, be more fruitful to think of prosody as the structural framework of syllables, feet, intonational phrases, etc., upon which the substantive features (segments and tones) are 'embroidered'. Explaining differential substitutions in Dutch speakers' English, James (1986) shows how the properties of a segment are determined by the totality of its suprasegmental context, with influence from the prosodic structure of L1. This suggests that the phonological grammar of L2 should therefore include at least three interrelated tiers of sound organization: the lexical (involving phonological words), the prosodic and the rhythmic (James, 1988).

In an experiment by Holden and Hogan (1993) English utterances that were given Russian intonation patterns were judged as by English listeners in emotionally negative terms. While attitude categories (such as *enthusiastic*, *impatient*, or *polite*) may be broadly applicable across some cultural boundaries, their prosodic correlates may patently differ. Listeners' perceptions of speakers' attitudes appear to be a function both of prosodic 'universals' – such as the 'involvement' implied by a wide intonational range, or the 'dominance' of a male's low pitch range (Cruttenden, 1986; Holden & Hogan, 1993; Ohala, 1984) – and patterning that is language-specific. Thus, Russian learners of English may prosodically misinterpret English 'politeness' for 'enthusiasm', and 'enthusiasm' for 'impatience' and 'skepticism' (Gibson, 1997).

Addressing aspects of the learner's L2 speech in discourse, Pennington (1992) has proposed the construct of *phonological fluency*, defined as 'sustained oral production in a natural context', and measured in terms of parameters such as speech rate (in syllables per second), length of runs (i.e. the average number of syllables between pauses), stalls and pauses, and so on (see Hieke, 1985). Such fluency parameters can be seen as the result of the *proceduralisation* of production (Dechert & Raupach, 1987).

Transfer from learned sound systems

The deviant forms in the L2 learner's productions have for a long time been explained, at least in part, in terms of the influence of the L1: *crosslinguistic influence* (Sharwood-Smith & Kellerman, 1986) or (negative) *transfer*. While the projection of L1 sound structure upon the L2 certainly seems to be one of the 'strategic solutions' available to learners (James, 1986, 1988; see also Tarone, 1978), the scope of the widely-used term *transfer* is not always made clear. Hammarberg (1988b, 1990) suggests that transfer can be understood as (1) a *strategy* – in terms of how the learner might go about resolving a phonological problem in L2; (2) a *process* – by which something is transferred; and (3) a *solution* – in the sense of the product of the strategy applied and the process which ensued Hammarberg (1990: 198–9).

The Contrastive Analysis Hypothesis (CAH) revolves around the claim that points of structural difference between L2 and L1 will give rise to difficulties (Lado, 1957). In the, 1960s research into the influence of the L1 in the acquisition of L2 speech was most often centred around a *contrastive analysis* of the phonologies of L1 and L2: this was expected to explain the kinds of errors learners made and the different degrees of difficulty they experienced with elements of the L2 sound system (for references see Leather & James, 1996; Major, 1998a; Major & Kim, 1999). One of the problems with the CAH is that it is not clear whether all differences between L2 and L1 are to be treated alike, or whether some differences are only critical if of a certain magnitude. Wode (1983) therefore proposed the notion of *critical similarity* (between L1 and L2) to determine what criteria need to be met for transfer from L1 to L2 to take place. Reflecting more recent concern with the longitudinal course of learning, the Similarity Differential Rate Hypothesis (Major & Kim, 1999) predicts that dissimilar phenomena will be more quickly acquired than similar phenomena, even if the absolute rates of acquisition differ.

It has long been observed (Polivanov, 1932; Trubetzkoy, 1958) that learners tend to map what they hear in L2 onto the sound system of their L1. Yet it is still far from fully understood exactly when and why they do. Flege's SLM (Flege, 1997: 82) postulates a number of factors that combine to determine whether a learner will discern (and so be able to act upon) the difference between an L2 sound and the most similar but non-identical sound in L1. Two factors relate to the phonetic systems of L1 and L2: the perceived (dis)similarity of an L2 sound in L2 from the closest sound in L1; and the nature of the means by which phonetic contrasts are realised in the L2. (Two other factors which are not language-specific are the state of development of the learner's L1 at the time the learning of L2 begins, and how much experience they have in the L2.) Hallé *et al.* (1999) argue from cross-language perception data that listeners may – at least some of the time – attend to detailed articulatory–phonetic properties of L1 and L2 phones, rather than base their perceptions only on the phonological contrasts of the two languages.

Cross-linguistic influence in phonology is clearly not limited to matching and substitutions between the segmental inventories of L2 and L1. It extends to phonotactics: learners from different L1 backgrounds use different strategies for consonant cluster simplification (Abrahamsson, 1997). It happens at the level of stress and syllabification (Trammell, 1999); and rhythmic structure as such (Kaltenbacher, 1997). It may not necessarily be confined within a single level of sound structure.

Kaltenbacher (1997) noted in the performance of Japanese learners of German the tendency (presumably due to their L1) to realise stress in terms of syllable duration, as might be predicted by the (somewhat controversial) theory of the *mora* as an abstract unit of isochrony. In studies of lexical tone learning by non-tonal (English and Dutch) speakers, Leather (1987, 1997) hypothesised a possible influence *across* structural levels: the ability of non-tonal learners to classify in non-random fashion tone stimuli based on minimal lexical pairs can be explained by reference to their experience of voice pitch patterning in intonation in their L1. Finally, cross-linguistic influence or transfer may not always be simple. Archibald (1997, 1998) shows with a range of data from language change, language typology and L2 and L1 acquisition that the reason why the acquisition of consonant clusters causes problems (e.g. for Korean L1 speakers) is not simply because particular clusters are not allowed in the learner's L1 but because the acquisition of clusters correlates with the acquisition of liquids: a complex interaction of the properties of the segmental inventory determine the feature geometry of a segment, which in turn determines which allowable sequences of segments are possible.

Other influences

It is now widely acknowledged that the learner's deviant phonological forms in L2 cannot be fully explained through simple comparison of the sound structures of L2 and L1 (see, e.g., Eliasson, 1984; James, 1989; Major, 1998a). The CAH fails signally to account for the developmental patterning of learning over time: Major and Kim (1999) point out in their review that the CAH does not have anything to say about order or rate of acquisition. Transfer theory in its various guises has failed to derive full explanations of learners' L2 performance from a phonological comparison of L1 and L2 as complete and closed systems. It is clear that the learner's processing strategies and longitudinal development need to be examined in relation also to universal typological preferences and the particular sociolinguistic, stylistic and discoursal contexts that inform the individual's learning environment (see James, 1996; Leather & James, 1996).

Orthography

L2 phonological development may interact with other linguistic levels of representation such as (for alphabetical systems) the orthographic (Giannini & Costamagna, 1997, García Lecumberri & Gallardo, this volume, Chapter 6). Young-Scholten (1997b) found an effect of orthographic exposure to L2 words during their learning and subsequent testing: English-speaking beginning learners of Polish who were confronted with a more complex syllable structure than in their L1 tended to retain rather than omit consonants in their pronunciations of words they saw in written form.

Markedness

Markedness Theory (see Major, 1996b; Moravcsik & Wirth, 1985) is one approach to constraining the range of potential structures that were generated by an over-abundance of binary features in the classic Chomsky and Halle (1968) design. Markedness expresses our intuitions in respect of likelihood, with 'marked' implying more, and 'unmarked' less likely states of affairs respectively (Mohanan, 1993: 61). In phonological theory markedness has been interpreted in terms of (1) frequency – _marked_ simply meaning less frequent – and (2) implicational hierarchies (for instance, voiced stops being _marked_ in relation to voiceless stops, since all languages have voiceless stops but not all have voiced stops as well). Major and Kim (1999: note 1) point out that the frequency definition is the less restrictive, since frequency in the total set of the world's languages does not necessarily entail presence in any particular language under consideration.

Eckman's (1977) Markedness Differential Hypothesis aims to explain some of an L2 learner's difficulties in terms of markedness differentials between L1 and L2: if implicationally related structures occur in L1 and L2, the L2 structure will be easier to acquire if it is *un*marked in relation to L1. There is some evidence that when the L1 processes fall within the category of unmarked tendencies transfer is a dominant strategy (see Cebrian, 1997, and citations therein). However, there are L2 speech data for which markedness relations cannot provide an adequate explanation (Hammarberg, 1988a) and, as Major and Kim (1999) found, the MDH does not longitudinally predict ease or difficulty of acquisition in terms of either (1) stages or (2) rate of learning. The study by Cichoki *et al.* (1999) of the acquisition of French consonants by Cantonese speakers only partly corroborates the MDH. Several of the patterns which the MDH incorrectly predicted – markedness 'reversals'- have been observed in primary language acquisition (and may be the result of an interplay between markedness and other developmental dynamics).

It appears, then, that markedness relations between languages apparently cannot predict all of the learner's difficulties. More differentiated proposals consider, as possible constraints on the transferability of forms from L1, such further factors as the relative integrity of the (prosodic) word (Cebrian, 1997), and markedness relations *within* the L2 as well as between L1 and L2 – as addressed by Carlisle's Intralingual Markedness Hypothesis (Carlisle, 1988, 2000). The phonetics exigencies of producing and perceiving particular speech sounds may also prevail over possible structural constraints imposed by markedness differentials. Thus, Stockman and Pluut (1999) examined the ranking of errors for consonants in four syllable position conditions in relation to the frequency distribution of errors reflecting the relative difficulty of the L1/L2 contrast. Anderson (1987) had found that these generally supported the Markedness Differential Hypothesis. However, Anderson's findings were not corroborated, possibly because of the phonetic-level difficulties of perception and production. Major and Kim (1999) hypothesise that the L2 learner is affected by the compound influence of typological markedness and the degree of phonetic similarity between L2 and L1.

Universals

Johansson (1973) found in the Swedish pronunciation of speakers of nine different L1s that 'the same vowels which appear as phonemes in children's speech and which are the most basic in the languages of the world, are also reproduced with the fewest phonetic deviations'. As Young-Scholten (1994, 1997b: 351) puts it, adult learners of an L2 'do not create rogue phonologies', but show evidence in their evolving L2 of 'direct access to the phonological principles of Universal Grammar'. Irrespective of the Universal Grammar associated particularly with Chomsky (e.g. 1986), there is evidence that universal (in the sense of language-independent) constraints on all language forms apply to a learner's evolving L2. This is the prediction of the Interlanguage Structural Conformity Hypothesis (SCH) proposed by Eckman (1991) and corroborated by data like those of Major (1996a) on the voicing of obstruents which reflected the markedness principles that are observed in primary language acquisition. Carlisle's studies (Carlisle, 1999, 2000) tested and failed to falsify the SCH, indicating that the implicational universals that obtain among the world's languages also obtain in L2 phonology, with more marked structures being more frequently modified than less marked ones. Archibald (1994), studying the acquisition of English metrical parameters by speakers of Polish, Hungarian and Spanish, found that both the representations (metrical structure) and processes (learning principles) evidenced in the L2 resembled those of native (L1) acquirers.

Since the CAH proved insufficient to account at all fully for the learner's performance in L2 there has been growing attention to the possible interplay of transfer – by definition specific to the L1–L2 combination – with universal constraints on language structures and processes. In the final stop devoicing behaviour of the adult Japanese students of English studied by Sekiya and Jo (1997) there was evident interaction between universals and L1 transfer.

Major's (1987) Ontogeny Model claims that the role of transfer processes in a learner's evolving L2 generally decreases over time, while the role of developmental processes (that reflect universal grammar) first increases then decreases. At the same time, on a moment-to-moment level the relative contributions of transfer and universal influences may vary in accordance with non-linguistic factors like the learner's attention to the language task in hand. Hancin-Bhatt (1997) formalises this in a 'dual-route' model: the learner may parse an L2 structure via (1) the L1-mediated route or (2) the direct route. This 'dual route' model is claimed to account for the variation that may be observed when a particular learner exhibits greater transfer in a low-attention than in a high-attention condition. Attention in this view may be the basis for what Paradis (1993) refers to as an 'activation threshold'.

Conclusion

L2 speech is a function of various local, specific factors – linguistic, social and psychological – and universal phonological constraints. To understand the course of phonological acquisition in a multilingual society, therefore, we must take account not only of formal features of the language(s) concerned but also the individual acquirer's circumstances (for instance, their age and its social consequences, their motivations and their prior linguistic experience). Subject to the influences which bear upon their individual life in society, the acquirer's perception and production of the new language will interrelate (in sometimes complex ways) in the process of developing the necessary phonetic representations and building phonological structure.

There are two clear implications for research. First, as phonological acquisition is gradual, only longitudinal designs can bring to light developmental processes – some of which may span long time frames (Leather & James, 1996; Major, 1998a). Revealing differences between individual learners at various stages in their progress, longitudinal studies can also identify developmental patterns that are obscured in group-averaged data (see, e.g., Leather, 1997). Second, while the disparate cultures of phonetic investigation (publishing in acoustic journals) and phonological analysis (in linguistics journals) may still be reluctant to interact, there are now increasingly examples of L2 speech research that address both phonetic and phonological concerns (e.g. Archibald, 1998; Riney & Flege, 1998). Recent symposia (e.g. James & Leather, 2000; Leather & James, 1997) and anthologies (e.g. James & Leather, 1997; Leather, 1999; Major, 1998b) constitute further evidence that the two – complementary – perspectives can be fruitfully integrated.

References

Abrahamsson, N. (1997) Vowel 'epenthesis' in Spanish and Spaniards' L2 production: Puzzle or evidence for natural phonology? In J. Leather and A. James (eds) *New Sounds 97: Proceedings of the Third International Symposium on the Acquisition of Second-Language Speech* (pp. 8–17). Klagenfurt: University of Klagenfurt.

Anderson, J. (1987) The Markedness Differential Hypothesis and syllable structure differences. In G. Youp and S. Weinberger (eds) *Interlanguage Phonology* (pp. 279–291). Rowley, MA: Newbury House.

Archangeli, D. (1988). Aspects of underspecification theory. *Phonology* 5, 183-, 207.

Archibald, J. (1992a) Adult abilities in L2 speech: Evidence from stress. In J. Leather and A. James (eds) New Sounds 92: *Proceedings of the, 1992 Amsterdam Symposium on the Acquisition of Second-Language Speech* (pp. 1–17). Amsterdam: University of Amsterdam.

Archibald, J. (1992b) Transfer of L1 parameter settings: Some empirical evidence from Polish metrics. *Canadian Journal of Linguistics* 37, 301–39.

Archibald, J. (1994) A formal model of learning L2 prosodic phonology. *Second Language Research* 10, 215–40.

Archibald, J. (1995) Phonological competence. In J. Archibald (ed.) *Phonological Acquisition and Phonological Theory* (pp. xiii-xxi). Hillsdale, NJ: Lawrence Erlbaum.

Archibald, J. (1997) The relationship between L2 segment and syllable structure. In J. Leather and A. James (eds) *New Sounds 97: Proceedings of the Third International Symposium on the Acquisition of Second-Language Speech* (pp.17–25). Klagenfurt: University of Klagenfurt.

Archibald, J. (1998) Second language phonology, phonetics, and typology. *Studies in Second Language Acquisition* 20, 189–211.

Barlow, J.A. and Gierut, J.A. (1999) Optimality theory in phonological acquisition. *Journal of Speech, Language, and Hearing Research* 42, 1482–98.

Baron-Cohen, S. and Staunton, R. (1994) Do children with autism acquire the phonology of their peers? An examination of group identification through the window of bilingualism. *First Language* 14, 241–8.

Beckman, M.E. and Edwards, J. (1992) Intonational categories and the articulatory control of duration. In Y. Tohkura, E. Vatikiotis-Bateson and Y. Sagisaka (eds) *Speech Perception, Production and Linguistic Structure* (pp. 359–75). Tokyo: Ohmsha.

Benson, B. (1988) Universal preference for the open syllable as an independent process in interlanguage phonology. *Language Learning* 38, 221–42.

Bongaerts, T. (1999) Ultimate attainment in L2 pronunciation: The case of very advanced late L2 learners. In D. Birdsong (ed.) *Second Language Acquisition and the Critical Period Hypothesis* (pp. 133–60). Mahwah, NJ: Lawrence Erlbaum.

Bongaerts, T., Summeren, C., Plancken B. and Schils E. (1995) Can late learners attain a native accent in a foreign language? In D. Singleton and Z. Lengyel (eds) *The Age Factor in Second Language Acquisition* (pp. 51–66). Clevedon: Multilingual Matters.

Bongaerts, T., Summeren, C., Plancken B. and Schils E. (1997) Age and ultimate attainment in the pronunciation of a foreign language. *Studies in Second Language Acquisition* 19, 447–65.

Bradlow, A., Pisoni, D., Yamada, R. and Tokhura, Y. (1996) Training Japanese listeners to identify English /r/ and /l/: IV. Some effects of perceptual learning on speech production. *Journal of the Acoustical Society of America* 101, 2299–310.

Brière, E. (1968) *A Psycholinguistic Study of Phonological Interference*. The Hague: Mouton.

Broselow, E. (1987) An investigation of transfer in second language phonology. In G. Ioup and S. Weinberger (eds) *Interlanguage Phonology: The Acquisition of a Second Language Sound System* (pp. 261–78). Cambridge, MA: Newbury House.

Broselow, E. (1988) Prosodic phonology and the acquisition of a second language. In S. Flynn and W. O'Neill (eds) *Linguistic Theory in Second Language Acquisition* (pp. 295–308). Dordrecht: Kluwer.

Broselow, E. and Finer, D. (1991) Parameter setting in second language phonology and syntax. *Second Language Research* 7, 35–59.

Broselow, E. and Park, H.-B. (1995) Mora conservation in second language prosody. In J. Archibald (ed.) *Phonological Acquisition and Phonological Theory* (pp. 151–68). Hillsdale, NJ: Erlbaum.

Broselow, E., Chen, S.-I. and Wang, C. (1998) The emergence of the unmarked in second language phonology. *Studies in Second Language Acquisition* 20, 261–80.

Broselow, E., Hurtig, R.R. and Ringen, C. (1987) The perception of second language prosody. In G. Ioup and S. Weinberger (eds) *Interlanguage Phonology: The Acquisition of a Second Language Sound System* (pp. 350–61). Rowley, MA: Newbury House.

Browman, C.P. and Goldstein, L.M. (1986) Towards an articulatory phonology. *Phonology Yearbook* 3, 219–52.

Browman, C.P. and Goldstein, L.M. (1992) Articulatory phonology: An overview. *Phonetica* 49, 155–80.

Carlisle, R.S. (1988) The effect of markedness on epenthesis in Spanish/English interlanguage phonology. *Issues and Developments in English and Applied Linguistics* 3, 15–23.

Carlisle, R.S. (1999) The modification of onsets in a markedness relationship: Testing the interlanguage structural conformity hypothesis. In J.H. Leather (ed.) *Phonological Issues in Language Learning* (pp. 59–94). Malden, MA: Blackwell.

Carlisle, R.S. (2000) The acquisition of two and three member onsets: Time III of a longitudinal study. In A. James and J. Leather (eds) *New Sounds, 2000: Proceedings of the Fourth International Symposium on the Acquisition of Second-Language Speech, University of Amsterdam, September, 2000* (pp. 42–47). Klagenfurt: University of Klagenfurt.

Cebrian, J. (1997) Markedness and phrasal domain in the transferability of voicing rules in Catalan–English interlanguage. In J. Leather and A. James (eds) *New Sounds 97: Proceedings of the Third International Symposium on the Acquisition of Second-Language Speech* (pp. 47–54). Klagenfurt: University of Klagenfurt.

Chomsky, N. (1986) *Knowledge of Language: Its Nature, Origin, and Use.* New York: Praeger.

Chomsky, N. and Halle, M. (1968) *The Sound Pattern of English.* New York: Harper and Row.

Cichoki, W., House, A.B., Kinloch, A.M. and Lister, A.C. (1999) Cantonese speakers and the acquisition of French consonants. In J.H. Leather (ed.) *Phonological Issues in Language Learning* (pp. 95–122). Malden, MA: Blackwell.

Clements, G.N. (1985) On the geometry of phonological features. *Phonology Yearbook* 2, 225–52.

Clements, G.N. (1990) The role of the sonority cycle in core syllabification. In J. Kingston and M. Beckman (eds) *Papers in Laboratory Phonology I* (pp. 283–333). Cambridge, UK: Cambridge University Press.

Clements, G.N. and Hume, E.V. (1995) The internal organization of speech sounds. In J. Goldsmith (ed.) *The Handbook of Phonological Theory* (pp. 245–306). New York: Blackwell.

Cruttenden, A. (1986) *Intonation.* Cambridge, UK: Cambridge University Press.

Cunningham-Anderson, U. (1997) Native speaker reactions to non-native speech. In A. James and J. Leather (eds) *Second-language Speech: Structure and process* (pp. 133–44). Berlin: Mouton de Gruyter.

Dechert, H. and Raupach, M. (1987) Prosodic patterns of proceduralized speech in second and first language narratives. In A. James and J. Leather (eds) *Sound Patterns in Second Language Acquisition* (pp. 81–102). Dordrecht: Foris.

Dinnsen, D.A. (1997) Nonsegmental phonologies. In M. J. Ball and R. Kent (eds) *The New Phonologies: Developments in Clinical Linguistics* (pp. 77–126). San Diego: Singular.

Donegan, P. (1978) On the Natural Phonology of vowels. *Ohio State University Working Papers in Linguistics.* Columbus, OH: Ohio State University.

Donegan, P. (1985) How learnable is phonology? In W.U. Dressler and L. Tonelli (eds) *Natural Phonology from Eisenstadt* (pp. 19–31). Padova: CLESP.

Donegan, P. and Stampe, D. (1979) The study of Natural Phonology. In D. Dinnsen (ed.) *Current Approaches to Phonological Theory* (pp. 126–73). Bloomington: Indiana University Press.

Dressler, W.U. (1984) Explaining natural phonology. *Phonology Yearbook* 1, 29–51.

Dressler, W.U. (1996) Principles of naturalness in phonology and across components. In B. Hurch and R. Rhodes (eds) *Natural Phonology: The State of the Art* (pp. 41–51). Berlin: Mouton.

Dupoux, E. and Mehler, J. (1990) Monitoring the lexicon with normal and compressed speech: Frequency effects and the prelexical code. *Journal of Memory and Language* 29, 316–35.

Dziubalska-Kołaczyk, K. (1987) Phonological rule typology and second language acquisition. In A. James and J. Leather (eds) *Sound Patterns in Second Language Acquisition* (pp. 193–206). Dordrecht: Foris.

Dziubalska-Kołaczyk, K. (1997) Syllabification' in first and second language. In J. Leather and A. James (eds) *New Sounds 97: Proceedings of the Third International Symposium on the Acquisition of Second-Language Speech* (pp. 68–78). Klagenfurt: University of Klagenfurt.

Eckman, F.R. (1977) Markedness and the contrastive analysis hypothesis. *Language Learning* 27, 315–30.

Eckman, F.R. (1991) The structural conformity hypothesis and the acquisition of consonant clusters in the interlanguage of ESL learners. *Studies in Second Language Acquisition* 13, 23–41.

Eckman, F.R. and Iverson, G.K. (1994). Pronunciation difficulties in ESL: Coda consonants in English interlanguage. In M. Yavas (ed.) *First and Second Language Phonology* (pp. 251–65). San Diego: Singular.

Edwards, J. (1994) *Multilingualism*. London: Routledge.

Eisenstein, M. (1983) Native reactions to non-native speech: A review of empirical research. *Studies in Second Language Acquisition* 5, 160–76.

Eliasson, S. (1984) Toward a theory of contrastive phonology. In S. Eliasson (ed.) *Theoretical Issues in Contrastive Phonology* (pp. 7–26). Heidelberg: Groos.

Elliott, A. (1995) Field independence/dependence, hemispheric specialization, and attitude in relation to pronunciation accuracy in Spanish as a foreign language. *Modern Language Journal* 79, 356–71.

Fant, G. (1987) Interactive phenomena in speech production. *Proceedings of the 11th International Congress of Phonetic Sciences* (pp. 376–81). Tallinn: Estonian Academy of Sciences.

Fathman, A. (1975) The relationship between age and second language productive ability. *Language Learning* 25, 245–53.

Ferguson, C.A. (1979) Phonology as an individual access system: Some data from language acquisition. In C.J. Fillmore, D. Kempler and W-S.Y. Wang (eds) *Individual Differences in Language Ability and Language Behavior*. New York: Academic Press.

Flege, J.E. (1988) Factors affecting degree of perceived foreign accent in English sentences. *Journal of the Acoustical Society of America* 84, 70–9.

Flege, J.E. (1995) Second-language speech learning: Findings, and problems. In W. Strange (ed.) *Speech Perception and Linguistic Experience: Theoretical and Methodological Issues* (pp. 233–73). Timonium, MD: York Press.

Flege, J.E. (1997) The role of category formation in second-language speech learning. In J. Leather and A. James (eds) *New Sounds 97: Proceedings of the Third International Symposium on the Acquisition of Second-Language Speech* (pp. 79–88). Klagenfurt: University of Klagenfurt.

Flege, J.E. and Liu, S. (2001) The effect of experience on adults' acquisition of a second language. *Studies in Second Language Acquisition* 23, 527–52.

Flege, J.E., Bohn, O.-S. and Jang, S. (1997a) The production and perception of English vowels by native speakers of German, Korean, Mandarin and Spanish. *Journal of Phonetics* 25, 437–70.

Flege, J.E., Frieda, A.M. and Nozawa, T. (1997b) Amount of native-language (L1) use affects the pronunciation of an L2. *Journal of Phonetics* 25, 169–86.

Flege, J.E., Munro, M.J. and MacKay, I.R.A. (1995) Factors affecting strength of perceived foreign accent in a second language. *Journal of the Acoustical Society of America* 97, 3125–34.

Fraser, H. (1997a) Phenomenological phonology and second language pronunciation. In J. Leather and A. James (eds) *New Sounds 97: Proceedings of the Third International Symposium on the Acquisition of Second-Language Speech* (pp. 89–95). Klagenfurt: University of Klagenfurt.

Fraser, H. (1997b) Phonology without tiers: Why the phonetic representation is not derived from the phonological representation. *Language Sciences*, 19, 101–37.

García Lecumberri, M.L. and Gallardo, F. (this volume) English FL sounds in school learners of different ages.

Giannini, S. and Costamagna, L. (1997) Language learning strategies in interlanguage phonology of Italian as L2: The acquisition of consonant length. In J. Leather and A. James (eds) *New Sounds 97: Proceedings of the Third International Symposium on the Acquisition of Second-Language Speech* (pp. 96–102). Klagenfurt: University of Klagenfurt.

Gibson, M. (1997) Non-native perception and production of English attitudinal intonation. In J. Leather and A. James (eds) *New Sounds 97: Proceedings of the Third International Symposium on the Acquisition of Second-Language Speech* (pp. 103–8). Klagenfurt: University of Klagenfurt.

Goldsmith J. (ed.) (1993) *The Last Phonological Rule*. Chicago: University of Chicago Press.

Greenberg, C. (1983) Syllable structure in second language acquisition. *CUNY Forum* (City University of New York) 9, 47–64.

Grosser, W. (1989) Akzentuierung und Intonation im englischen Erwerb österreichischer Lerner. *Salzburger Studien zur Anglistik und Amerikanistik*, Vol. 9. Salzburg: University of Salzburg.

Guion, S.G., Flege, J.E. and Loftin, J.D. (2000) The effect of L1 use on pronunciation in Quichua–Spanish bilinguals. *Journal of Phonetics* 28, 27–42.

Gussenhoven, C. and Rietveld, T. (1998) On the speaker-dependence of the perceived prominence of F peaks. *Journal of Phonetics* 26, 371–80.

Hallé, P., Best, C.T. and Levitt, A. (1999) Phonetic versus phonological influences on French listeners' perception of American English appointments. *Journal of Phonetics* 27, 281–306.

Hammarberg, B. (1988a) Acquisition of phonology. *Annual Review of Applied Linguistics* 9, 23–41.

Hammarberg, B. (1988b) *Studien zur Phonologie des Zweitspracherwerbs*. Stockholm: Almqvist and Wiksell International.

Hammarberg, B. (1990) Conditions on transfer in phonology. In J. Leather and A. James (eds) *New Sounds 90: Proceedings of the, 1990 Amsterdam Symposium on the Acquisition of Second-Language Speech* (pp. 198–215). Amsterdam: University of Amsterdam.

Hancin-Bhatt, B. (1994) Segment transfer: A consequence of a dynamic system. *Second Language Research* 10, 241–69.

Hancin-Bhatt, B. (1997) Extended full transfer/full access in L2 sound patterns. In J. Leather and A. James (eds) *New Sounds 97: Proceedings of the Third International Symposium on the Acquisition of Second-Language Speech* (pp. 109–17). Klagenfurt: University of Klagenfurt.

Hancin-Bhatt, B. and Bhatt, R. (1992) On the nature of L1 filter and cross-language transfer effects. In J. Leather and A. James (eds) *New Sounds 92: Proceedings of the, 1992 Amsterdam Symposium on the Acquisition of Second-Language Speech* (pp. 18–28). University of Amsterdam.

Hancin-Bhatt, B. and Bhatt R. (1997) Optimal L2 syllables. Interactions of transfer and developmental factors. *Studies in Second Language Acquisition,* 19, 331–78.

Hardison, D. (1999) Bimodal speech perception by native and nonnative speakers of English: Factors affecting the McGurk effect. In J.H. Leather (ed.) *Phonological Issues in Language Learning* (pp. 213–84). Malden, MA: Blackwell.

Harley, B. and Hart, D. (1997) Language aptitude and second language proficiency in classroom learners of different starting ages. *Studies in Second Language Acquisition* 19, 379–400.

Harley, B., Howard, J. and Hart, D. (1995) Second language processing at different ages: Do younger learners pay more attention to prosodic cues to sentence structure? *Language Learning* 45, 43–71.

Haugen, E. (1956) *Bilingualism in the Americas: A Bibliography and Research Guide.* Baltimore, MD: American Dialect Society.

Hazan, V. and Barrett, S. (2000) The development of phonemic categorization in children aged 6–12. *Journal of Phonetics* 28, 377–96.

Hernandez, A.E. and Bates, E. (1999). Bilingualism and the brain. In *MIT Encyclopedia of Cognitive Sciences* (pp. 80–1). Cambridge, MA: MIT Press.

Hieke, A.E. (1985) A componential approach to oral fluency evaluation. *Modern Language Journal* 69, 135–42.

Hodne, B. (1985) Yet another look at interlanguage phonology: The modification of English syllable structure by native speakers of Polish. *Language Learning* 35, 405–22.

Holden, K. and Hogan, J. (1993) The emotive impact of foreign intonation: An experiment in switching English and Russian intonation. *Language and Speech* 36, 67–88.

Holm, A. and Dodd, B. (1999) A longitudinal study of the phonological development of two Cantonese–English bilingual children. *Applied Psycholinguistics,* 20, 349–76.

Husby, O. (1997) Rhythmical features in Norwegian spoken by adult Vietnamese. In J. Leather and A. James (eds) *New Sounds 97: Proceedings of the Third International Symposium on the Acquisition of Second-Language Speech* (pp. 144–53). Klagenfurt: University of Klagenfurt.

Ioup G., Boustagui, E., El Tigi, E. and Moselle, M. (1994) A case of successful adult second language acquisition in a naturalistic environment. *Studies in Second Language Acquisition* 16, 73–98.

James, A.R. (1986) *Suprasegmental Phonology and Segmental Form.* Tübingen: Niemeyer.

James, A.R. (1988) *The Acquisition of a Second Language Phonology.* Tübingen: Narr.

James, A.R. (1989) Linguistic theory and second language phonological learning: A perspective and some proposals. *Applied Linguistics* 10, 367–81.

James, A.R. (1996) Second language phonology. In P. Jordens and J. Lalleman (eds) *Investigating Second Language Acquisition* (pp. 293–3, 20). Berlin: Mouton de Gruyter.

Age and the Acquisition of English as a Foreign Language
James, A.R. and Leather, J.H. (eds) (1997) *Second-Language Speech: Structure and Process*. Berlin: Mouton de Gruyter.

James, A.R. and Leather, J.H. (2000) *New Sounds, 2000: Proceedings of the Fourth International Symposium on the Acquisition of Second-Language Speech*, University of Amsterdam, September, 2000. Klagenfurt: University of Klagenfurt.

Jenkins, J.J. (1979) Four points to remember: A tetrahedral model of memory experiments. In L.S. Cermak and F.I.M. Craik (eds) *Levels of Processing in Human Memory* (pp. 429–46). Hillsdale, NJ: Erlbaum.

Johansson, S. (1973) *Immigrant Swedish Phonology*. Lund, Sweden: Gleerup.

Johnson, J. and Newport, E. (1989) Critical period effects in second language learning: The influence of maturational state on the acquisition of English as a second language. *Cognitive Psychology* 21, 60–99.

Johnson, K., Strand, E.A. and D'Imperio, M. (1999) Auditory-visual integration of talker gender in vowel perception. *Journal of Phonetics* 27, 359–84.

Kachru, B.B. (1996) The paradigms of marginality. *World Englishes* 15, 241–55.

Kaisse, E.M. and Shaw, A. (1985) On the theory of lexical phonology. *Phonology Yearbook* 2, 1–30.

Kaltenbacher, E. (1997) German speech rhythm in L2 acquisition. In J. Leather and A. James (eds) *New Sounds 97: Proceedings of the Third International Symposium on the Acquisition of Second-Language Speech* (pp. 158–66). Klagenfurt: University of Klagenfurt.

Karpf, A. (1991) Universal Grammar needs organisation. *Folia Linguistica* 25, 339–60.

Kerschhofer-Puhalo, N. (1997) Vowel substitutions in German as a foreign language. In J. Leather and A. James (eds) *New Sounds 97: Proceedings of the Third International Symposium on the Acquisition of Second-Language Speech* (pp. 167–75). Klagenfurt: University of Klagenfurt.

Kløve, M. (1992) Principles and constraints in SLA phonology. In J. Leather and A. James (eds) *New Sounds 92: Proceedings of the, 1992 Amsterdam Symposium on the Acquisition of Second-Language Speech* (pp. 113–21). Amsterdam: University of Amsterdam.

Kohler, K. (1981) Contrastive phonology and the acquisition of phonetic skills. *Phonetica* 38, 213–26.

Koster, C.C. and Koet, T. (1993) The evaluation of accent in the English of Dutchmen. *Language Learning* 43, 69–92.

Krashen, S. (1985) *The Input Hypothesis: Issues and Implications*. New York: Longman.

Kuhl, P.K. (1992) Speech prototypes: Studies on the nature, function, ontogeny and phylogeny of the 'centers' of speech categories. In Y. Tohkura, E. Vatikiotis-Bateson and Y. Sagisaka (eds) *Speech Perception, Production and Linguistic Structure* (pp. 239–64). Tokyo: Ohmsa.

Kuhl, P.K. (1993) An examination of the 'perceptual magnet' effect. *Journal of the Acoustical Society of America* 93, 2423.

Labov, W. (1972) *Sociolinguistic Patterns*. Philadelphia: University of Pennsylvania Press.

Ladefoged, P. (1975) *A Course in Phonetics*. New York: Harcourt.

Lado, R. (1957) *Linguistics across Cultures*. Ann Arbor: University of Michigan Press.

Laeufer, C. (1997) Towards a typology of bilingual phonological systems. In A. James and J. Leather (eds) *Second-Language Speech: Structure and Process* (pp. 325–42). Berlin: Mouton de Gruyter.

Lamendella, J. (1977) General principles of neurofunctional organization and their manifestation in primary and non-primary language acquisition. *Language Learning* 27, 155–96.

Lave, J. and Wenger, E. (1991). *Situated Learning: Legitimate Peripheral Participation.* Cambridge: Cambridge University Press.

Leather, J.H. (1983) Speaker normalization in perception of lexical tone. *Journal of Phonetics* 11, 373–82.

Leather, J.H. (1987) F pattern inference in the perceptual acquisition of second-language tone. In A. James and J. Leather (eds) *Sound Patterns in Second Language Acquisition* (pp. 59–80). Dordrecht: Foris.

Leather, J.H. (1997) Interrelation of perceptual and productive learning in the initial acquisition of second-language tone. In A. James and J. Leather (eds) *Second-Language Speech: Structure and Process* (pp. 75–101). Berlin: Mouton de Gruyter.

Leather, J.H. (ed.) (1999) *Phonological Issues in Language Learning.* Malden, MA: Blackwell.

Leather, J.H. (2002) Modelling the acquisition of speech in a 'multilingual' society An ecological approach. In C. Kramsch (ed.) *Language Acquisition, Language Socialization* (pp. 47–67). London: Continuum Press.

Leather, J.H. and James, A.R. (1991) The acquisition of second language speech. *Studies in Second Language Acquisition* 13, 305–41.

Leather, J.H. and James, A.R. (1996) Second language speech. In W. C. Ritchie and Tej K. Bhatia (eds) *Handbook of Second Language Acquisition* (pp. 269–316). New York: Academic Press.

Leather, J.H. and James, A.R. (eds) (1997) *New Sounds 97: Proceedings of the Third International Symposium on the Acquisition of Second-Language Speech.* Klagenfurt: University of Klagenfurt.

Leather, J.H. and Van Dam, J. (2003) Towards an ecology of language acquisition. In J.H. Leather and J. Van Dam (eds) *Ecology of Language Acquisition* (pp. 261–78). Dordrecht: Kluwer Academic.

Lenneberg, E. (1967) *Biological Foundations of Language.* New York: Wiley.

Liouw, S.J.R. and Poon, K.K.L. (1998) Phonological awareness in multilingual Chinese children. *Applied Psycholinguistics*, 19, 339–62.

Logan, J.S., Lively, S.E. and Pisoni, D.B. (1991) Training Japanese listeners to identify /r/ and /l/: A first report. *Journal of the Acoustical society of America* 89, 874–86.

MacEachern, M.R. (2000) On the visual distinctiveness of words in the English lexicon. *Journal of Phonetics* 28, 367–76.

Magen, H.S. (1998) The perception of foreign-accented speech. *Journal of Phonetics* 26, 381–400.

Mairs, J.L. (1989) Stress assignment in interlanguage phonology: An analysis of the stress system of Spanish speakers learning English. In S.M. Gass and J. Schachter (eds) *Linguistic Perspectives on Second Language Acquisition* (pp. 260–83). Cambridge: Cambridge University Press.

Major, R. (1987) The natural phonology of second language acquisition. In A. James and J. Leather (ed.) *Sound Patterns in Second Language Acquisition* (pp. 207–24). Dordrecht: Foris.

Major, R. (1996a) Markedness and second language acquisition of consonant clusters. In R. Preston and R. Bayley (eds) *Variation Linguistics and Second Language Acquisition* (pp. 75–96). Amsterdam: Benjamins.

Major, R. (1996b) Markedness universals. *Studies in Second Language Acquisition* 18, 69–90.

Major, R. (1998a) Interlanguage phonetics and phonology: An introduction. *Studies in Second Language Acquisition* 20, 131–7.

Major, R. (ed.) (1998b) *Studies in Second Language Acquisition* 20 (special issue on interlanguage phonetics and phonology).

Major, R. and Kim, E. (1999) The similarity differential rate hypothesis. In J.H. Leather (ed.) *Phonological Issues in Language Learning* (pp. 151–84). Malden, MA: Blackwell.

Markham, D. (1997) Phonetic imitation, accent, and the learner. *Travaux de l'Institut de Linguistique de Lund 33*. Lund: Lund University Press.

Markham, D. (2000) Individual differences in the acquisition of second-language speech. In A. James and J. Leather (eds) *New Sounds 2000: Proceedings of the 4th International Symposium on the Acquisition of Second-language Speech* (pp. 236–39). Klagenfurt: University of Klagenfurt.

Markham, D. and Nagano-Madsen, Y. (1996) Input modality effects in foreign accent. In H.T. Bunnell and W. Idsardi (eds) *International Conference on Spoken Language Processing '96* (Vol. 3, pp. 1473–6). Philadelphia: Applied Science and Engineering Laboratories, Alfred E. duPont Institute.

Matthews, J. (1997) The influence of pronunciation training on the perception of second-language contrasts. In J. Leather and A. James (eds) *New Sounds 97: Proceedings of the Third International Symposium on the Acquisition of Second-Language Speech* (pp. 223–9). Klagenfurt: University of Klagenfurt.

McAllister, R., Flege, J.E. and Piske, T. (2000) The feature hypothesis applied to the acquisition of Swedish quantity. In A. James and J. Leather (eds) *New Sounds, 2000: Proceedings of the Fourth International Symposium on the Acquisition of Second-Language Speech*. Klagenfurt: University of Klagenfurt.

McLaughlin, Barry (1985) *Second Language Acquisition in Childhood. Volume 2: School-Age Children*. Hillsdale, NJ: Lawrence Erlbaum.

Mehler, J. and Christophe, A. (1992) Speech processing and segmentation in Romance languages. In Y. Tohkura, E. Vatikiotis-Bateson and Y. Sagisaka (eds) *Speech Perception, Production and Linguistic Structure* (pp. 221–38). Tokyo: Ohmsha.

Mohanan, K. (1993) Fields of attraction in phonology. In J. Goldsmith (1993) (ed.) *The Last Phonological Rule* (pp. 61–116). Chicago: University of Chicago Press.

Moravcsik, E.A. and Wirth, J.A. (1985) Markedness: An overview. In F. R. Ekman, E. A. Moravcsik and J.A. Wirth (eds) *Markedness* (pp. 1–11). New York: Plenum Press.

Moyer, A. (1999) Ultimate attainment in L2 phonology: The critical factors of age, motivation, and instruction. *Studies in Second Language Acquisition* 21, 81–108.

Munro, M.J. and Derwing T.M. (1999) Foreign accent, comprehensibility, and intelligibility in the speech of second-language learners. In J. Leather (ed.) *Phonological Issues in Language Learning* (pp. 285–310). Malden, MA: Blackwell.

Nakai, S. (1997) Perceptual factors in the acquisition of FL vowels. In J. Leather and A. James (eds) *New Sounds 97: Proceedings of the Third International Symposium on the Acquisition of Second-Language Speech* (pp. 249–56). Klagenfurt: University of Klagenfurt.

Nayar, P.B. (1994) Whose English is it? *TESL-EJ* 1, (1), F1.

Nemser, W. (1971) *An Experimental Study of Phonological Interference in the English of Hungarians*. Bloomington, IN: Indiana University Press.

Neufeld, G. (1988) Phonological asymmetry in second-language learning and performance. *Language Learning* 38, 531–60.

Neufeld, G. (1997) Phonological asymmetry in L2 perception and production. In J. Leather and A. James (eds) *New Sounds 97: Proceedings of the Third International Symposium on the Acquisition of Second-Language Speech* (pp. 257–61). Klagenfurt: University of Klagenfurt.

Ochs, E. and Schieffelin, B. (1983) *Acquiring Conversational Competence*. London: Routledge.

Ohala, J.J. (1984) An ethological perspective on common cross-language utilization of F0 of voice. *Phonetica* 41, 1–16.

Ohala, J.J. (1986) Consumer's guide to evidence in phonology. *Phonology Yearbook* 3, 3–26.

Ohala, J.J. and Jaeger, J. (eds) (1986) *Experimental Phonology*. Orlando, FL: Academic Press.

Paradis, M. (1993) Linguistic, psycholinguistic and neurolinguistic aspects of the 'interference' in bilingual speakers: The Activation Threshold Hypothesis. *International Journal of Psycholinguistics* 9: 133–45.

Patkowski, M.S. (1990) Age and accent in a second language: A reply to James Emil Flege. *Applied Linguistics* 11, 73–89.

Penfield, W. and Roberts, L. (1959) *Speech and Brain Mechanisms*. Princeton, NJ: Princeton University Press.

Pennington, M. (1992) Discourse factors related to L2 phonological proficiency: An exploratory study. In J. Leather and A. James (ed.) *New Sounds 92: Proceedings of the, 1992 Amsterdam Symposium on the Acquisition of Second-Language Speech* (pp. 137–55). Amsterdam: University of Amsterdam.

Pertz, D. and Bever, T. (1975) Sensitivity to phonological universals in children and adults. *Language* 51, 149–62.

Phillipson, R. and Skutnabb-Kangas, T. (1996) English only worldwide or language ecology? *TESOL Quarterly* 30: 429–52.

Piske, T. and MacKay, I.R.A. (1999) Age and L1 use effects on degree of foreign accent in English. In J. J. Ohala, Y. Hasegawa, M. Ohala, D. Granville and A.C. Bailey (eds) *Proceedings of the 14th International Congree of Phonetic Sciences* (pp. 1433–6). Berkeley: University of California.

Piske T., MacKay, I.R.A. and Flege, J.E. (2001) Factors affecting degree of foreign accent in an L2: A review. *Journal of Phonetics* 29, 191–215.

Plaut, D.C. and Kello, C.T. (1999) The emergence of phonology from the interplay of speech comprehension and production: A distributed connectionist approach. In B. MacWhinney (ed.) *The Emergence of Language* (pp. 381–415). Mahwah, NJ: Erlbaum.

Polivanov, E. (1932) The subjective nature of the perception of sounds. In A. Leontev (ed.) *E. D. Polivanov: Selected Writings* (D. Armstrong, trans.) (pp. 223–37). The Hague: Mouton. (Original work published, 1932.)

Prince, A.S. and Smolensky, P. (1993) Optimality theory: Constraint interaction in generative grammar (*Technical Report No. 2*). Piscataway, NJ: Cognitive Sciences Center, Rutgers University.

Repp, B. (1984) Categorical perception: Issues, methods, findings. In N. J. Lass (ed.) *Speech and Language: Advances in Basic Research and Practice* (Vol. 10). New York: Academic Press.

Rice, K. (1992) On deriving sonority: A structural account of sonority relationships. *Phonology* 9, 61–99.

Riney, T.J. and Flege, J.E. (1998) Changes over time in global foreign accent and liquid identifiability and accuracy. *Studies in Second Language Acquisition*, 20, 213–43.

Ritchie, W. (1968) On the explanation of phonic interference. *Language Learning* 18, 183–97.

Rochet, B. (1995) Perception and production of L2 speech sounds by adults. In W. Strange (ed.) *Speech Perception and Linguistic Experience: Theoretical and Methodological Issues* (pp. 379–410). Timonium, MD: York Press.

Romaine, S. (1996) Bilingualism. In W.C. Ritchie and Tej K. Bhatia (eds) *Handbook of Second Language Acquisition* (pp. 571–604) New York: Academic Press.

Rubach, J. (1984) Rule typology and phonological interference. In S. Eliasson (ed.) *Theoretical Issues in Contrastive Phonology* (pp. 37–50). Heidelberg: Groos.

Sato, C. (1984) Phonological processes in second language acquisition: Another look at interlanguage syllable structure. *Language Learning* 34, 43–57.

Scherer, K.R. and Giles, H. (eds) (1979) *Social Markers in Speech*. Cambridge: Cambridge University Press.

Schmid, S. (1997) Phonological processes in Spanish–Italian interlanguages. In J. Leather and A. James (eds) *New Sounds 97: Proceedings of the Third International Symposium on the Acquisition of Second-Language Speech* (pp. 286–93). Klagenfurt: University of Klagenfurt.

Schnitzer, M. (1990) Critique of linguistic knowledge. *Language and Communication* 10, 95–126.

Schnitzer, M. and Krasinksi, E. (1994) The development of segmental phonological production in a bilingual child. *Journal of Child Language* 21, 585–622.

Schnitzer, M. and Krasinksi, E. (1996) The development of segmental phonological production in a bilingual child: A contrasting second case. *Journal of Child Language* 23, 547–71.

Scovel, T. (1969) Foreign accents, language acquisition and cerebral dominance. *Language Learning*, 19, 245–53.

Scovel, T. (1988) *A Time to Speak: A Psycholinguistic Inquiry into the Critical Period for Human Speech*. New York: Newbury House.

Sekiya, Y. and Jo, T. (1997) The interlanguage syllable structure of intermediate Japanese learners of English: Influence of markedness and L1 acquisition processes. In J. Leather and A. James (eds) *New Sounds 97: Proceedings of the Third International Symposium on the Acquisition of Second-Language Speech* (pp. 294–304). Klagenfurt: University of Klagenfurt.

Sekiyama, K. and Tohkura, Y. (1993) Inter-language differences in the influence of visual cues in speech perception. *Journal of Phonetics* 21, 427–44.

Selinker, L. (1972) Interlanguage. *International Review of Applied Linguistics* 10, 209–31.

Selkirk, E. (1984) On the major class features and syllable theory. In M. Aronoff and R. Oehrle (eds) *Language Sound Structure* (pp. 107–36). Cambridge, MA: MIT Press.

Sharwood-Smith, M. and Kellerman, E. (1986) Crosslinguistic influence in second language acquisition: An introduction. In E. Kellerman and M. Sharwood-Smith (eds) *Crosslinguistic Influence and Second Language Acquisition* (pp. 1–9). Oxford: Pergamon Press.

Singleton, D. (1989) *Language Acquisition: The Age Factor*. Clevedon: Multilingual Matters.

Singleton, D. (2001) Age and second language acquisition. *Annual Review of Applied Linguistics* 21, 77–89.

Singleton, D. and Lengyel, Z. (eds) (1995) *The Age Factor in Second Language Acquisition: A Critical Look at the Critical Period Hypothesis*. Clevedon: Multilingual Matters.

Skehan, P. (1989) *Individual Differences in Second-Language Learning.* London: Edward Arnold.

Smit, U. and Dalton-Puffer, C. (1997) EFL pronunciation learning and motivation research. In J. Leather and A. James (eds) *New Sounds 97: Proceedings of the Third International Symposium on the Acquisition of Second-Language Speech* (pp. 321–30). Klagenfurt: University of Klagenfurt.

Steriade, D. (1987) Redundant values. *Chicago Linguistic Society* 23, 339–62.

Stockman, I.J. and Pluut, E. (1999) Segment composition as a factor in the syllabification errors of second-language speakers. In J.H. Leather (ed.). *Phonological Issues in Language Learning* (pp. 185–212). Malden, MA: Blackwell.

Strange, W. (1992) Learning non-native phoneme contrasts: Interactions among subject, stimulus and task variables. In Y. Tohkura, E. Vatikiotis-Bateson and Y. Sagisaka (eds) *Speech Perception, Production and Linguistic Structure* (pp., 197–219). Tokyo: Ohmsha.

Strange, W. (ed.) (1995) *Speech Perception and Linguistic Experience: Theoretical and Methodological Issues.* Timonium, MD: York Press.

Tarone, E. (1972) A suggested unit for interlingual identification in pronunciation. *TESOL Quarterly* 6, 325–31.

Tarone, E. (1978) The phonology of interlanguage. In J. Richards (ed.) *Understanding Second and Foreign Language Learning* (pp. 15–33). Rowley, MA: Newbury House.

Tarone, E. (1980) Some influences on the syllable structure of interlanguage phonology. *International Review of Applied Linguistics* 16, 143–63.

Texeira-Rebello, J. (1997) The acquisition of English initial / s / clusters by Brazilian EFL learners. In J. Leather and A. James (eds) *New Sounds 97: Proceedings of the 3rd International Symposium on the Acquisition of Second-language Speech* (pp. 336–42). Klagenfurt: University of Klagenfurt.

Tomlin, R. and Villa, E. (1994) Attention in cognitive science and SLA. *Studies in Second Language Acquisition* 16, 185–204.

Trammell, R. L. (1999) English ambisyllabic consonants and half-closed syllables in language teaching. In J.H. Leather (ed.). *Phonological Issues in Language Learning.* (pp. 311–56). Malden, MA: Blackwell.

Tropf, H. (1983) Variation in der Phonologie des ungesteuerten Zweitspracherwerbs (Bd 1, Bd 2). Unpublished doctoral dissertation, University of Heidelberg.

Tropf, H. (1987) Sonority as a variability factor in second language phonology. In A. James and J. Leather (eds) *Sound Patterns in Second Language Acquisition* (pp. 173–91). Dordrecht: Foris.

Trubetzkoy, N. (1958) Grundzüge der Phonologie (Travaux du cercle linguistique de Prague 7). Göttingen: Vandenhoek and Ruprecht. (Original work published, 1939.)

Varonis, E.M. and Gass, S. (1982) The comprehensibility of nonnative speech. *Studies in Second Language Acquisition* 4, 114–36.

Watson, I. (1991) Phonological processing in two languages. In E. Bialystok (ed.) *Language Processing in Bilinguals* (pp. 25–48) Cambridge: Cambridge University Press.

Weinberger, S. (1987) The influence of linguistic context on syllable simplification. In G. Ioup and S. Weinberger (eds) *Interlanguage Phonology: The Acquisition of a Second Language Sound System* (pp. 401–17). Rowley, MA: Newbury House.

Weinberger, S. (1997) Minimal segments in second language phonology. In A. James and J. Leather (eds) *Second-Language Speech: Structure and Process* (pp. 263–311). Berlin: Mouton de Gruyter.

Weinreich, U. (1953) *Languages in Contact*. The Hague: Mouton.

Weinreich, U. (1957) On the description of phonic interference. *Word* 13, 1–11.

Wingfield, A. and Byrnes, D. (1981) *The Psychology of Human Memory*. New York: Academic Press.

Wode, H. (1983) Phonology in L2 acquisition. In H. Wode (ed.) *Papers on Language Acquisition, Language Learning and Language Teaching* (pp.175–87). Heidelberg: Gross.

Yamada, R., Tokhura, Y., Bradlow, A. and Pisoni, D. (1996). Does training in speech perception modify speech production? *Proceedings of the International Conference on Spoken Language Processing 1996*. Piscataway, NJ: IEEE.

Yeni-Komshian, G., Flege, J.E. and Liu, H. (1997) Pronunciation proficiency in L1 and L2 among Korean–English bilinguals: The effect of age of arrival in the US. *Journal of the Acoustical Society of America*, 92, S102A.

Young-Scholten, M. (1994) On positive evidence and ultimate attainment in L2 phonology. *Second Language Research* 10, 193–214.

Young-Scholten, M. (1997a) Interlanguage and postlexical transfer. In A. James and J. Leather (eds) *Second-Language Speech: Structure and Process* (pp. 187–210). Berlin: Mouton de Gruyter.

Young-Scholten, M. (1997b) Second-language syllable simplification: Deviant development or deviant input? In J. Leather and A. James (eds) *New Sounds 97: Proceedings of the Third International Symposium on the Acquisition of Second-Language Speech* (pp. 351–60). Klagenfurt: University of Klagenfurt.

Zborowska, J. (1997) The acquisition of phonostylistics in a second language: Innateness or self-organization. In J. Leather and A. James (eds) *New Sounds 97: Proceedings of the Third International Symposium on the Acquisition of Second-Language Speech* (pp. 361–9). Klagenfurt: University of Klagenfurt.

Chapter 3

Know your Grammar: What the Knowledge of Syntax and Morphology in an L2 Reveals about the Critical Period for Second/ Foreign Language Acquisition

STEFKA H. MARINOVA-TODD

> It is a truth universally acknowledged, that a single man in possession
> of a good fortune, must be in want of a wife. (Jane Austen, *Pride and Prejudice*)

If Jane Austen were to consider current sentiments about age and ultimate attainment in a foreign language, she might write: 'It is a truth *still* universally acknowledged, that a young child exposed to a foreign language, must master it to native-like proficiency'. As a keen observer of human character and a clever critic of Georgian society, Jane Austen was expressing a common opinion of her time that she believed to be questionable, if not absurd. Likewise, in our times, a commonly expressed view that young children learn foreign languages (FL)[1] quickly and easily is questioned and debated by researchers and the factors affecting the process of second language acquisition (SLA) are far more complex than commonly recognised. Age of arrival in the second language (L2) environment has proven to be merely one among many factors that mutually contribute to determine the ultimate attainment in an L2. Recent research points to the importance of factors other than age of arrival and emphasises the necessity of focusing carefully on developing foreign language programmes that provide the best environment in which learners of all ages can efficiently utilise their cognitive abilities in order to achieve the highest possible proficiency in their L2s.

The time during childhood when learning a language is possible, usually achieved relatively easily and with great degree of success, is referred to as *the critical period for language acquisition*. Once this period is over, usually postulated to be sometime during puberty, it is assumed that a person who begins to learn an L2 will be unable to achieve native-like competence and performance in it. The idea of a critical period was first introduced by Penfield and Roberts (1959) and later further developed by Lenneberg (1967) who examined the neurological development of the brain and proposed that, during puberty, the human brain becomes lateralised (i.e. the left and right hemispheres assume different functions) and the centre for language-processing becomes localized in the left hemisphere (at least in the majority of right-handed individuals). Thus, he proposed that a critical period for language acquisition exists and, once the functions of the brain are lateralised, the mastering of a language becomes more difficult and less successful. As research accumulated in the area, Lamandella (1977) argued that Lenneberg's conclusion regarding the critical period was too strong and introduced the term *sensitive period*[2] to represent the time when language acquisition is most efficient, usually during childhood, but not impossible after the period of heightened sensitivity.

Today it is generally agreed that a critical period does exist for first language (L1) acquisition but the hypothesis is not as uniformly accepted as applicable to SLA. Research evidence has been diverse and the debate regarding the existence of a critical period for SLA is as heated today as ever. Studies examining different aspects of linguistic competence have provided evidence in support of either side of the debate but no conclusive argument has been reached yet!

When considering separately the time required for L2 learning and the ultimate success achieved in the L2, some researchers suggested a compromise conclusion that *older is faster but younger is better* (Krashen *et al.*, 1979). Larsen-Freeman and Long's (1991) review of the literature revealed that L2 learning over an extended period of time benefited only very young children who were able to achieve native-like proficiency in all areas of language (phonology, syntax and semantics). However, at the initial stages of L2 acquisition, older learners were at an advantage in rate of acquisition but only in limited aspects.

In this chapter we will review relevant research in the field of L2 acquisition revealing that the degree of ultimate success in an L2 does not solely depend on biological factors, such as age. Instead, it will be argued that L2 acquisition is a more complex phenomenon determined by many social, psychological and experiential factors. Knowledge of syntax and morphology (which together comprise grammar) has been determined as one of the more reliable measures of L2 proficiency. We will examine studies in support of the critical period hypothesis showing that older learners achieve limited success in L2 grammar. However, we will also review studies that have emphasised the greater variability in the ultimate attainment of older learners, some of whom achieve native-like proficiency in the L2. Finally, it will be argued that not the age of the learner but the availability of and access to good L2 input and instruction must be considered in producing best outcomes in the L2.

The Importance of Grammar

In the last 20 years numerous studies have been conducted that examined the age differences in SLA in various areas of linguistic competence (e.g. in phonology: Bongaerts, 1999; Bongaerts *et al.*, 1995; Flege, 1992, 1995, 1999; in morphosyntax: Birdsong, 1992, 1999; Johnson & Newport, 1989; in semantics: Liu *et al.*, 1992; in pragmatics: House, 1996, just to mention some of the more recent and significant contributions). The outcomes showed various degrees of L2 success for older learners, fuelling the ongoing heated debate about the critical period hypothesis (CPH).

In a recent critical review of the CPH literature, Marinova-Todd *et al.* (2000) observed that, despite general perceptions that older learners are slower L2 learners, the research has long revealed that, in fact, older learners are faster in the process of L2 acquisition, especially at the initial stages (Snow, 1987: Snow & Hoefnagel-Höhle, 1977, 1978). As a result, the task taken by CPH supporters has been to show that older L2 learners, despite accelerated rates of language acquisition, achieve significantly poorer ultimate attainment in the L2 relative to younger learners. Many factors have been proposed to explain the inability of most post-pubertal learners to achieve native-like competence in the L2 (for a review see Birdsong, 1999).

The basic assumption of a biologically determined critical period is that some essential capacities of younger children are not available to adult learners. One such capacity is the learner's access to universal grammar (UG), that is, the innate system of linguistic categories, mechanisms and constraints shared by all human languages (Chomsky, 1995). The often expressed notion is that 'if there is a critical period for L1, then L2 grammars should fall outside of the range of grammars permitted by UG, whereas if there is no critical period, then these grammars should be UG constrained' (Eubank & Gregg, 1999: 79). In other words, if a person is exposed to an L2 before the critical period has ended, he or she will have 'access' to the UG and thus will be more likely to acquire the L2 similarly to an L1; but if an L2 is introduced after the completion of the critical period, the learner will not have access to UG, and thus, the L2 will be learned differently from the L1.

While many studies have been conducted, the results have been inconclusive. There is evidence in support of the 'no-access hypothesis', which states that adult L2 grammars are not constrained by UG (Bley-Vroman, 1989; Schachter, 1989), and evidence in support of the 'full-access hypothesis', namely, that adult L2 grammars are fully constrained by UG (Schwartz & Sprouse, 1996). Somewhere in the middle falls a relatively recent study (White & Genesee, 1996) in which the authors argue that despite observed age of acquisition effects (75% of their young learners achieved near-native proficiency in the L2, while only 33% of the older learners reached that level of ultimate attainment), the poorer performance of the older L2 learners was not due to a decline in access to UG, since a third of them achieved near-native proficiency in the L2. As a result, the 'partial-access hypothesis' was suggested which argued that *some* aspects of UG remain available to older L2 learners, thus leading to greater variability in the ultimate attainment of an L2 (Epstein *et al.*, 1996).

Since morphosyntax has been the area in which older learners seem to excel the most, especially when compared to pronunciation (Flege, 1999; Oyama, 1976; Patkowski, 1990; Scovel, 1988), many studies using various methods have tested the learners' proficiency in L2 grammar. The review of the literature presented here is an attempt to provide an updated and focused account of the research to date which provides evidence in support and against the CPH, especially in the area of grammar or, more specifically, morphosyntactic L2 knowledge. I will conclude with a discussion of the relevance of the CPH to the practice of foreign language learning and teaching.

Doomed to Failure, So Why Bother?

There seems to be abundant research as well as anecdotal evidence showing that, typically, older learners, usually the ones exposed to the L2 after puberty, tend to be poorer language 'achievers' than children. This accepted fact is used by many as evidence to quickly jump to the conclusion that older learners can *never* achieve native-like competence/performance in their L2s. This conclusion, although incorrect, is not surprising because most studies have examined L2 learners' performance on average across age groups, instead of emphasising the great variation among the older learners' achievements in the L2 (Marinova-Todd *et al.*, 2000).

In morphosyntax, the area where older learners tend to achieve highest levels of success, studies have shown that, on average, older learners' performance is below that of the younger learners (Patkowski, 1980). In a notable study Coppieters (1987) compared the performance of adult native speakers of French to that of near-native speakers from varying L1 backgrounds on a grammaticality-judgement test in French. Results showed that the group of native speakers performed significantly better than the group of near-native speakers and the native speakers performed more consistently on the test than the near-natives, who showed greater variation in their performance.

A different renowned study by Johnson and Newport (1989) was based on the assumption that once children achieve general problem-solving strategies, their ability to acquire new languages diminishes. They studied native speakers of Chinese and Korean who had been first exposed to English either before puberty (15 years and younger) or after puberty (17 years and older). A grammaticality-judgement test which measured different rule types of English grammar was used. The authors argued that the L1 did not have a measurable effect on the acquisition of an L2 and claimed that their results supported the maturational state hypothesis for a critical period, according to which 'early in life, humans have a superior capacity for acquiring languages . . . [which] disappears or declines with maturation' (Johnson & Newport, 1989: 64), in both their L1 and L2.

This study has been regarded as the best evidence in support of the critical period in L2 learning (Long, 1990). Others (Bialystok & Hakuta, 1994; Birdsong & Molis, 2001) have raised problems with the selection of the subjects involved, the grammatical structures examined in the test and the tasks that were used to assess proficiency in the L2. Bialystok and Hakuta (1994) argued that a deeper examination of the correlation between age of arrival to the L2 environment and scores on the grammaticality-judgement test shows that deterioration in L2 proficiency occurred for learners older than 20, much later than 15, the age proposed by Johnson and Newport (1989). Age-related effects are reported to occur for only some of the structures examined, particularly the ones that differ greatly between English and both Chinese and Korean (e.g. determiners, plurals and subcategorisation of verbs). Finally, in a later study, Johnson (1992) presented a written version of the same test to the same subjects and found fewer age-related effects on proficiency in the L2. These last results should be particularly puzzling to supporters of the CPH since if the critical period is biologically determined its effect should be apparent under different testing conditions.

Finally, Johnson *et al.* (1996) applied the same methodology used in the earlier study by Johnson and Newport (1989) to test the consistency of the L2 knowledge of learners who had been exposed to their L2 at different ages. Johnson *et al.* (1996) gave their subjects the same test twice, and the re-test session was administered 10 days after the original test. Their results indicated that while the younger learners achieved very high scores on both tests, so that their performance did not increase significantly on the re-test, the older learners showed a significant improvement on the re-test, which was considered an indication of the inconsistency of their L2 knowledge.

Theoretically, if the critical period for L2 acquisition exists, and older learners are strictly at a disadvantage due to age and some biological or maturational constraints, then *all* late L2 learners should be performing well below the younger learners. However, many studies, whether supporting or challenging the CPH, have shown that younger learners tend to perform fairly similarly to one another, while generally older learners show greater variation in their L2 performance (Asher & Garcia, 1969; Birdsong, 1992; Bongaerts *et al.*, 1995; Coppieters, 1987; Johnson & Newport, 1989; Oyama, 1976, Riney & Flege 1998; Singleton, 1995; White & Genesee, 1996). Very few of the studies (Birdsong, 1992; Coppieters, 1987) report details on the individual performance of their subjects and, thus, the noteworthy performance of the older learners who achieve native or near-native proficiency in the L2 remains unnoticed.

A significant problem in psycholinguistic theory has been the lack of a uniformly accepted theory of SLA. Attempting to resolve this problem, researchers have turned their attention toward neuroscience in the hope of finding new and more conclusive evidence on which they could base more coherent theories of L2 acquisition (Danesi, 1994). Generally, studies within the field of neurobiology have provided evidence confirming the existence of the critical period for L2 learning. Weber-Fox and Neville (1999) have performed a series of experiments using a combined behavioural–electrophysiological approach and different linguistic stimuli, and their results have consistently shown different brain patterns among younger and older learners. In a study of syntactic features, Weber-Fox and Neville (1996), on one hand, collected data from measures of self-rated proficiency and from standardised tests of knowledge of English grammar; and on the other hand, observed the ERP (Event-Related Brain Potential) patterns in L2 learners of different ages. Their results indicated that during detection of semantic anomalies, an altered response was observed across all age groups but the effect was most prominent in subjects who were first exposed to the L2 after the age of 11. Reactions to grammatical anomalies resulted in delayed response, which was only observed in subjects who were exposed to the L2 after the age of 11. As a result, Weber-Fox and Neville (1996) concluded that their findings were consistent with the idea of the critical period for L2 acquisition and showed that different parts of the brain, specialised for processing different aspects of language, display different sensitive periods.

Thus far, we have reviewed studies showing that older learners generally tend to perform more poorly on morphosyntactic tests when compared to younger learners. A myriad of explanations have been proposed ranging from arguments based on pure linguistic theory (e.g. access to UG), through behavioural explanations justified with maturational constraints, to scientific reasoning based on neuroimaging techniques which seem to imply different localisation and processing of L1 and L2. Given these findings, if one accepts the notion of a critical period for SLA, the more interesting question remains: why are there people who seem to evade the effects of a critical period? As will be discussed later, although older learners typically achieve more limited levels of success in the L2, there are some individuals who achieve native-like competence in their performance in the L2, and thus challenge the CPH.

Some Do Better, So Why Not All?

It has been suggested that the way to disprove the CPH 'would be to produce learners who have demonstrably attained native-like proficiency despite having begun exposure well after the closure of the hypothesised sensitive periods' (Long, 1990: 274). At the time this statement was made, there was virtually no published evidence showing that such learners existed. However, since then the number of studies showing the existence of such very proficient older learners has been constantly growing. Originally, a study by Birdsong (1992) replicated the study by Coppieters (1987) mentioned earlier, and its results were surprising. While, on average, near-native speakers performed at a lower level than native speakers, Birdsong observed that there were some near-native speakers who performed well above some of the native speakers. In addition, the native group did not perform as consistently as previously reported (Coppieters, 1987). Birdsong's results contribute to the critical period debate in three important ways: first, the variability in the performance of the native speakers raises the issue of what is considered a 'native' standard of grammar (similar to the issue of 'standard accent') at which the L2 learners should aim; second, his results demonstrated the existence of older learners of L2 who can achieve native-like proficiency in the target language despite the late age at which they acquired the L2; and lastly, he showed that age effects were still evident well after the critical period has ended, a fact which contradicts predictions made by the CPH (Johnson & Newport, 1989). In his discussion, Birdsong pointed out that it is important to study these most advanced L2 learners in order to gain insight into the factors that have contributed to their ultimate success in the L2.

Very recently, Birdsong (2003) has theoretically considered the temporal and geometric features of maturationally determined critical periods and has discussed the types of age effects that are observed in L2 acquisition to date. In reviewing the behavioural studies of age effects in L2 acquisition, he argued that the construct of a critical period is a poor fit for the L2 data and that it cannot be considered independently from incidences of native-like attainment in the L2.

Since Birdsong's pivotal 1992 study, there has been new evidence confirming the existence of older learners who achieve native-like proficiency in their L2s, though they only represent a small part of the total population of late L2 learners (Birdsong, 1999). Some of the more recent studies have reported near-native achievement for some older learners in the area of morphosyntax (Birdsong, 1992; Juffs & Harrington, 1995; White & Genesee, 1996), and in pronunciation (Bongaerts, 1999) as well as semantic and pragmatic competence (Ioup *et al.*, 1994). These adult L2 learners should be of particular interest to researchers interested in resolving the debate over the CPH. As Long (1990) pointed out, the existence of these very successful adult L2 learners deeply challenges, if not completely refuting, the existence of a biologically based critical period for SLA. Then, the more interesting issue to be discussed is not whether there is a critical period, but what are the factors, in addition to age of first exposure to an L2, that contribute to the high levels of proficiency achieved by some older learners. A closer examination of the linguistic and biographical profiles of these learners may provide some long-needed answers about the nature of beneficial L2 environments and the quality of effective foreign language (FL) teaching practices. Therefore, the main focus of FL educators would shift from providing *early* FL instruction to a more *quality-oriented* FL instruction that is focused on diminishing the wide variation in outcomes for older learners.

When developing FL teaching programmes designed to assist older learners in achieving native-like L2 proficiency, one must account for the effect of the degree of similarity between the L1 and L2 of the learner. Older learners generally have a more sophisticated knowledge of their L1 that could influence their learning of an L2. Young children, however, are usually still developing their L1 when they are faced with the task of learning an L2, and thus, their unstable knowledge of L1 may interfere less with their learning of an L2 (Bialystok & Hakuta, 1999). Research has confirmed that the degree of morphosyntactic similarity between L1 and L2 has an effect on structures at different levels of linguistic analysis, varying from abstract rules of UG (e.g. subjacency constraint: Juffs & Harrington, 1995; Schachter, 1989) to surface structures sharing similarity between the two languages (e.g. number, determiners, negation: Bialystok & Miller, 1999). Results have shown that on grammaticality-judgement tests older learners tend to successfully transfer their knowledge from their L1 and, thus, perform better on items that are shared across the two languages.

As a general learning process, the acquisition of a foreign language progresses along the shape of a learning curve, where the person initially achieves high levels of L2 proficiency at a very quick rate (the curve is very steep) up to a point when the rate of improvement slows down and the learning curve becomes nearly flat (a state in SLA called *fossilisation*, Selinker, 1972). Behavioural evidence suggests that the L2 proficiency of older learners fossilises at different levels, some closer to and some further away from the standards of the target language. The fossilisation of L2 proficiency in older learners could result from lack of access to feedback (about pronunciation, grammar or word choice) after a certain point in L2 development. As long as the meaning of their utterances is understood, their grammar or pronunciation may not be corrected. As a result, the older learners may never become aware of their errors. However, as some studies have shown (Ioup *et al.*, 1994), if the learners are made conscious of the errors, and it is important to them to correct them, they have the potential to achieve native or near-native proficiency in their L2s.

So far, we have presented evidence showing that, on average, older learners tend to achieve lower levels of L2 proficiency when compared to younger learners, although a small proportion of older learners perform at native-like levels. We have also discussed some possible factors, other than age, that could explain why some older learners tend to do better than others.

A Learner is a Learner, No Matter How Old

On the theoretical level the debate surrounding the CPH is interesting and meaningful. On the practical level, however, the truly important issue for both FL teachers and their students is the direct application of the age-based argument to foreign language teaching and learning. The general public wants to know when is the best time to learn a new language and what are the circumstances that generate the highest proficiency in it.

Considering both theoretical and behavioural evidence we have argued that 'instead of focusing on the limited success of older learners, it is more productive to examine the factors that lead to very high levels of proficiency in the L2 for learners of any age (Marinova-Todd *et al.*, 2001). Recent research indicates that the earlier one is exposed to an L2, in an optimal environment rich in L2 input and interaction, the better the outcome (e.g. Birdsong & Molis, 2001; Flege, 1999; Flege *et al.*, 1997, 1999). Of course, it is not surprising that the more time a learner spends at a task, the better he or she will be at it, a fact consistent with research findings that the length of residence in an L2-dominated environment is a better predictor of ultimate attainment in the L2 than the age of arrival in the L2 environment (Slavoff & Johnson, 1995).

In addition to length of exposure, the quality of the L2 input needs to be native-like, if the aim of the instruction is native-like proficiency. It is just as reasonable to expect that learners may not strive for native-like proficiency in their L2 and be satisfied with proficiency at the level necessary for communicating competently during their daily routines. Proving that older learners have the potential for native-like ultimate attainment in the L2 may be of significance only to SLA theoreticians. In real life, the main purpose of language is to function as a tool for communication. As long as its purpose is achieved, it is not practically advantageous to aim at higher levels of performance in the L2 when a person could reapply his or her resources toward alternative goals, such as establishing a network of friends, developing new skills likely to improve employment opportunities, assuring a constant and smooth flow of daily routines necessary to sustain life, all of which tend to be less of an issue for younger learners. In the case study mentioned earlier, Ioup *et al.* (1994) examined the acquisition process of one very successful adult L2 learner. They studied a woman who was a native speaker of English and who achieved native-like proficiency in her L2 – Arabic. She was first exposed to Arabic when she was in her early twenties, married to a native speaker of Arabic and lived in Egypt, and she had a high degree of motivation to achieve high levels of proficiency in her L2. The results from the study revealed that the subject had achieved native-like proficiency in her L2 based on the quality of her speech production, her ability to recognise accents in the L2 and her knowledge of syntactic rules for which she had not received explicit feedback. The success in L2 learning was attributed to her high degree of motivation to learn the language, her exposure to a naturalistic environment and her conscious attention to grammatical form.

In addition to this case study, the effects of the L2 learning process, on the one hand, and the type of L2 learning environment, on the other hand, have been studied more formally on a larger scale. It has been argued that if adults are able to learn an L2 implicitly in more natural settings, similar to the way children learn language, then they may achieve similar levels of performance at a faster rate (Neufeld, 1979; Snow & Hoefnagel-Hohle, 1977, 1978).

Ellis (1993) reported a study that was focused on the effects of implicit versus explicit L2 learning. He devised an experimental procedure within which he taught three groups of adult subjects the grammar and vocabulary of an L2 under three different treatment conditions:

(1) explicitly teaching the grammatical rules;
(2) implicitly, wherein the subjects were presented only with instances without strict formulation of the rules; and

(3) combined, where the subjects were taught the rules and given ample examples to apply them.

Then he tested the subjects' L2 knowledge on a grammaticality-judgement test. Ellis' (1993) results showed that the implicit group learned the least and the explicit group only learned the rules but was unable to appropriately apply them. The combined group, although the slowest in the learning process, was most successful on the grammaticality-judgement test. The necessity for some explicit instruction (Ellis, 1993), as well as the need for conscious attention to grammatical form (Ioup *et al.*, 1994), may be characteristics of greater value to the older learner. It is unlikely and unreasonable to expect that older learners would learn an L2 in a naturalistic setting similar to young children. Therefore, it is important for FL instruction to consider the various exogenous factors when developing FL programmes. The inclusion of some explicit instruction, which seems necessary for older learners, together with copious opportunity for practice in as natural settings as possible should be important considerations when designing FL programmes for older learners.

Conclusion

Ultimate attainment in L2 morphosyntax has been well researched. Even 15 years ago, after reviewing the relevant literature, Snow argued: 'In contrast to the predictions of the CPH, perhaps the most striking aspect of the data is the degree to which older children and adults reveal their potential for fast, natural, and successful language learning' (Snow, 1987: 205). Today, although the general sentiment still is that, on average, late learners do not tend to realize levels of success as high as those of younger learners, new evidence continues to show that late learners definitely have the capacity to learn L2 grammar, and indeed some do, to near-native level. It appears that older learners benefit from some formal instruction of grammatical rules and thus tend to accelerate at least in the initial stages of L2 learning (see some of the studies in the second part of this volume). It is not surprising that the best setting for learning an L2, whether learners are young or old, is an environment where the L2 is the language of dominant discourse. Research has shown that in the limited setting of a formal classroom early L2 instruction does not prove advantageous unless followed by well-designed and implemented FL instruction building on previous knowledge (Singleton, 1997). In order to maximise the benefits for FL learners it is important that the educators designing FL programmes consider and incorporate the knowledge acquired from empirical research. An ideal FL instruction programme does not need to mainly focus on the age at which the L2 is introduced, especially if its introduction is likely to jeopardise the students' attainment in other content areas (such as mathematics or science). Since older students have the capacity to learn an L2 proficiently, high-quality FL instruction could be offered to them at a stage when they are most highly motivated to learn the language, and thus, are likely to continue learning and using it, beyond the scope of formal instruction.

Even in Jane Austen's times, regardless of social expectations, single rich gentlemen were not necessarily in need of a marriage partner. Undisputedly, many single men of limited means were also 'in want of a wife'. Likewise, today, young children do not necessarily develop native-like proficiency in an L2 quickly and easily, regardless of what is widely believed. And, as we have seen here, there are older learners who achieve 'native-likeness' in their L2s. Under the right circumstances and with excellent instruction, the chances of achieving native-like competence in an L2 are similarly increased for both younger and older learners.

Acknowledgement

I would like to thank Catherine E. Snow and David Birdsong who gave me constructive feedback on earlier versions of this chapter. Special thanks to Maria Pilar García-Mayo for her thorough editorial comments, which helped me polish the final draft.

Notes

1. In the field of L2 acquisition, the term 'foreign language' is used to describe a language that is usually learned in a formal setting after a native language has been acquired. 'Second language', however, is used more broadly to refer to the acquisition of a language other than the native language but more strictly, L2 is learned in a more natural environment similar to the way a native language is acquired. In my discussion I will use the broader definition of L2 and only refer to FL when indeed it relates to language acquisition in the classroom context.
2. In recent thinking about the issue few, if any, take the view that there is an 'absolute' critical period. The term *critical period* is used in the field to describe a *sensitive period* in which younger learners are advantaged vis-à-vis older learners.

References

Asher, J. and Garcia, R. (1969) The optimal age to learn a foreign language. *Modern Language Journal* 53, 344–51.

Bialystok, E. and Hakuta, K. (1994) *In Other Words: The Science and Psychology of Second-Language Acquisition*. New York: Basic Books.

Bialystok, E. and Hakuta, K. (1999) Confounded age: Linguistic and cognitive factors in age differences for second language acquisition. In D. Birdsong (ed.) *Second Language Acquisition and the Critical Period Hypothesis* (pp. 161–81). Mahwah, NJ: Erlbaum.

Bialystok, E. and Miller, B. (1999) The problem of age in second language acquisition: Influences from language, task, and structure. *Bilingualism: Language and Cognition* 2, 127–45.

Birdsong, D. (1992) Ultimate attainment in second language acquisition. *Language* 68, 706–55.

Birdsong, D. (1999) Introduction: Whys and why nots of the critical period hypothesis. In D. Birdsong (ed.) *Second Language Acquisition and the Critical Period Hypothesis* (pp. 1–22). Mahwah, NJ: Erlbaum.

Birdsong, D. (2003) Interpreting age effects in second language acquisition. In J. Kroll and A. DeGroot (eds) *Handbook of Bilingualism: Psycholinguistic Perspectives.* Cambridge: Cambridge University Press. In press.

Birdsong, D. and Molis, M. (2001) On the evidence for maturational constraints in second-language acquisition. *Journal of Memory and Language* 44, 235–49.

Bley-Vroman, R. (1989) What is the logical problem of foreign language learning? In S. Gass and J. Schachter (eds) *Linguistic Perspectives on Second Language Acquisition* (pp. 41–68). Cambridge: Cambridge University Press.

Bongaerts, T. (1999) Ultimate attainment in L2 pronunciation: The case of very advanced late L2 learners. In D. Birdsong (ed.) *Second Language Acquisition and the Critical Period Hypothesis* (pp. 133–59). Mahwah, NJ: Erlbaum.

Bongaerts, T., Planken, B. and Schils, E. (1995) Can late starters attain a native accent in a foreign language? A test of the critical period hypothesis. In D. Singleton and Z. Lengyel (eds) *The Age Factor in Second Language Acquisition* (pp. 30–50). Clevedon: Multilingual Matters.

Chomsky, N. (1995) *The Minimalist Program.* Cambridge, MA: MIT Press.

Coppieters, R. (1987) Competence differences between native and near native speakers. *Language* 63, 544–73.

Danesi, M. (1994) The neuroscientific perspective in second language acquisition research: a critical synopsis. *Lenguas Modernas* 21, 145–68.

Ellis, N. (1993) Rules and instances in foreign language learning: Interactions of explicit and implicit knowledge. *European Journal of Cognitive Psychology* 5, 289–318.

Epstein, S., Flynn, S. and Martohardjono, G. (1996) Second language acquisition: Theoretical and experimental issues in contemporary research. *Behavioral and Brain Sciences* 19, 677–758.

Eubank, L. and Gregg, K. (1999) Critical periods and (second) language acquisition: Divide et impera. In D. Birdsong (ed.) *Second Language Acquisition and the Critical Period Hypothesis* (pp. 65–99). Mahwah, NJ: Erlbaum.

Flege, J.E., (1992) Speech learning in a second language. In C. Ferguson, L. Menn and C. Stoel-Gammon (eds) *Phonological Development: Models, Research, Implications* (pp. 565–604). Timonium, MD: York Press.

Flege, J.E. (1995) Second language speech learning. Theory, findings, and problems. In W. Strange (ed.) *Speech Perception and Linguistic Experience: Issues in Cross-Language Research* (pp. 233–77). Timonium, MD: York Press.

Flege, J.E. (1999) Age of learning and second language speech. In D. Birdsong (ed.), *Second Language Acquisition and the Critical Period Hypothesis* (pp. 101–31). Mahwah, NJ: Erlbaum.

Flege, J., Frieda, E. and Nozawa, T. (1997) Amount of native language (L1) use affects the pronunciation of an L2. *Journal of Phonetics* 25, 169–86.

Flege, J.E., Yeni-Komshian, G. and Liu, S. (1999) Age constraints on second language learning. *Journal of Memory and Language* 41, 78–104.

House, J. (1996) Developing pragmatic fluency in English as a foreign language. *Studies in Second Language Acquisition* 18, 225–52.

Ioup, G., Boustagui, E., Tigi, M. and Moselle, M. (1994) Reexamining the critical period hypothesis: A case of successful adult SLA in a naturalistic environment. *Studies in Second Language Acquisition* 16, 73–98.

Johnson, J. (1992) Critical period effects in second language acquisition: The effect of written versus auditory materials on the assessment of grammatical competence. *Language Learning* 42, 217–48.

Johnson, J. and Newport, E. (1989) Critical period effects in second language learning: the influence of the maturational state on the acquisition of English as a second language. *Cognitive Psychology* 21, 60–99.

Johnson, J., Shenkman, K., Newport, E. and Medin, D. (1996) Indeterminacy in the grammar of adult language learners. *Journal of Memory and Language* 35, 335–52.

Juffs, A. and Harrington, M. (1995) Parsing effects in second language sentence processing: Subject and object asymmetries in wh-extraction. *Studies in Second Language Acquisition* 17, 483–516.

Krashen, S., Long, M. and Scarcella, R. (1979) Age, rate and eventual attainment in second language acquisition. *TESOL Quarterly* 13, 573–82.

Lamandella, J. (1977) General principles of neurofunctional organization and their manifestations in primary and non-primary language acquisition. *Language Learning* 27, 155–96.

Larsen-Freeman, D. and Long, M. (1991) *An Introduction to Second Language Acquisition Research*. London: Longman.

Lenneberg, E. (1967) *Biological Foundations of Language*. New York: John Wiley.

Liu, H., Bates, E. and Li, P. (1992) Sentence interpretation in bilingual speakers of English and Chinese. *Applied Psycholinguistics* 13, 451–84.

Long, M. (1990) Maturational constraints on language development. *Studies in Second Language Acquisition* 12, 251–85.

Marinova-Todd, S.H., Marshall, D.B and Snow, C.E. (2000) Three misconceptions about age and L2 learning. *TESOL Quarterly* 34, 9–34.

Marinova-Todd, S.H., Marshall, D.B. and Snow, C.E. (2001) Missing the point: A response to Hyltenstam and Abrahamsson. *TESOL Quarterly* 35, 171–6.

Neufeld, G. (1979) Towards a theory of language learning ability. *Language Learning* 29 (2), 227–41.

Oyama, S. (1976) A sensitive period in the acquisition of a non-native phonological system. *Journal of Psycholinguistic Research* 5, 261–85.

Patkowski, M. (1980) The sensitive period for the acquisition of syntax in a second language. *Language Learning* 30, 449–72.

Patkowski, M. (1990) Age and accent in a second language: A reply to James Emile Flege. *Applied Linguistics* 11, 73–89.

Penfield, W. and Roberts, L. (1959) *Speech and Brain Mechanisms*. Princeton, NJ: Princeton University Press.

Riney, T. and Flege, J.E. (1998) Changes over time in global foreign accent and liquid identifiability and accuracy. *Studies in Second Language Acquisition* 20, 213–43.

Schachter, J. (1989) Testing a proposed universal. In S. Gass and J. Schachter (eds) *Linguistic Perspectives on Second Language Acquisition* (pp. 73–88). Cambridge: Cambridge University Press.

Schwartz, B.D. and Sprouse, R.A. (1996) L2 cognitive states and the Full Transfer/Full Access model. *Second Language Research* 12, 40–72.

Scovel, T. (1988) *A Time to Speak: A Psycholinguistic Inquiry into the Critical Period for Human Speech.* Rowley, MA: Newbury House.

Selinker, L. (1972) Interlanguage. *International Review of Applied Linguistics* 10, 209–31.

Singleton, D. (1995) Introduction: a critical look at the critical hypothesis in second language acquisition research. In D. Singleton and Z. Lengyel (eds) *The Age Factor in Second Language Acquisition* (pp. 1–29). Clevedon: Multilingual Matters.

Singleton, D. (1997) Second language in primary school: The age dimension. *The Irish Yearbook of Applied Linguistics* 15, 155–16.

Slavoff, G. and Johnson, J. (1995) The effects of age on the rate of learning a second language. *Studies in Second Language Acquisition* 17(1), 1–16.

Snow, C. (1987) Relevance of the notion of a critical period to language acquisition. In M. H. Bornstein (ed.) *Sensitive Periods in Development: Interdisciplinary Perspectives* (pp. 183–209). Hillsdale, NJ: Lawrence Erlbaum.

Snow, C. and Hoefnagel-Höhle, M. (1977) Age differences in pronunciation of foreign sounds. *Language and Speech* 20, 357–65.

Snow, C. and Hoefnagel-Höhle, M. (1978) The critical period for language acquisition: Evidence from second language learning. *Child Development* 49, 1114–28.

Weber-Fox, C. and Neville, H. (1996) Maturational constraints on functional specializations for language processing: ERP and behavioural evidence in bilingual speakers. *Journal of Cognitive Neuroscience* 8, 231–56.

Weber-Fox, C. and Neville, H. (1999) Functional neural subsystems are differentially affected by delays in second language immersion: ERP and behavioural evidence in bilinguals. In D. Birdsong (ed.) *Second Language Acquisition and the Critical Period Hypothesis* (pp. 23–38). Mahwah, NJ: Erlbaum.

White, L. and Genesee, F. (1996) How native is near-native? The issue of ultimate attainment in adult second language acquisition. *Second Language Research* 12, 233–65.

Part 2

Fieldwork in Bilingual Communities

Chapter 4

The Influence of Age on the Acquisition of English: General Proficiency, Attitudes and Code-mixing

JASONE CENOZ

The Effect of Age on Foreign Language Acquisition in Formal Contexts

The early introduction of foreign languages (FLs) in kindergarden and primary school has expanded in Europe in the last 15 years. The European Commission's White Paper 'Teaching and Learning: Towards the Learning Society' (1995) considers that European citizens should be proficient in three community languages and recommends foreign language teaching at pre-school level in order to allow for second foreign languages in secondary school. As Blondin *et al.* (1998) point out, foreign-language teaching in pre-secondary education presents great diversity. Some projects are at the stage of small-scale experiments while others have been generalised. Projects also differ in terms of the age of introduction, the intensity, the specific teaching methodology used and many other contextual factors.

The early introduction of a foreign language in the school curriculum increases the total amount of time that learners have at their disposal and many parents and educators also consider that young children are specially gifted to learn foreign languages. The idea is expressed very clearly by Hieghington, a teacher of French on the Surrey Primary French Project developed in the United Kingdom when referring to primary school children:

> They have no awkwardness or inhibitions with the new language and are not at all bothered about making mistakes. Most significant of all, they soak up new language and ideas rather as a sponge does water. (Heighington, 1996: 57)

Are young children really sponges when learning second and foreign languages? Do they present better attitudes than older children? Apart from the interest that the possible responses to these questions have for research in second/foreign language acquisition, research that analyses the early introduction of a foreign language in the school context also has important educational implications. An analysis of the effectiveness of early foreign language teaching can cover different areas such as ultimate school achievement, rate of achievement, the development of attitudes and motivation, code-mixing and code-switching, the development of metalinguistic awareness or the influence of contextual factors.

When studying the effect of age it is important to distinguish between second and foreign language situations, that is, between situations in which there is exposure to the target language with or without formal instruction and situations in which exposure to the language is limited to the school context and usually to very few hours per week. Learners in foreign language contexts have very limited exposure to the language and typically have non-native teachers and no communicative need to use the foreign language outside the classroom. These specific conditions are different from those of learners immersed in a second language context from a very early age who generally achieve native-like competence in the second language (Birdsong, 1999; Harley & Wang, 1997; Singleton, 2001; Singleton & Lengyel, 1995).

Foreign language learners in school contexts cannot possibly achieve native or native-like proficiency in the foreign language and therefore as it is impossible to compare the ultimate achievement of younger and older learners we can only study rate of achievement or ultimate school achievement (see also Muñoz, 2000; Singleton, 1995).

Most studies comparing learners who have started learning a foreign language at different ages in the school context do not focus on ultimate achievement in the school context but on comparisons between early and late starters made in the early years of secondary school. In general terms, the evidence supporting the advantage of learners who have been taught a foreign language for a longer period of time (early starters) is weak and if there are advantages, they tend to disappear over time (see Blondin *et al.*, 1998; Burstall, 1977). Nevertheless, some of the studies present problems because beginners and non-beginners are mixed in the same classes (Singleton, 1995). Some studies have reported some advantages for younger learners in listening comprehension and some communicative abilities but not in grammatical control (see Blondin *et al.*, [1998] for a review).

When the rate of acquisition has been the focus of the comparison and the time for learning is held constant, older learners present advantages over younger learners (Burstall, 1977; Holmstrand, 1982; Muñoz, 2000). Research conducted in natural settings has also reported that older learners progress faster in the first stages of language acquisition and there is the possibility that in the case of formal contexts the advantages presented by older learners could be due to the fact that there is not enough exposure to go beyond the first stages of foreign language acquisition. Genesee (1987) and Harley (1986) also report that learners who experience intensive exposure to the second language in late immersion in the first year(s) of secondary school present similar levels of proficiency in the second language as children who have experienced more exposure to the second language in early immersion programmes.

Therefore, in general terms research studies do not support the idea that children are 'sponges' when acquiring a second/foreign language, at least, as far as rate of achievement is concerned. However, teachers and researchers report that younger children present very positive attitudes towards learning foreign languages and are very motivated (Blondin *et al.*, 1998; Burstall, 1975; Cenoz & Lindsay, 1994; Clyne *et al.*, 1995; Donato *et al.*, 2000; Hawkins, 1996; Hurrell & Satchwell, 1996; Johnstone, 1996; Nikolov, 1999; Satchwell, 1996; Taechner, 1991). Younger learners could be motivated because the teaching methodology used in kindergarten and primary school focuses on communicative skills rather than on the formal structures of the language. Younger learners could also present more positive attitudes and be more motivated because of their general positive attitude towards learning as opposed to the rejection of the school system typically associated with older learners. Nevertheless, in a study conducted in Barcelona, Muñoz and Tragant (2001) found no differences in motivation between learners who started learning English as a third language in the third and sixth years of primary school.

As has already been mentioned, English is the most common foreign language but for many European children, English is not a second language but a third language (or even a fourth language). For example, many children who live in bilingual/multilingual communities or who have a family language that is not spoken at the community level are exposed to English as a third language in kindergarten or primary school (see Cenoz & Jessner, 2000). When foreign-language teaching starts at a very early age, these educational situations pose several questions: Will three languages at an early age be too many? Will young children get the languages mixed? Research on early trilingual development in natural contexts is still very limited but it indicates that children do not usually mix languages and that they are able to use different languages according to their interlocutors' linguistic repertoire (see, for example, Quay, 2001). However, research on the relationship between the introduction of foreign-language teaching at different ages and code-mixing is still very limited but results indicate that younger learners do not mix codes more often than older learners (Cenoz, 2001).

The Early Introduction of English as a Third Language in the Basque Autonomous Community

The increasing role of English in Europe has also developed a growing interest in learning English in the Basque Country. Interest in the improved quality of English is very strong in the Basque Autonomous Community and great effort has been made in recent years to reinforce and improve the teaching of English within the context of bilingual education. English is a third language in the Basque educational system which is bilingual with Basque and Spanish either as languages of instruction or school subjects (see Cenoz [1998] for a description).

The Spanish Educational Reform implemented in 1993 pays specific attention to the role of foreign languages in the curriculum. In accordance with the Reform, foreign languages are introduced in the third year of primary school at the age of eight, three years earlier than previously. The Reform also considers important changes at the methodological level including communicative competence, positive attitudes and metalinguistic awareness as desired goals for foreign-language teaching.

The Basque Government has also tried to improve the quality of English teaching by encouraging the adoption of new instructional approaches, especially those that emphasise the acquisition of oral skills, the use of learner-centred syllabuses and the integration of curricula for the three languages (Cenoz & Lindsay, 1994). Some schools have adopted a different approach in order to intensify the role of English in the curriculum within bilingual education and are using English as the language of instruction at the end of primary school and in secondary school (Cenoz, 1998). Nevertheless, the most popular project is the early introduction of English as a third language in the second year of kindergarten to 4-year-old children.

The early introduction of English in kindergarten was initiated on an experimental basis in several private Basque schools, or 'ikastolak', in 1991. These schools were model D schools with Basque as the language of instruction and Spanish as a school subject and their pupils are native speakers of Basque or Spanish and, in some cases, early bilinguals in Basque and Spanish. Similar initiatives have been developed in many other ikastolak (Basque-speaking schools) and also in a large number of state schools. When English is introduced in kindergarten it is taught for four or five sessions per week (between 2 and 3 hours). The teacher of English only uses English in the classroom and all the activities are oral. The methodology used is based on story-telling, songs and other oral activities and requires the children's active participation by means of collective dramatisation and play.

The Effect of Age on Third Language Acquisition in the Basque Country: Research Perspectives

Taking into account the expansion of pre-secondary foreign-language teaching and the limited number of research studies on the effect of the introduction of a foreign language at different ages the 'Research in English Applied Linguistics' (REAL) research group at the University of the Basque Country decided to conduct a study in order to analyse the effect of the age of introduction of English as a third language on general proficiency in English and on attitudes and motivation towards learning English. The research study combines longitudinal and cross-sectional designs and aims at comparing:

(1) ultimate school achievement by learners who have started learning English at different ages and have received different amount of instruction;
(2) rate of acquisition by learners who have started at different ages but have received the same amount of instruction and
(3) the development of attitudes and motivation.

Data collection started in 1996 and, apart from general proficiency in English and attitude/motivation, specific studies are being carried out on phonetics (see García Lecumberri & Gallardo, this volume, Chapter 6), lexis (Cenoz, 2001), syntax (see García Mayo, this volume, Chapter 5) and writing skills (see Lasagabaster and Doiz, this volume chapter 7).

English is taught as a third language to all the learners who have participated in this project. The English language was traditionally introduced in the sixth year of primary school (11 years old) but when the Spanish Educational Reform was implemented in 1993, foreign languages were introduced in the third year of primary school when children are eight years old. The school collaborating with this study has taken part in a specific project to introduce the teaching of English in the second year of kindergarten at the age of four. This programme started in 1991. Therefore, this school provides the possibility of comparing groups of children who have started their English classes at three different ages within the same bilingual programme and school curriculum. All the children in this research study come from the same geographical area and similar social backgrounds. The subjects included in this research study were selected on the condition that they did not receive instruction or were not exposed to English outside school (private classes, academies, summer courses, etc.).

This chapter reports some of the data obtained in this project and focuses on the effect of the introduction of English as a foreign language at different ages on the rate of achievement, the development of attitudes and motivation and code-mixing. Specifically, the research questions were:

(1) Is the general rate of acquisition higher for older or younger children when the time for learning is held constant?
(2) Are attitudes and motivation more or less positive when the foreign language is taught from an early age?
(3) Do younger children mix codes more often than older children?

Methodology

Sample

All the participants in this research study (N = 135) were primary and secondary school children from a school in Gipuzkoa. This school has Basque as the language of instruction (D model) and it serves both as a total immersion programme for students whose first language is Spanish and a first language maintenance programme for students whose first language is Basque (Cenoz, 1998). Spanish and English are taught as school subjects but Basque is the main language of communication at school. Some subjects use only Basque at home, others only Spanish and others both Basque and Spanish but the use of the Basque language is slightly more common than the use of Spanish at home for the subjects in our sample. The distribution of male and female subjects is quite balanced: 48.4% male subjects and 51.6% female subjects.

All the participants in this study had received 600 hours of instruction in English but instruction had started at different ages: in kindergarten (4 years old), in grade 3 (8 years old), and in grade 6 (11 years old) as can be seen in Table 1.

Table 1 Characteristics of the sample

	Primary 5	*Secondary 2*	*Secondary 5*
Mean age	10.1	12.9	16.3
Starting age	Kindergarten 2 (4 years old)	Primary 3 (8 years old)	Primary 6 (11 years old)
Hours of English	600	600	600

Instruments

The specific data for the comparisons reported in this chapter were collected in the years 1998 and 1999. Before the tests were administered all the subjects in each of the classes in which data were going to be collected completed a short questionnaire and subjects who had received additional instruction in English or had been exposed to English outside school were excluded from the sample. The following tests and questionnaires were administered:

Background questionnaire
    This questionnaire was designed to obtain information about gender, age, socioeducational background, degree of bilingualism in Basque and Spanish and the use of Basque and Spanish.

Tests of English proficiency
The Frog Story: The picture story *'Frog, Where Are You?'* (Mayer, 1969) was used as a measure of oral production. The Frog story consists of 24 pictures with no text and the interviewer asks the learner to describe the pictures. It has been used in a large number of contexts all over the world with different languages both with children and adults (Berman & Slobin, 1994; MacWhinney, 2000).

Second Story: Apart from the story *'Frog, Where Are You?'* participants were also asked to tell another story that was related to the learners' class activities. This story was different in the different age levels but presents the advantage of using a tool that is closely related to the classroom activities.

Listening comprehension: Students also completed a listening comprehension test which consisted of three parts. In the first part, participants listened to a song and had to put some pictures in order (max = 8 points). In the second part participants were asked to listen to a passage and identify eight characters (max = 8) and in the third part they had to choose an adverb to describe the eating habits of four characters (max = 20). The maximum score is 36 points.

Cloze test: In this test participants were asked to fill in 34 blanks by using the appropriate words in a text which was the very well-known story 'Little Red Riding Hood'. This test measures lexical, grammatical and discursive aspects of language production. The maximum score is 34 points.

Reading comprehension/grammar test: This test consists of three parts. In the first part, participants were asked to look at four pictures and to match the different parts of a dialogue (max = 8). In the second part, participants were asked to fill in some blanks by using the appropriate word (auxiliaries, pronouns, quantifiers, etc., max = 15). The third part is similar to the first and participants were asked to put the different parts of a dialogue in order (max = 8). The maximum score is 31 points.

Composition: Participants were also asked to write a composition with a maximum length of 250 words. In the composition, students were asked to write a letter to an English family telling them about their own family, their school and their hobbies. The maximum score for the composition is 100 points.

Attitudes and motivation questionnaires

Participants were also asked to complete an attitude questionnaire based on Gardner's (1985) and Baker's (1992) questionnaires in order to measure their attitudes towards English, Basque and Spanish. The questionnaire had an Osgood format and included eight adjectives and their opposites and students were asked to express their feelings towards learning the three languages. Each of the items had a score ranging from one to seven and the total score is 56 points.

Motivation towards learning the language was measured by a scale based on Gardner (1985) including a combination of the three components of motivation as proposed by Gardner: desire to learn the language, effort and attitudes towards learning the language. The motivation questionnaire included 13 items and had a Likert format asking students to identify with one of the five positions ranging from 'I strongly agree' to 'I strongly disagree'.

Procedure

The stories were recorded, transcribed and analysed in order to examine different aspects of oral production. First, an overall evaluation of the oral production including pronunciation, vocabulary, grammar, fluency and content was carried out. The composition was graded according to the holistic approach proposed by Jacobs *et al.*'s (1981). This system uses scales corresponding to content, organisation, vocabulary, language use and mechanics. The reliability of the scores was achieved by the combination of objective and holistic criteria and the collaboration of two evaluators in the holistic evaluations. Once the results of the tests were codified and the oral tests were fully transcribed, analyses were conducted by using the Statistical Package for the Social Sciences (SPSS).

Results

Rate of acquisition and age

In order to measure the effect of age on the general rate of acquisition the measures of English proficiency were analysed. The comparisons after 600 hours of exposure included three groups of subjects: fifth year of primary school, second year of secondary school and fifth year of secondary school.

ORAL PROFICIENCY

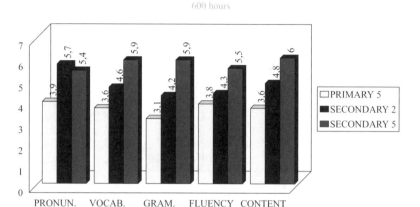

Figure 1 Oral proficiency

Figure 1 includes the results of the Anova analyses comparing the five components of oral production after 600 hours of exposure.

The results of the Anova analyses indicate that there are significant differences in the five measures of oral proficiency: pronunciation ($F = 24.1$, $S = 0.00$), vocabulary ($F = 20.1$, $S = 0.00$), grammar ($F = 31.4$, $S = 0.00$), fluency ($F = 12.3$, $S = 0.00$) and content ($F = 23.1$, $S = 0.00$). In all the measures, the scores obtained by secondary school students were higher than those obtained by younger learners. The Scheffé procedure was carried out in order to know the specific differences between the means of the three different combinations of two groups. The results indicate that the differences between the fifth year of primary school and the second year of secondary school are significant for all the components of oral proficiency except fluency while the differences between the fifth year of primary and the fifth year of secondary are significant for all the components. When the means between the two older groups are compared the results indicate that the differences are significant for all the components except pronunciation. Learners in the fifth year of primary school only completed the oral test and the attitudes/motivation questionnaire so the rest of the analyses of English language proficiency only include the older groups.

Figure 2 includes the scores obtained by the second year of secondary and the fifth year of secondary school in the five dimensions of the composition:

The results of the T-tests analyses indicate that there are significant dif-

COMPOSITION

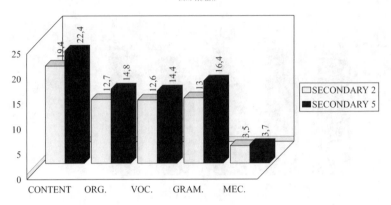

Figure 2 Composition

ferences in four of the five measures: content ($T = -4.4$, $S = 0.00$), organization ($T = -3.9$, $S = 0.00$), vocabulary ($T = -4.0$, $S = 0.00$) and grammar ($T = -4.5$, $S = 0.00$). The older group (fifth year of secondary school) obtained significantly higher scores than the younger group (second year of secondary school) in these four scales. There were no significant differences when the means corresponding to the mechanics of writing were compared ($T = -1.2$, $S = 0.20$).

The scores obtained by the two groups in listening comprehension, cloze test and reading comprehension are presented in Figure 3.

The results of the T-test analyses indicate that the differences between the groups are significant in the three tests: listening comprehension ($T = -2.7$, $S = 0.00$), cloze test ($T = -8.9$, $S = 0.00$) and reading comprehension ($T = -6.7$, $S = 0.00$). Older learners (fifth year of secondary school) obtained significantly higher scores than younger learners (second year of secondary school) in the three tests.

Attitudes, motivation and age

The scores obtained in the attitudes and motivation questionnaires after 600 hours of exposure are presented in Figure 4.

The results of the Anova analyses indicate that the differences between the means are significant both for attitudes ($F = 8$, $S = 0.00$) and motivation ($F = 5.2$, $S = 0.00$). Learners in the fifth year of primary school obtained the highest scores both in attitudes and motivation. The Scheffé procedure in-

LISTENING, CLOZE, READING

600 hours

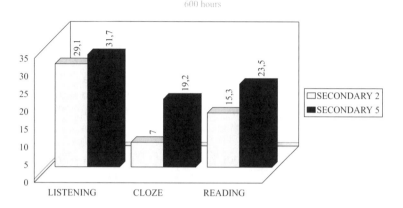

Figure 3 Listening, cloze and reading

ATTITUDES AND MOTIVATION

600 hours

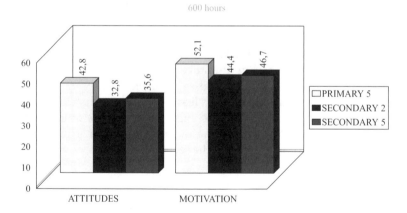

Figure 4 Attitudes and motivation

dicates that there are significant differences in attitudes when the fifth year of primary school is compared to the second year of secondary school and also when the fifth year of primary school is compared to the fifth year of secondary school. There are also significant differences in motivation when the fifth year of primary school is compared to the fifth year of secondary school but the differences in motivation between the fifth year of primary school and the fifth year of secondary school are only marginally significant. The differences between the scores obtained in attitudes and motivation by the two secondary school groups are not significant.

Code-mixing and age

The data corresponding to code-mixing in oral production are presented in Tables 2 and 3. The results in Table 2 indicate the average number of terms (or expressions) transferred from Basque and Spanish into English and the percentage of subjects who transfer terms (or expressions) from these languages. The data indicate that learners who started learning English in kindergarten, at the age of four, do not mix codes more often than learners who started learning English at the age of 8 or at the age of eleven.

Following Cenoz (2001), all the terms and expressions transferred from Basque and Spanish were divided into interactional strategies, code-switching and transfer. Interactional strategies refer to direct or indirect appeals to the interlocutor in order to get help to produce a specific term in English. Code-switching includes whole sentences produced in Basque or Spanish when the speaker is not appealing to the interlocutor for help and transfer refers to the use of one or more terms (but not whole sentences) in Basque or Spanish as part of an utterance produced in English. The distribution of the different categories in given in Table 3.

The results indicate that there is no clear pattern in the distribution of the three categories that can be related to age. In fact, the use of interactional strategies and transfer by the youngest and the oldest groups is very similar and differs from the group in the second year of secondary school.

Table 2 Cross-linguistic influence from Basque and Spanish in English oral production

	Average number of transferred terms or expressions per subject	*Percentage of subjects who transfer (%)*
Primary 5	6.32	77
Secondary 2	9.43	81
Secondary 5	5.98	85

Table 3 Functions of code-mixing in English oral production

	Interactional (%)	*Code-switching (%)*	*Transfer (%)*
Primary 5	62.6	0.8	36.6
Secondary 2	49	2.5	48.3
Secondary 5	57	6.4	36.6

Discussion and Implications

The first research question focuses on the comparison of the level of English proficiency between groups of learners who have had the same amount of exposure (600 hours) but started learning English at different ages. The results indicate that older learners obtain significantly higher results than younger learners in most of the measures of English proficiency. The only differences that are not significant are the mechanics of writing in the composition. The fact that there are no significant differences between the second year of secondary and the fifth year of secondary school in pronunciation and in the mechanics of writing can be due to fossilisation in the case of pronunciation and to the control that both groups have of the basic elements of punctuation and orthography. It is important to notice that the mechanics of writing only accounts for 5% of the composition score. Even though only the two older groups completed all the tests, the general trend observed after 600 hours of exposure is that the oldest group (fifth year of secondary school) presents the highest level of proficiency in English followed by the intermediate group (second year of secondary school) and the lowest scores correspond to the youngest group (fifth year of primary school).

These results confirm the poor results obtained by young students in educational contexts in previous studies conducted in other settings (Burstall, 1977; Ekstrand, 1976; Oller & Nagato, 1974) and also the results obtained by Muñoz in a similar context when comparing learners who had started in the third year of primary to learners who had started in the sixth year of primary (Muñoz, 2000).

Some possible explanations for these results are related to cognitive maturity and type of input. Cognitive maturity could explain the higher linguistic development of the secondary school children as well as their higher scores in content and could also be linked to higher developed test-taking strategies.

Another possible explanation of the results is linked to the type of input. The more traditional approaches used with older learners could explain the higher lexical and syntactic complexity of their production and their higher scores on the written tests (composition, cloze test, reading-grammar test). The effect of the type of input has also been found in comparisons of early and late immersion (Harley, 1986) and can explain our results in written tests. However, the type of input cannot explain the better results obtained by older learners in oral proficiency because the methodological approach used with younger learners in this study emphasises oral activities.

The second research question aims at comparing the attitudes and motivation of learners who have received the same amount of exposure but started learning English at different ages (Figure 4).

The results of the statistical analyses indicate that younger learners tend to present significantly more positive attitudes and are more motivated than older learners after 600 hours of exposure. It is also interesting to see that there are no significant differences between the two secondary school groups.

The more positive attitudes and motivation presented by primary school learners can be explained as linked to psychological and educational factors. Psychological factors associated with age could explain a rejection of the school system and have a negative effect on the attitudes and motivation scores obtained by secondary school subjects. This explanation is consistent with the findings reported in Cenoz (2002) who observed that attitudes towards English, Spanish and Basque were less positive among older students. An alternative explanation is related to educational factors and particularly to input and teaching methods used in secondary school as compared to primary school. Learners seem to enjoy their English classes when an oral-based approach and a very active methodology based on drama and storytelling is used. Their attitudes and motivation are less positive when more attention is devoted to grammar and vocabulary learning in secondary school.

It is interesting to see that scores in social psychological factors (attitudes and motivation) and in language proficiency go in opposite directions. Attitudes and motivation have been associated with second/foreign language development (Gardner, 1985) but their influence can be indirect or less prominent than that of other factors (Dörnyei, 1998).

The third research question aims at examining whether younger children mix their languages more often than older children. Our data only include oral production in English but they indicate that the early introduction of third language at the age of four is not associated with a higher level of language mixing than for the introduction of a foreign language at the age of eight or eleven. These results confirm those reported in Cenoz (2001) and also confirm the ability to maintain linguistic boundaries observed in multilingual acquisition in natural contexts (Quay, 2001). The data also indicate that cross-linguistic influence has different functions. This specific context is towards the bilingual/multilingual end of the language mode continuum as proposed by Grosjean (1998) and a strategy such as asking for help in Basque or Spanish is very common when learners tell a story in English. It is also interesting to observe that there are important individual differences in cross-linguistic interaction and some learners do not transfer from Basque and Spanish when speaking English.

In sum, this study provides more evidence to confirm that older learners learn more quickly than younger learners (see also Muñoz, this volume, Chapter 8) but it also proves that younger learners present more positive attitudes and are more motivated and that they do not mix languages more than older learners. The study presented here is part of a project and only includes the data corresponding to a specific point in the development of English proficiency. In order to get a complete picture of the effect of the early introduction of English it is necessary to complete the longitudinal study so as to compare the three groups of students at several points in their development of English skills. The pursuit of this specific area of research has important implications for language planning and also for the study of the age factor in foreign language contexts and the specific characteristics of third language acquisition.

Acknowledgements

This research was carried out with the assistance of the research grants, DGES PB97–0611, BFF–2000–0101 from the Spanish Ministry of Education and the Ministry of Science and Technology and grant PI–1998–96 from the Basque Government.

References

Baker, C. (1992) *Attitudes and Language*. Clevedon: Multilingual Matters.

Berman, R.A. and Slobin, D.I. (1994) *Relating Events in Narrative: A Crosslinguistic Developmental Study*. Hillsdale, NJ: Erlbaum.

Birdsong, D. (ed.) (1999) *Second Language Acquisition and the Critical Period Hypothesis*. Mahwah, NJ: Erlbaum.

Blondin, C., Candelier, M., Edelenbos, P., Johnstone, R., Kubanek-German, A. and Taeschner, T. (1998) *Foreign Language in Primary and Pre-school Education*. London: CILT, Centre for Information on Language Teaching.

Burstall, C. (1975) Factors affecting foreign-language learning: A consideration of some recent research findings. *Language Teaching and Linguistics* 8, 5–25.

Burstall, C. (1977) Primary French in the balance. *Foreign Language Annals* 10, 245–52.

Cenoz, J. (1998) Multilingual education in the Basque Country. In J. Cenoz and F. Genesee (eds) *Beyond Bilingualism: Multilingualism and Multilingual Education* (pp. 175–91). Clevedon: Multilingual Matters.

Cenoz, J. (2001) The effect of linguistic distance, L2 status and age on crosslinguistic influence in the third language. In J. Cenoz, B. Hufeisen and U. Jessner (eds) *Crosslinguistic Influence in Third Language Acquisition: Psycholinguistic Perspectives* (pp 8–20). Clevedon: Multilingual Matters.

Cenoz, J. (2002) Three languages in contact: language attitudes in the Basque Country. In D. Lasagabaster and J. Sierra (eds) *Language Awareness in the Foreign Language Classroom* (pp. 37–60). Leioa: Universidad del País Vasco.

Cenoz, J. and Lindsay, D. (1994) Teaching English in primary school: A project to introduce a third language to eight year olds. *Language and Education* 8, 201–10.

Cenoz, J. and Jessner, U. (eds) (2000) *English in Europe: The Acquisition of a Third Language*. Clevedon: Multilingual Matters.

Clyne, M., Jenkins, C., Chen, I.Y., Tsokalidou, R. and Wallner, T. (1995) *Developing Second Language from Primary School: Models and Outcomes*. Deakin: National Languages and Literacy Institute of Australia.

Donato, R., Tucker, G.R., Wudthayagorn, J. and Igarashi, K. (2000) Converging evidence: Attitudes, achievements, and instruction in the later years of FLES. *Foreign Language Annals* 33, 377–93.

Dörnyei, Z. (1998) Motivation in second and foreign language learning. *Language Teaching* 31, 117–35.

Ekstrand, L. (1976) Age and length of residence as variables related to the adjustment of migrant children, with special reference to second language learning. In G. Nickel (ed.) *Proceedings of the Fourth International Congress of Applied Linguistics* (Vol. 3) (pp. 179–98). Stuttgart: Hochschulverlag.

European Commission (1995) *Teaching and Learning: Towards the Learning Society. White Paper*. Brussels: European Commission.

García Lecumberri, M.L. and Gallardo, F. (this volume) English FL sounds in school learners of different ages.

García Mayo, M.P. (this volume) Age, length of exposure and grammatically judgements in the acquisition of English as a foreign language.

Gardner, R. (1985) *Social Psychology and Second Language Learning*. London: Arnold.

Genesee, F. (1987) *Learning through Two Languages*. Cambridge, MA: Newbury House.

Grosjean, F. (1998) Studying bilinguals: Methodological and conceptual issues. *Bilingualism: Language and Cognition* 1, 131–49.

Harley, B. (1986) *Age in Second Language Acquisition*. Clevedon: Multilingual Matters.

Harley, B. and Wang, B. (1997) The critical period hypothesis: Where are we now? In A.M.B. de Groot and J.F. Kroll (eds) *Tutorials in Bilingualism: Psycholinguistic Perspectives* (pp. 19–51). Mahwah, NJ: Lawrence Erlbaum.

Hawkins, E. (ed.) (1996) *Thirty Years of Language Teaching*. London: CILT.

Heighington, S. (1996) Case study 5. Taking up the challenge. In A. Hurrell and P. Satchwell (eds) *Reflections on Modern Languages in Primary Education* (pp. 55–61). London: CILT.

Holmstrand, L.S.E. (1982) *English in the Elementary School*. Stockholm/Uppsala: Almqvist & Wiksell International.

Hurrell, A. and Satchwell, P. (eds) (1996) *Reflections on Modern Languages in Primary Education*. London: CILT.

Jacobs, H.L., Zinkgraf, S.A., Wormuth, D.R., Hartfiel, V.F. and Hughey, J.B. (1981) *Testing ESL Composition*. Newbury: Rowley.

Johnstone, R. (1996) The Scottish initiatives. In E. Hawkins (ed.) *Thirty Years of Language Teaching* (pp. 171–175). London: CILT.

Lasagabaster, D. and Doiz, A. (this volume) Maturational constraints on foreign language written production.

MacWhinney, B. (2000) *The CHILDES Project: Tools for Analysing Talk, Third Edition* (Vols 1 and 2). Mahwah, NJ: Lawrence Erlbaum.

Mayer, M. (1969) *Frog, Where Are You?* New York: The Dial Press.

Muñoz, C. (2000) Bilingualism and trilingualism in school students in Catalonia. In J. Cenoz and U. Jessner (eds.) *English in Europe: The Acquisition of a Third Language* (pp. 157–178). Clevedon: Multilingual Matters.

Muñoz, C. (this volume) Variation in oral skills development and age of onset.

Muñoz, C. and Tragant, E. (2001) Motivation and attitudes towards L2: Some effects of age and instruction. In S. Foster-Cohen and A. Nizegorodcew (eds) *Eurosla Yearbook* (pp. 211–24). Amsterdam: John Benjamins.

Nikolov, M. (1999) 'Why do you learn English?' 'Because the teacher is short.' A study of Hungarian children's foreign language learning motivation. *Language Teaching Research* 3, 33–56.

Oller, J. and Nagato, N. (1974) The long-term effect of FLES: An experiment. *Modern Language Journal* 58, 15–19.

Quay, S. (2001) Managing linguistic boundaries in early trilingual development. In J. Cenoz and F. Genesee (eds) *Trends in Bilingual Acquisition* (pp. 149–199). Amsterdam: John Benjamins.

Satchwell, P. (1996) The present position in England. In E. Hawkins (ed.) *Thirty Years of Language Teaching* (pp. 171–75). London: CILT.

Singleton, D. (1995) Introduction: A critical look at the critical period hypothesis in second language acquisition research. In D. Singleton and Z. Lengyel (eds) *The Age Factor in Second Language Acquisition* (pp. 1–29). Clevedon: Multilingual Matters.

Singleton, D. (2001) Age and second language acquisition. *Annual Review of Applied Linguistics* 21, 77–89.

Singleton, D. and Lengyel, Z. (1995) *The Age Factor in Second Language Acquisition*. Clevedon: Multilingual Matters.

Taechner, T. (1991) *A Developmental Psycholinguistic Approach to Second Language Teaching*. Norwood, NJ: Ablex.

Chapter 5

Age, Length of Exposure and Grammaticality Judgements in the Acquisition of English as a Foreign Language

MARÍA DEL PILAR GARCÍA MAYO

Introduction

Second-language learners vary on a number of individual factors such as personality, motivation , learning style, aptitude and age. It is precisely this last dimension, age, one of the variables that has been most frequently considered in discussions of individual differences in second language acquisition (SLA) (Bialystok, 1997; Bialystok & Miller, 1999; Dulay *et al.*, 1982; Hatch, 1983; Marinova-Todd *et al.*, 2000; Scovel, 2000; Singleton 1989, 1997, 2001; Singleton & Lengyel, 1995).

The main concern of age-related research is whether the age at which someone is first exposed to a second language (L2), in the classroom or naturalistically, affects acquisition of that language in any way. As Larsen-Freeman and Long (1991) point out, some writers claim that SLA is the same process and just as successful whether the learner begins as a child or an adult and / or that adults are really better learners because they start off faster (Ellis, 1985; Flege, 1987). Others consider the data obtained in research ambiguous and that adults are at a disadvantage only in a few areas, especially phonology (McLaughlin, 1984). A third group is convinced that younger learners are at an advantage, particularly where ultimate levels of attainment are concerned (Harley, 1986; Patkowski, 1980)[1].

The reasons for this interest in the age issue relate not only to theoretical matters, such as whether children or adults go about acquisition similarly or differently or whether an innate language faculty continues to function beyond a particular maturational point (Martohardjono & Flynn, 1995), but also to very practical issues such as when L2 instruction should begin at school.

Research findings suggest that the *success* and *rate* of SLA appear to be strongly influenced by the age of the learners. Where success is concerned, the general finding is, not surprisingly, that *the longer the exposure to the L2, the more native-like L2 proficiency becomes* (Burstall, 1975). Success in SLA also appears to be strongly related to the age when SLA is commenced (*the younger the better*) (Johnson & Newport, 1989).

Where rate is concerned, there is evidence to suggest that *older learners are better*. That is, if learners at different ages are matched according to the amount of time they have been exposed to the L2, it is the older learners who reach higher levels of proficiency. Thus, older children acquire a foreign language faster than younger children in early states of morphological and syntactic development where time and exposure are held constant (Krashen *et al.*, 1979).

However, the bulk of research carried out on the age issue concerns learning situations where the second language is in active use within the community, that is, second language learning settings (e.g. learning English in the USA or England, Swedish in Sweden, etc.). Needless to say, those situations have very little in common with those of a foreign-language learning environment in which the language is taught in the classroom but not readily available in the world outside (e.g. learning English in Spain, French in the USA, etc.) (Cook, 1999).

The study reported in this chapter was carried out in a foreign-language environment with bilingual (Basque/Spanish) subjects of different age groups that were learning English as a third language (L3). We were interested in analysing the results obtained by these groups in a specific type of task, namely, a grammaticality-judgement task[2] targeting structures related to the so-called *pro-drop* parameter (Jaeggli & Safir, 1989). Our research questions were the following:

(1) Does length of exposure in a foreign language setting have any influence on target-like performance in a grammaticality judgement task?
(2) Does an earlier exposure to the language mean more target-like performance in that type of task?
(3) Is higher cognitive development related to higher degree of metalinguistic awareness?

The rest of the chapter is structured as follows: the second section briefly introduces the concepts of grammaticality judgement and metalinguistic awareness and it also provides some background information about the *pro-drop* parameter. The next two sections feature information on the subjects, the materials and the hypotheses of the study and provides the results obtained. The final section discusses the possible implications of those results.

Background

Grammaticality judgements

As Gass (1983) mentions, intuitions, particularly judgements of grammaticality, have played an important role in the development of theoretical linguistics but the study of their nature with L2 learners has not received much attention until quite recently (Davies & Kaplan, 1998; Ellis, 1990; Gass, 1994; Hedgcock, 1993; McDonald, 2000; Munnich *et al.*, 1994; Murphy, 1997). Gass mentions two reasons for this fact: the exclusive focus on production data and the uncertainty regarding what is involved in providing judgements have led to a mistrust of this research instrument among some researchers (Ellis, 1991) in the field of SLA.[3] The most important factor leading to this mistrust concerns the learners' overall ability in the target language. There is clearly a difference between L1 judgement data and L2 judgement data. In the case of L2 judgements, one is asking learners to make judgements about the language being learned at a stage in which their knowledge of the system is incomplete. Here, there may be a mismatch between the two systems (the target system and learners' internalised one) with respect to particular phenomena.

As is well known (Eubank *et al.*, 1995; Selinker, 1972), the language L2 learners use (*interlanguage*) is an independent system. If we assume that L2 learners' interlanguages are natural languages, we would suppose that they could be investigated through the same methods as other types of natural languages for which a main methodological device is the use of native speakers' intuitions. Given the competence–performance distinction (Chomsky, 1965), any observations made about how L2 learners construct L2 mental grammars are necessarily made through the evidence provided by their performance. The learners' mental grammars cannot be accessed directly and their properties must be inferred from performance data (Hawkins, 2001: 23).

Schütze (1996) reports that, throughout much of the history of linguistics, linguistic intuitions have been the most important source of evidence in constructing grammars. Major types of intuition include canonical grammaticality judgements, intuitions about derivational morphology, relationships among words, intuitions about correspondences among different utterance types (e.g. question/answer pairs), identification of structural versus lexical ambiguity, and discrimination of the syntactic status of superficially similar word strings, among many others (Chomsky, 1981).

Birdsong (1989) points out that there is a theoretical distinction to be made between *grammaticality judgements* and *acceptability judgements*, despite the fact that the terms are often used interchangeably. As mentioned by Gass (1994: 303) 'the former, in strict linguistic terms, involve those sentences that are generated by the grammar, whereas the latter involve those sentences about which speakers have a feel of well-formedness. As a theoretical construct, grammaticality judgements are not directly accessible but are inferred through acceptability judgements.' Birdsong (1989: 60) also notes that there is a danger of attributing to metalinguistic performance a 'straightforward relationship to linguistic competence.'

Grammaticality judgements are, therefore, not a direct reflection of competence, for competence is an abstraction and it is not measurable. However, there is no question that they provide performance data: the assumption is that a sentence which is judged to be grammatical is in agreement with the learners' interlanguage grammar and that the evolution of learners' intuitions largely reflects the development of interlanguage knowledge (Sorace, 1985).

There are a number of ways in which grammaticality judgements have been used. Gass (1994) summarises them in three main areas:

(1) researchers differ in whether or not they ask learners to correct the sentences that are judged ungrammatical (e.g. Munnich *et al.*, 1994);
(2) sometimes learners judge individual sentences, some others they are asked to provide preference judgements (i.e. select the more appropriate sentence among the ones provided) (Lakshmanan & Teranishi, 1994); and
(3) learners are given a number of possible responses to choose from (responses may be dichotomous – a sentence can be either grammatical or ungrammatical; or there may be a range of possibilities that include the degree of confidence a learner has in making responses).

Besides these three main areas, researchers vary widely in (1) whether they use a standard grammaticality judgement, in which subjects are allowed as much time as necessary to complete the task, they may be asked to correct sentences considered ungrammatical and even to explain why they think so, versus a timed grammaticality judgement task, like the Magnitude Estimation technique reported on in Sorace (1996), and (2) the number of sentences subjects are asked to give judgements about, ranging from 30 or 40 to more than 200.

The grammaticality-judgement elicitation technique is just one of the methods of obtaining information about the knowledge L2 learners have and, as other performance measures, is not without its limitations (Cowan & Hatasa, 1994; Davies & Kaplan, 1998; García Mayo, 2003; García Mayo & Lázaro Ibarrola, 2001; Goss *et al.*, 1994). Sorace (1996: 376–7) mentions a variety of extralinguistic factors that may influence the validity of L1 intuitions but can apply to non-native judgements as well: parsing strategies, context and mode of presentation and pragmatic considerations, among others. However, as Hedgcock (1993: 16) points out:

> One aspect of the L2 knowledge base which researchers may control for is the manner and content of subjects' training in the L2. Holding this factor constant would ensure that subjects had available to them roughly the same amount, and essentially the same type, of instructional input. Thus, to the extent that subjects' learning and use of L2 is primarily tutored (and probably formal) in nature, and is of comparable duration, it is not unreasonable to assert that the L2 data made available to learners may contribute to an L2 knowledge base which is similarly constructed across all subjects (although learner-to-learner variation would certainly have to be allowed for).

As we will see later, the subjects in our study have the same amount and the same type of instructional input and they were matched for number of hours of exposure to the foreign language they were learning. The grammaticality-judgement task was added as another test among the battery they had to take (see Cenoz, Chapter 4), as a complementary measure in the study of the subjects' interlanguage.

Metalinguistic awareness

Besides the performance information grammaticality judgements provide, there is yet another additional aspect to be considered. Galambos and Hakuta (1988: 141) define the ability to think about language, *metalinguistic awareness*, as 'the ability to attend and reflect upon the properties of languages'. Baker (1993: 122) defines it as 'the ability to think about and reflect upon the nature and functions of language'.

Metalinguistic activities encompass a wide range of phenomena part of which are linguistic intuitions (including grammaticality judgements). A common aspect emphasised in most definitions of metalinguistic awareness is the ability on the part of the speaker to view language in and of itself, and to be able to perform certain operations on it. In this sense, grammaticality judgements are crucial in determining this ability. Gass (1983) claims that metalinguistic awareness has an important function for L2 learners, allowing them to make comparisons between native language and target language, self-correct and perhaps even monitor their output. Investigating a learner's ability to judge grammaticality, Gass claims, is therefore essential to an understanding of learner development.

For Bialystok (1981) simple grammaticality-judgement tasks reflect information about implicit knowledge, that is, the intuitive knowledge of language, but additional tasks, such as correction of errors, reflect explicit, analysed knowledge that represents consciously held insights about language. In this chapter we will be examining both implicit and explicit knowledge.

The pro-drop parameter

Although Spanish and Basque are languages with very different origins (the former is a Latin-based language while the latter has non-Indoeuropean roots), they both belong to the group of so-called *pro-drop* languages (Ortiz de Urbina, 1989). According to Chomsky (1981), Jaeggli (1982), Jaeggli and Safir (1989) and Rizzi (1982, 1986), the *pro-drop* parameter differentiates, for instance, Spanish and Italian from English with respect to the properties in the following list.[4]

(A) Spanish and Basque, unlike English, can have missing subjects, as shown in (1) and (2), where following standard practice an asterisk indicates ungrammaticality:

    (1) Spanish: Llegaron   a   las   seis
                 arrive 3pl PAST   a t   the   six
                 'They arrived at six'

          Basque: Seietan   iritsi   ziren
                 six-LOC   arrive   3pl PAST
                 'They arrived at six'

          English: *Arrived at six versus They arrived at six

    (2) Spanish: Llovió   mucho   ayer
                 rain 3sg PAST   a lot   yersterday
                 'It rained a lot yesterday'

          Basque: Atzo   euri   asko   egin   zuen
                 yesterday   rain   a lot   make AUX–3s
                 'It rained a lot yesterday'

          English: *Rained a lot yesterday versus It rained a lot yesterday

(B) Spanish and Basque, unlike English, can have free subject-verb inversion, as shown in (3):

    (3) Spanish: Han   venido   mis amigos
                 have 3pl   come-PP   my friends
                 'My friends have come'

Basque: Etorri dira   nire   lagunak
         come AUX 3pl   I-GEN   friend-ABS-PL
         'My friends have come'

English: *Have come my friends versus My friends have come

(C) Spanish and Basque can have apparent violations of the so-called *that-trace filter*. The filter accounts for the fact that extraction of a *wh*-phrase from the subject position next to a lexically filled complementiser is excluded in English, as illustrated in (4):

(4) Spanish: ¿Quién dijiste   que ____ llegó   tarde?
             who say–2nd sg.   that   arrive–3rd sg. late
             'Who did you say arrived late?'

Basque: Nor esan   zenuen   berandu   iritsi
        Who say-PF   AUX 2sg.   late   arrive-PF AUX- 3sg-
        PAST

        zela?
        that
        'Who did you say arrived late?'

English: *Who did you say that ____ arrived late? versus Who did you say arrived late?

As already mentioned, our subjects speak two *pro-drop* languages, Basque and Spanish, and are learning a non-*pro-drop* one, English.

Subjects, Design and Material

Subjects

The subjects of this study were two groups of Basque/Spanish bilinguals who were studying English as an L3 at the same school. Participants were given proficiency tests to assure adequate competence in the two languages (Sierra & Olaziregui, 1991). The groups were matched for number of hours of exposure and type of instruction received but, crucially, they differed in the age of first exposure to English (8–9 versus 11–12). The subjects' knowledge of English came exclusively from classroom exposure. Table 1 illustrates the composition of the groups which will be briefly described in the following lines.

Group A was made up of 30 11–12-year-old subjects who were first exposed to English when they were 8–9. Group B was made up of 30 14–15-year-old subjects who were first exposed to English when they were 11–12.

Table 1 Subjects participating in the study[5]

Academic year	Group	Number of subjects	Age at time of testing (mean)	Age of first exposure	Years	Hours
1996–97	A	30	11–12 (11.3)	8–9	4	396
1996–97	B	30	14–15 (14.26)	11–12	4	396
1998–99	C	26	13–14 (13.15)	8–9	6	594
1998–99	D	18	16–17 (16.3)	11–12	6	594

At the time the task was performed, both groups were in their fourth year of exposure to the language (approximately 396 hours). Group C and Group D are actually Groups A and B, respectively, but now in their sixth year of exposure to the language (approximately 594 hours).

Design and materials

Students were given a grammaticality-judgement (GJ) task with 17 sentences related to the *pro-drop* parameter and 13 distractors. The test based on White (1985)[6] – see Appendix – consisted of the following items.

(1) six ungrammatical sentences with missing subjects (*We will be late for school if don't take this bus);
(2) five ungrammatical sentences with subject–verb inversion (*Slept the baby for three hours);
(3) six sentences relevant to the *that-trace* effect: two were ungrammatical in English (*Who did you say that arrived late?) and four were grammatical with *that* omitted (Who do you think will win the prize?)

Students received task instructions in Basque and were asked to decide which sentences were correct, and which ones incorrect and to say 'don't know' for those they had doubts about. If they thought the sentence was incorrect, they were asked to make the relevant changes.[7]

Research questions and contrasts analysed

In the present chapter we want to answer the following research questions:

(1) Does *length of exposure* in a foreign-language setting have any influence on target-like performance in a grammaticality-judgement task?,
(2) What about its influence on metalinguistic awareness?

In order to answer these two questions, we analysed the results obtained by the same group of subjects at Time 1 (396 hours of exposure) and Time 2 (594 hours of exposure). That is, we analysed the contrasts between Group

A vs Group C and Group B versus Group D: the same two groups before and after 198 extra hours of exposure. The working hypothesis was that the longer the exposure to the L2, the more target-like proficiency would become and the more metalinguistically aware learners would be.

(3) Does an *earlier exposure* to the language mean a better performance in a grammaticality-judgement task? Does it mean that subjects who have had an earlier exposure to the language would be more metalinguistically aware?

In order to answer this question we analysed the results obtained by Group C and Group D whose members had been first exposed to English at different ages (Group C, 8–9; Group D, 11–12) but had the same number of hours of instruction (594, approximately).[8] Based on previous research (García Mayo, 1999), the working hypothesis was that, where time and exposure are held constant, older children would be more target-like and more metalinguistic aware than younger ones.

Results

The contrasts related to grammaticality judgements are featured first, followed by the contrasts related to metalinguistic awareness.

Grammaticality judgements

Tables 2 and 3 show the results for Groups A and C and Tables 4 and 5 those for Groups B and D (recall that A/C and B/D are the same group of subjects after 198 extra hours of exposure).[9]

Interestingly, the same pattern can be observed when Time 1 (T1) and Time 2 (T2) are compared in the two groups and the same comments apply for both. There are statistically significant differences between T1 and T2 in both groups as far as:

Table 2 Grammaticality-judgement task: Group A

	Don't know (%)	*Correct (%)*	*Incorrect (%)*
*Ø-subject	44[a]	47	9[a]
*V–S[a]	40[a]	44	16[a]
*that-trace	62[a]	30	8[b]
Ø-trace	52[a]	34[b]	14

[a] $p \approx 0$; [b] $p < 0.05$

Table 3 Grammaticality-judgement task: Group C

	Don't know (%)	Correct (%)	Incorrect (%)
*Ø-subject	14[a]	57	29[a]
*V–S	11[a]	41	48[a]
*that-trace	12[a]	67	21[b]
Ø-trace	14[a]	68[b]	18

[a] $p \approx 0$; [b] $p < 0.05$

Table 4 Grammaticality-judgement task: Group B

	Don't know (%)	Correct (%)	Incorrect (%)
*Ø-subject	44[a]	20	36[b]
*V–S	47[a]	23	30[a]
*that-trace	53[b]	43	4[b]
Ø-trace	61[a]	36[c]	3

[a] $p \approx 0$; [b] $p < 0.05$; [c] $p < 0.10$

Table 5 Grammaticality-judgement task: Group D[5]

	Don't know (%)	Correct (%)	Incorrect (%)
*Ø-subject	15[a]	37	48[b]
*V–S	9[a]	21	70[a]
*that-trace	6[b]	69	25[b]
Ø-trace	10[a]	46[c]	44

[a] $p \approx 0$; [b] $p < 0.05$; [c] $p < 0.10$.

(1) the correct identification of ungrammatical sentences as incorrect with:

   (a) null subjects (A: 9% vs C: 29%; B: 36% vs D: 48%)
   (b) subject-verb inversion (A: 16% vs C: 48%; B: 30% vs D: 70%)
   (c) *that-trace (A: 8% vs C: 21%; B: 4% vs D: 25%)

(2) the correct identification of grammatical sentences as correct with *that* omitted (A: 34% versus C: 68%; B: 36% versus D: 46%)

(3) the decrease in the 'don't know' answers in all four aspects of the *pro-drop* parameter tested.

In view of these results, we conclude that length of exposure to the foreign language seems to have a positive effect in the target-like performance of these subjects. Thus, it appears that in a foreign language setting evidence can also be found to support the hypothesis that the longer the exposure to the L2, the more native-like L2 performance becomes.

In order to answer research question (3) (Does an earlier exposure to the language mean a more target-like performance in a grammaticality-judgement task?), we analysed the results obtained by Group C and Group D whose subjects had been first exposed to English at different ages (Group C: 8–9, Group D, 11–12). Tables 6 and 7 show the results corresponding to Groups C and D:

Statistically significant differences between the two groups are found as far as:

(1) the incorrect identification of ungrammatical sentences as correct with missing subjects (C: 57% versus D: 37%); and subject–verb inversion (C: 41% versus D: 21%); and
(2) the correct identification of the ungrammatical sentences as incorrect with missing subjects (C: 29% versus D: 48%) and subject–verb inversion (C: 48% versus D: 70%).

That is, the statistically significant differences are in favour of the older learners: they behave in a more target-like fashion as far as providing accurate grammaticality judgements of the sentences under study. There are no significant differences in those aspects related to *that*-trace effects, a pattern that has already been reported in previous work with adult EFL learners (García Mayo, 1997, 1998).

Table 6 Grammaticality-judgement task: Group C

	Don't know (%)	*Correct (%)*	*Incorrect (%)*
*Ø-subject	14	57[b]	29[b]
*V–S	11	41[b]	48[b]
*that-trace	12	67	21
Ø-trace	14	68	18

[a] $p < 0.05$

Table 7 Grammaticality-judgement task: Group D

	Don't know (%)	*Correct (%)*	*Incorrect (%)*
*Ø-subject	15	37[b]	48[b]
*V–S	9	21[b]	70[b]
*that-trace	6	69	25
Ø-trace	10	46	44

[b] $p < 0.05$

Metalinguistic awareness

In order to answer research question (2) (Is higher cognitive development related to higher degree of metalinguistic awareness?), we carried out the same contrasts as before as to (i) the percentage of sentences recognized as ungrammatical by the different groups and (ii) how many out of the sentences recognised as ungrammatical were appropriately corrected. Tables 8 and 9 illustrate the contrasts between Groups A and C, on one hand, and B and D, on the other.

Table 8 shows the results obtained by the learners whose first exposure to English was when they were eight years old; the only significant difference after 168 extra instructional hours is the one related to the percentage of appropriate corrections made. Table 9 shows the results for the group whose first exposure to the language was when they were 11 years old. The contrasts are significant both as to the percentage of sentences recognised as ungrammatical and as to the ones appropriately corrected.

Table 10 shows the contrast between two groups with the same number of hours of exposure but with different ages of first exposure to English. Both contrasts are significant, which seems to indicate that Group D (age of first exposure 11–12) has a greater sensitivity to deviance, that is, that subjects in this group have a greater ability to pinpoint the troublespot in each sentence and provide a correction for the problems they find.

Table 8 Recognition and correction of ungrammatical sentences (Group A versus Group C)

	Group A (%)	*Group C (%)*
Percentage of sentences recognised as ungrammatical	30	32
Out of those sentences recognised as ungrammatical, total appropriately corrected	9^b	30^b

^{b} $p < 0.05.$

Table 9 Recognition and correction of ungrammatical sentences (Group B versus Group D)

	Group B (%)	*Group D (%)*
Percentage of sentences recognized as ungrammatical	47^b	52^b
Out of those sentences recognised as ungrammatical, total appropriately corrected	59^b	73^b

^{b} $p < 0.05.$

Table 10 Recognition and correction of ungrammatical sentences (Group C versus Group D)

	Group B (%)	Group D (%)
Percentage of sentences recognized as ungrammatical	32[a]	52[a]
Out of those sentences recognized as ungrammatical, total appropriately corrected	30[a]	73[a]

[b] $p < 0.05$.

Discussion

Considering the data analysed here, and as for our first research question, we concluded that the length of exposure to the foreign language (English) seems to have a positive effect on the subjects' performance, at least with respect to grammaticality-judgement tasks. As we have seen, there is a significant increase in the correct identification of ungrammatical sentences as incorrect and a significant decrease in the percentage of 'don't know' answers. Thus, it appears that evidence can also be found in a foreign language setting in favour of the hypothesis that the longer the exposure to the L2, the better performance becomes.

As for the question regarding earlier timing of first exposure, we found that older subjects who had been first exposed to English at 11–12 perform more successfully than the younger group, whose first exposure to the language was at age 8–9. These results support research carried out in a similar project (Celaya *et al.*, 2001; Fullana, 1998; Fullana & Muñoz, 1999; Muñoz, 1999, this volume, Chapter 8; Pérez Vidal *et al.* 2000; Victori & Tragant, this volume, Chapter 9) in which the older subjects obtained significantly higher scores than the younger ones in several different types of task (grammar, cloze, dictation, written composition and minimal pair discrimination). Thus, it seems that an earlier start does not produce significantly better results in a situation of instructed foreign-language acquisition, that is, the earlier is not the better, at least in this context (García Mayo, 2000; García Mayo *et al.*, 2001a, b, c, 2002; Lázaro Ibarrola *et al.*, 2001). Considering the results reported in García Mayo (1999), in which the older group did better than the younger one (Group A), it seems that 198 extra hours of exposure do not seem to be sufficient for the younger learners to improve to the level of the older ones.

What about metalinguistic awareness? The contrast between Groups C and D showed a greater sensitivity to deviance by the older group (i.e. the one exposed to the language later in life), and the contrasts between Groups A/C and B/D revealed an overall ability to make appropriate corrections in those sentences identified as ungrammatical at Time 2, after more hours of instruction.[10]

The literature on the validity and reliability of grammaticality judgements emphasises the idea that caution must be applied when interpreting the data elicited in this way. Although we realised that there may be problems such as indeterminacy (Gass, 1994; Sorace, 1988) with the items related to the *that*-trace effect (that is, there were few items and they could be beyond the level of the learners), we also want to emphasise the interesting significant differences between younger and older subjects which are shown by the grammaticality-judgement task. The results obtained by this research instrument support research carried out using other instruments (see Cenoz, this volume, Chapter 4; García Lecumberri & Gallardo del Puerto, this volume, Chapter 6; Lasagabaster & Doiz, this volume, Chapter 7). A possible explanation for the older learners' better performance could be their greater cognitive ability (Felix, 1981; Harley, 1986; Krashen *et al.* 1979; Piaget & Inhelder,1969). Krashen *et al.* (1979) have already argued that older learners were better and quicker than younger ones, specifically in the acquisition of the morphological aspects of language. We need to examine the progress of these children further and see whether the older learners continue to do better than the younger ones or whether the younger ones eventually surpass them..

The results presented here, which are part of a larger longitudinal research project on the issue of age and the acquisition of English as an L3 in the Basque Country, are also supported by those obtained in a similar research project in Catalonia (Muñoz, 1999). When one considers the overall picture emerging from these studies, it seems clear that the early introduction of the English language in classroom settings will not lead to appropriate results if instructional hours are not used effectively and there is no increase in the number of hours of exposure. As for the former, plans should be made to use the language as a means of instruction *and* communication in class: students should be given the opportunity to have communicative and significant interaction. Regarding the increase in hours of exposure, content-based teaching should be considered a possibility and work should also be done on the area of changing motivation and attitudes toward the study of a foreign language. As Lightbown (2000: 449) observes:

> If the total amount of time of instruction is limited, it is likely to be more effective to begin instruction when learners have reached an age at which they can make use of a variety of learning strategies, including their L1 literacy skills, to make the most of that time.

A call for more research on age-related issues needs to be made so that L2/L3 acquisition in instructed foreign language settings is considered in more detail. Otherwise, we would run the risk of overgeneralising the findings to contexts where no research has been done yet.

Acknowledgements

This study is part of a larger longitudinal research project carried out under research grants DGICYT PS95–0025, DGES PB97–0611, BFF–2000–0101 (Spanish Ministry of Science and Technology), PI–1998–96 (Basque Government) and 9/UPV 00103.130–13578/2001 (University of the Basque Country). Those grants are hereby gratefully acknowledged. Shorter versions of this chapter were presented at the XXIV International AEDEAN Conference (Ciudad Real, 14–16 December 2000) and at the Third International Symposium on Bilingualism (Bristol, 18–20 April 2001). I thank the audiences there for useful comments. I also wish to thank Stefka H. Marinova-Todd for comments and suggestions to improve earlier versions of this chapter and Vicente Núñez Antón (Department of Econometrics and Statistics, University of the Basque Country) for the statistical analysis of the data. All errors remain my responsibility.

Notes

1. A detailed review of the main positions can be found in Birdsong (1999) and Singleton (1989) and is well beyond the scope of this chapter.
2. As Gass (1994: 303; 2001: 229) points out, there is a difference between acceptability judgements and grammaticality judgements, the latter being the term commonly in use. In linguistically-based second language acquisition research, one asks the subjects about the (un)acceptability of sentences and infers from the answer whether the sentence is grammatical (i.e. whether it is generated by the grammar).
3. Chaudron (1983) in his literature review on the subject pointed out that grammaticality judgements are complex behavioural activities that must be used with caution and with full understanding of their limitations. For a review of linguistic and extralinguistic variables in judgement tasks see Hedgcock (1993), Schütze (1996) and Sorace (1996).
4. The *pro-drop* parameter allows for the personal pronoun to be omitted in languages where the verbs are inflected to reflect that pronoun. Accounts of this parameter differ considerably as to the number of properties that cluster with the presence or absence of null subjects (White, 1989: 84ff). For an analysis of the evolution of research on the *pro-drop* parameter see Liceras (1997a, b).
5. Group A: sixth grade, primary school; Group B: third Compulsory secondary; Group C: second Compulsory secondary; Group D: 1st non-compulsory secondary. The Spanish educational system starts when children are three years old. From three to six, they attend pre-primary school; primary school covers the period from 6 to 12; compulsory secondary education (Educación Secundaria Obligatoria) goes from the period of 12 to 16 and non-compulsory secondary (bachillerato) from 16 to 18.
6. Although White (1989: 88) herself admits that there are problems with some of

the items, we used a similar test in order to be able to establish comparisons with previous research.

7. The Magnitude Estimation technique (Sorace, 1993, 1996) was not considered a possibility in this context due to the difficulty in making sure that informants understand and apply the concept of ratio (Sorace, 1993: footnote 19).

8. The contrast between Groups A and B has already been analysed in previous work (García Mayo, 1999).

9. Correct = subjects' judgement of sentences as correct.
   Incorrect = subjects' judgement of sentences as incorrect
   *Ø-subject = ungrammatical sentences with null subjects (*We will be late for school if don't take this bus)
   *V–S = ungrammatical sentences with subject-verb inversion (*Slept the baby for three hours)
   *that-trace: ungrammatical sentences with extraction of the embedded subject and the complementiser I intact (*Who did you say that arrived late?)
   Ø-trace = grammatical sentences with *that* omitted (Who do you think will win the prize?)
   Letters next to percentages indicate that there are statistically significant differences between the two groups contrasted (A versus C; B versus D; C versus D). The statistical (non-) significance was established by means of the two-sample binominal test. Statistical data are based on actual numbers and not on percentages, used here for the sake of simplicity.

10. Although we have not focused here on the results regarding the *pro-drop* parameter, it is worth mentioning that the same split of properties observed in García Mayo (1999) when Groups A and B were contrasted could now be observed in the contrast between Groups C and D: there are significant differences in favour of the older learners as far as the correct identification as ungrammatical of sentences with missing subjects and subject–verb inversion but no significant differences as far as those effects having to do with *that-trace and Ø-trace. When the same groups were contrasted after more hours of instruction, significant differences were also observed in sentences with *that*-trace and Ø-trace. However, the results related to these two properties should be considered with caution due to the low number of relevant items included in the test.

References

Baker, C. (1993) *Foundations of Bilingual Education and Bilingualism*.Clevedon: Multilingual Matters.

Bialystok, E. (1997) The structure of age: In search of barriers to second language acquisition. *Second Language Research* 13, 116–37.

Bialystok, E. (1981) The role of linguistic knowledge in second language use. *Studies in Second Language Acquisition* 4(1), 31–45.

Bialystok, E. and Miller, B. (1999) The problem of age in second language acquisition: Influences from language, structure and task. *Bilingualism: Language and Cognition* 2(2), 127–45.

Birdsong, D. (1989) *Metalinguistic Performance and Interlinguistic Competence*. Berlin: Springer.

Birdsong, D. (ed.) (1999) *Second Language Acquisition: The Critical Period Hypothesis*. Mahwah, NJ: Lawrence Erlbaum.

Burstall, C. (1975) Factors affecting foreign language learning: A consideration of some recent research findings. *Language Teaching and Linguistics Abstracts* 8, 5–25.

Celaya, M.L., Torras, M.R. and Pérez Vidal, C. (2001) Short and mid-term effects of an earlier start: An analysis of EFL written production. In S. Foster-Cohen and A. Nizegorodcew (eds) *EUROSLA Yearbook* (pp. 195–209). Amsterdam: John Benjamins.

Ceñoz, J. (this volume) The influence of age on the acquisition of English: General proficiency, attitudes and code-mixing.

Chaudron, C. (1983) Research on metalinguistic judgements: A review of theory, methods and results. *Language Learning* 33(3), 343–77.

Chomsky, N. (1965) *Aspects of the Theory of Syntax*. Cambridge, MA: MIT Press.

Chomsky, N. (1981) *Lectures on Government and Binding*. Dordrecht: Foris.

Cook, V. (1999) Using SLA research in language teaching. *International Journal of Applied Linguistics* 9(2), 267–84.

Cowan, R. and Hatasa, Y. (1994) Investigating the validity and reliability of native speaker and second language judgements about sentences. In E. Tarone, S. Gass and A. Cohen (eds) *Research Methodology in Second Language Acquisition* (pp. 287–302). Hillsdale, NJ: Lawrence Erlbaum.

Davies, W. D. and Kaplan, T. I. (1998) Native speaker vs L2 learner grammaticality judgements. *Applied Linguistics* 19(10), 183–203.

Dulay, H., Burt, M. and Krashen, S. (1982) *Language Two*. Oxford: Oxford University Press.

Ellis, R. (1985) *Understanding Second Language Acquisition*. Oxford: Oxford University Press.

Ellis, R. (1990) Grammaticality judgements and learner variability. In H. Burmeister and P. Rounds (eds) *Variability in Second Language Acquisition: Proceedings of the Tenth Meeting of the Second Language Research Forum* (pp. 25–60). Eugene: Department of Linguistics. University of Oregon.

Ellis, R. (1991) Grammaticality judgements and second language acquisition. *Studies in Second Language Acquisition* 13, 161–86.

Eubank, L., Selinker, L. and Sharwood-Smith, M. (eds) (1995) *The Current State of Interlanguage*. Amsterdam: John Benjamins.

Felix, S. (1981) On the (in)applicability of Piagetian thought to language learning. *Studies in Second Language Acquisition* 3(2), 201–20.

Flege, J. (1987) A critical period for learning to pronounce foreign languages? *Applied Linguistics* 8(2), 162–77.

Fullana, N. (1998) El efecto de la edad y cantidad de exposición a la L2 (inglés) sobre la percepción y producción de los fonemas del inglés. Paper presented at the II Trobada Internacional sobre l'adquisició de les llengües de L'Estat. Universitat de Barcelona, 2–4 September.

Fullana, N. and Muñoz, C. (1999) The development of auditory discrimination skills in EFL learners of different ages. *Proceedings of the XXIII International AEDEAN Conference*. León: Universidad de León . CD-ROM format.

Galambos, S.J. and Hakuta, K. (1988) Subject-specific and task-specific characteristic of metalinguistic awareness in bilingual children. *Applied Psycholinguistics* 9, 141–62.

García Lecumberri, M.L. and Gallardo, F. (this volume) English FL sounds in school learners of different ages.

García Mayo, M.P. (1997) Parametric variation in adult L2 acquisition: The *pro-drop* parameter. In P. Guardia and J. Stone (eds) *Proceedings of the XXth International AEDEAN Conference* (pp. 189–97). Barcelona: Universitat de Barcelona.

García Mayo, M.P. (1998) The null subject parameter in adult second language acquisition. *Atlantis* XX(1), 47–58.

García Mayo, M.P. (1999) Grammaticality judgements, metalinguistic awareness and the age factor in EFL. In P. Gallardo and E. Llurdá (eds) *Proceedings of the XXII International AEDEAN Conference* (pp. 561–66). Lleida: Universitat de Lleida.

García Mayo, M.P. (2000) Juicios de gramaticalidad y el factor edad en inglés como lengua extranjera. Plenary lecture, XIX Summer Courses, The University of the Basque Country (Course: *El factor edad en la adquisición de lenguas extranjeras,* San Sebastián, 10–12 July.)

García Mayo, M.P. (2003) Native vs non-native strategies in rendering grammaticality judgements. *Revista Canaria de Estudios Ingleses* [under review].

García Mayo, M.P. and Lázaro Ibarrola, A. (2001) Strategies in rendering grammaticality judgements in L1 and L2 . In L. Iglesias Rábade and S. Doval Suárez (eds.) *Proceedings of the II International Conference on Contrastive Linguistics* (pp.445–453). Santiago: Universidad de Santiago de Compostela.

García Mayo, M.P., Lázaro Ibarrola, A. and Liceras, J.M. (2001a) La forma *is* y los pronombres débiles como morfemas de concordancia en la interlengua inglesa de niños bilingües castellano/euskera. In L. González Romero, M. Martínez Vázquez, B. Rodríguez Arrizabalaga and P. Ron Vaz (eds) *Recent Approaches to English Grammar* (pp. 77–89). Huelva: Universidad de Huelva.

García Mayo, M.P., Lázaro Ibarrola, A. and Liceras, J.M. (2001b) Comodines *is* y *he* en el inglés/euskera-castellano. In M.R. Pérez and I. Doval (eds) *Adquisición y enseñanza de lenguas, bilingüismo y traducción.* Vigo: Universidad de Vigo [in press].

García Mayo, M.P., Lázaro Ibarrola, A. and Liceras, J.M. (2001c) The English interlanguage of bilingual (Basque–Spanish) children: Evidence for Full Transfer and delay in feature assignment. Paper presented at the 11th EUROSLA conference, Paderborn (Germany), 26–29 September.

García Mayo, M.P., Lázaro Ibarrola, A. and Liceras, J.M. (2002) Agreement in the interlanguage of Basque/Spanish bilingual children: A minimalist farewell to *pro.* Paper presented at the 12th EUROSLA conference. Basel (Switzerland), 18–21 September.

Gass, S.M. (1983) The development of L2 intuitions. *TESOL Quarterly* 17(2), 273–91.

Gass, S.M. (1994) The reliability of second language grammaticality judgements. In E. Tarone, S. Gass and A. Cohen (eds) *Research Methodology in Second Language Acquisition* (pp. 303–22). Mahwah, NJ: Earlbaum.

Gass, S.M. (2001) Innovations in second language research methods. *Annual Review of Applied Linguistics* 21, 221–32.

Goss, N., Ying-Hua, Z. and Lantolf, J. (1994) Two heads may be better than one: Mental activity in second language grammaticality judgements. In E. Tarone, S.M. Gass and A. Cohen (eds) *Research Methodology in Second Language Acquisition* (pp. 263–86). Hillsdale, NJ: Lawrence Erlbaum.

Harley, B. (1986) *Age and Second Language Acquisition.* Clevedon: Multilingual Matters.

Hatch, E. (1983) *Psycholinguistics: A Second Language Perspective.* Rowley, MA: Newbury House.

Hawkins, R. (2001) *Second Language Syntax: A Generative Introduction.* Oxford: Blackwell.

Hedgcock, J. (1993) Well-formed vs ill-formed strings in L2 metalinguistic tasks: Specifying features of grammaticality judgements. *Second Language Research* 9, 1–21.

Jaeggli, O. (1982). *Topics in Romance Syntax*. Dordrecht: Foris.
Jaeggli, O. and Safir, K. (1989) The null subject parameter and parametric theory. In O. Jaeggli and K. Safir (eds) *The Null Subject Parameter* (pp. 1–44). Dordrecht: Foris.
Johnson, J. and Newport, E. (1989) Critical period effects in second language learning: The influence of maturational state on the acquisition of ESL. *Cognitive Psychology* 21, 60–99.
Krashen, S., Long, M. and Scarcella, R. (1979) Age, rate and eventual attainment in second language acquisition. *TESOL Quarterly* 9, 573–82.
Lakshmanan, U. and Teranishi, K. (1994) Preference versus grammaticality judgements: Some methodological issues concerning the governing category parameter in second language acquisition. In E. Tarone, S. Gass and A. Cohen (eds) *Research Methodology in Second Language Acquisition* (pp. 185–206). Mahwah, NJ: Erlbaum.
Larsen-Freeman, D. and Long, M. (1991) *An Introduction to Second Language Acquisition Research*. New York: Longman.
Lasagabaster, D. and Doiz, A. (this volume) Maturational constraints on foreign language written production.
Lázaro Ibarrola, A., García Mayo, M.P. and Liceras, J.M. (2001) Age and the acquisition of English as an L3 by bilingual (Basque–Spanish) children: Is the earlier the better? *Proceedings of the Second International Conference on Third Language Acquisition and Trilingualism*. CD-ROM document.
Liceras, J.M. (1997a) The now and then of L2 growing pains. In L. Diaz and C. Pérez (eds) *Views on the Acquisition and Use of a Second Language* (pp. 65–85). Barcelona: Universitat Pompeu Fabra.
Liceras, J. M. (1997b) La evolución del concepto de parámetro en la teoría lingüística y las consecuencias para la gramática comparada. In P. Fernández Nistal and J.M.Bravo Gozalo (eds) *Aproximaciones a los Estudios de Traducción* (pp. 71–113).Valladolid: Servicio de Apoyo a la Enseñanza.
Lightbown, P. (2000) Classroom second language acquisition research and second language teaching. *Applied Linguistics* 21(4), 431–82.
Marinova-Todd, S.H., Bradford Marshall, D. and Snow, C.E. (2000) Three misconceptions about age and L2 learning. *TESOL Quarterly* 34(1), 9–35.
Martohardjono, G. and Flynn, S. (1995) Is there an age factor for Universal Grammar? In D. Singleton and Z. Lengyel (eds) *The Age Factor in Second Language Acquisition* (pp. 135–53). Clevedon: Multilingual Matters.
McDonald, J.L. (2000) Grammaticality judgements in a second language: Influence of age of acquisition and native language. *Applied Psycholinguistics* 21, 395–423.
McLaughlin, B. (1984) *Second Language Acquisition in Childhood*. Hillsdale, NJ: Lawrence Erlbaum.
Munnich, E., Flynn, S. and Martohardjono, G. (1994) Elicited imitation and grammaticality judgment tasks: What they measure and how they relate to each other. In E. Tarone, S. Gass and A. Cohen (eds) *Research Methodology in Second Language Acquisition* (pp. 227–43). Mahwah, NJ: Erlbaum.
Muñoz, C. (1999) The effects of age on instructed foreign language acquisition. In S. González-Fernández Corugedo, R. Baldeón, D. García, A. Ojanguren, M. Urdiales and A. Antón (eds) *Essays in English Language Teaching: A Review of the Communicative Approach* (pp. 1–22). Oviedo: Universidad de Oviedo.
Muñoz, C. (this volume) Variation in oral skills development and age of onset.
Murphy, V.A. (1997) The effect of modality on a grammaticality judgment task. *Second Language Research* 13(1), 34–65.
Ortiz de Urbina, J. (1989) *Parameters in the Grammar of Basque*. Dordrecht: Foris.

Patkowski, M. (1980) The sensitive period of the acquisition of syntax in a second language. *Language Learning* 30, 449–72.

Pérez Vidal, C., Torras, M.R. and Celaya, M.L. (2000) Age and EFL written performance by Catalan–Spanish bilinguals. *Spanish Applied Linguistics* 4(2), 267–90.

Piaget, J. and Inhelder, B. (1969). *The Psychology of the Child.* London: Routledge and Kegan Paul.

Rizzi, L. (1982) *Issues in Italian Syntax.* Dordrecth: Foris.

Rizzi, L. (1986) Null objects in Italian and the theory of *pro. Linguistic Inquiry* 17, 501–57.

Schütze, D.T. (1996) *The Empirical Base of Linguistics. Grammaticality Judgements and Linguistic Methodology.* Chicago: The University of Chicago.

Scovel, T. (2000) A critical review of the critical period hypothesis. *Annual Review of Applied Linguistics* 20, 213–23.

Selinker, L. (1972) Interlanguage. *International Review of Applied Linguistics* 10, 209–31.

Sierra, J. and Olaziregi, I. (1991) *HINE: Hizkuntza Idatziaren Neurketa Eskolen* (Measurement of written proficiency in school contexts). Gasteiz: Basque Government Press Service.

Singleton, D. (1989) *Language Acquisition: The Age Factor.* Clevedon: Multilingual Matters.

Singleton, D. (1997) Age and second language learning. In R. Tucker and D. Corson (eds) *Encyclopedia of Language and Education* (pp. 43–50). Dordrecht: Kluwer.

Singleton, D. (2001) Age and second language acquisition. *Annual Review of Applied Linguistics* 21, 77–98.

Singleton, D. and Lengyel, Z. (eds) (1995) *The Age Factor in Second Language Acquisition.* Clevedon: Multilingual Matters.

Sorace, A. (1985) Metalinguistic knowledge and language use in acquisition-poor environments. *Applied Linguistics* 6(3), 239–54.

Sorace, A. (1988) Linguistic intuitions in interlanguage development: The problem of indeterminacy. In J. Parkhurst, M. Sharwood-Smith and P. Van Buren (eds) *Learnability and Second Languages* (pp. 167–91). Dordrecht: Foris.

Sorace, A. (1993) Incomplete vs divergent representations of unaccusativity in non-native grammars of Italian. *Second Language Research* 9 , 22–47.

Sorace, A. (1996) The use of acceptability judgements in second language acquisition research. In W.C. Ritchie and T.K. Bathia (eds) *Handbook of Second Language Acquisition* (pp. 375–409). New York: Academic Press.

Victori, M. and Tragant, E. (this volume) Learner strategies: A cross-sectional and longitudinal study of primary and high-school EFL learners.

White, L. (1985) The pro-drop parameter in adult second language acquisition. *Language Learning* 35, 47–62.

White, L. (1989) *Universal Grammar and Second Language Acquisition.* Amsterdam: John Benjamins.

Appendix

Read the following sentences and indicate whether they are *correct, incorrect* or you *don't know*. If you think they are incorrect, make the changes that you consider necessary.

(1)   We will be late for school if don't take this bus.
(2)   Seems that Patricia is sad.

(3) The policeman did not know when escape the prisoner.
(4) My sister is very tired because came home late last night.
(5) Who do you think will win the prize?
(6) There looked a strange man through the window.
(7) Slept the baby for three hours.
 (8) Who did you say that arrived late?
 (9) Which men did she say would marry her?
(10) Which movie do you think that will be on television this evening?
(11) Francis is in trouble because did not do his homework.
(12) Walked the boy very far.
(13) John is bad-mannered. Eats like a pig.
(14) What programme did you say that John watched last night?
(15) The mailman came. Have arrived three letters.
(16) Who do you believe will be the next president of the USA?
(17) Is raining very hard today.

Chapter 6

English FL Sounds in School Learners of Different Ages

MARÍA LUISA GARCÍA LECUMBERRI and FRANCISCO GALLARDO

Introduction

In recent decades there has been a vindication of the role of pronunciation in foreign language (FL) effective communication and a considerable increase in research addressing the mechanisms of second language (L2) speech learning and the reasons for foreign accents.

The traditional view of native language (NL) transfer as the main reason for learner errors (Stockwell & Bowen, 1965) has been strongly contested in recent years. Nevertheless most authors (Altenberg & Vago, 1983; Eckman, 1977; Ellis, 1994; Flege, 1992, 1999; García Lecumberri & Cenoz, 1997; Ioup, 1984; Major, 1987a, 2001; Scholes, 1986; Wode, 1980) believe that phonetic/ phonological mistakes are very often due to first language (L1) influences, more so than errors at other levels (Ellis, 1994; Ioup, 1984; Leather & James, 1991) and mediated by factors such as markedness (Carlisle, 1994; Eckman, 1977), universal tendencies (Altenberg & Vago, 1983; Wode, 1980), stage of L2 acquisition (Fox *et al.*, 1995; Hammarberg, 1990; Major, 1987b; Wenk, 1986), degree of L1 maintenance (Flege, 1999; Thompson, 1991) etc. (see Leather, this volume, for more details).

Additionally, learners' personal characteristics such as age, motivation, sociolinguistic and affective factors (Bongaerts, 1999; Bongaerts *et al.*, 1995, 1997; Cenoz & García Lecumberri, 1999a, 1999b; Guiora *et al.*, 1980; Major, 1987a; Purcell & Suter, 1980; Singleton, 1989, Thompson, 1991) and the characteristics of the learning process such as its context, the amount and type of L2 sound exposure (Bongaerts *et al.*, 1995; Krashen *et al.*, 1982; Singleton, 1989) and instruction types employed (Blanco *et al.*, 1997; Ioup, 1995) have proved to have a bearing on the weight that transfer may have and on the level of FL phonetic development. Accordingly, transfer is generally accepted to be particularly important in the acquisition of an FL sound system, although mediated by the above mentioned factors and just one of the strategies learners may employ (Odlin, 1989).

Learners' Age

Let us now concentrate briefly on one of the factors that may have an influence on FL acquisition: – learners' age (see Singleton, this volume, Chapter 1, for a more detailed account). When talking of age in the FL acquisition context, it is important to make the following distinction: on the one hand, there is the influence of age as a broad issue which concerns any effects which may correlate with learners' age, either at the beginning of acquisition, at a specific point or in the long term and it refers to any age from birth to senescence (Cook, 1995). On the other hand, there is *one* age effect which has been extensively discussed in the literature and which is commonly known as the Critical Period (CP) for language acquisition. Accordingly, the CP is not synonymous with the influence of age *per se*, but is instead one of the possible aspects of age as a factor.

It has often been observed that adults may acquire a FL to a high level of proficiency but nevertheless retain a foreign accent, whereas children are able to acquire a FL – including its pronunciation – with a native or near-native competence. Observations such as these prompted the critical period hypothesis (CPH) (see Singleton (Chapter 1) and Leather (Chapter 2), this volume) which has received particular support in the case of FL pronunciation (Patkowski, 1990; Pennington, 1998; Scovel, 1988; Strozer, 1994). Scovel (1988) even suggests that pronunciation may be the only linguistic ability to have a critical period because it involves neuro-muscular skills. However, authors such as Klein (1986) only mention the influence of physiological factors for cases of very mature learners whose auditory and neuromuscular deterioration is well advanced.

Explanations for the effect of age on L2 speech acquisition often refer to the establishment of the L1 sound system, suggesting the progressive development of a selective tuning mechanism towards NL sounds as a result of exposure to them. Such accounts can be found in theories like Kuhl's Prototypes (1993), Best's Perceptual Assimilation Model (1994) and Flege's Speech Learning Model (Flege, 1992). In these views, the ability to perceiving other contrasts is not unavoidably lost after a certain age, but it becomes more difficult to access.[1]

Without adhering to the actual CPH, many researchers have suggested that age is an important factor in language acquisition in that the earlier the starting age, the greater the possibility of successful phonological acquisition (Asher & García, 1969; Flege, 1999; Flege *et al.*, 1995; Munro *et al.*, 1996; Oyama, 1976; Thompson, 1991). This position, which we may call 'early advantage', has also been criticised by studies showing that adults may outperform young learners at initial stages of FL acquisition (Burstall, 1975; Muñoz, 2000; Olson & Samuels, 1973; Snow & Hoefnagel-Höhle, 1977; Thogmartin, 1982). However , it has been demonstrated that this initial 'older advantage' may be turned around in the long term, because learners who start acquiring the language early, often end up surpassing adult learners (Cook, 1991; Krashen *et al.*, 1982; Snow & Hoefnagel-Höhle, 1977, 1978).

Some laboratory experiments have shown that adults can be trained to perceive FL sounds and sound sequences and even produce them in such a way that they are indistinguishable from native pronunciations (Neufeld, 1979). However, the methodology of these experiments and their applicability to real life circumstances has been questioned (Long, 1990). There is also evidence showing that adult learners may attain high FL competence even to native or near-native levels (Bohn & Flege, 1992; Bongaerts, 1999; Bongaerts *et al.*, 1995, 1997; Markham, 1997). Nevertheless, these studies often deal with NLs and FLs which are typologically close and phonetically/phonologically similar (as Bongaerts *et al.* admit), often in multilingual societies where the FL is nearly a national L2 (such as is the case for English in Holland). In addition, some studies employ native judges whose accents are very different to the learners' model ones, and who may have little experience in accents even in their own NL, so that their judgements may not be very accurate since they may interpret foreign pronunciations as NL variants (as Markham [1997] notes).

To conclude this discussion on age, we may say that defendants of the existence of early age advantages often use arguments concerning pronunciation acquisition whilst detractors often make the exception of pronunciation as the only linguistic component which may be affected by starting age since it involves not only cognitive development but also neuromuscular coordination skills (Scovel, 1988). Even those who maintain that older learners show an initial advantage, frequently make an exception for oral skills. (Singleton, 1989).

The Significance of Exposure

Let us now consider one of the most important factors in language acquisition, which has been found to interact crucially with age: exposure. With the term 'exposure', we are referring to all the very diverse types of contact that learners have with the TL, including passive listening to real speech, listening to the media, real interactions, classroom instruction, reading, etc. Obviously, for pronunciation acquisition, sources of aural exposure are particularly relevant. It is useful to classify aural exposure along scales of quantity and quality. As far as quantity is concerned, we could talk of a scale where one end represents minimal aural exposure (for instance in old fashioned FL teaching methods based solely on grammar and translation) and the other end represents total immersion in the TL natural context, with 100% of the learners' information and interaction being carried out in the TL. As for quality, single-source non-native heavily NL marked pronunciations of the TL would occupy the lowest end of the scale, whereas very diverse, natural and native speech would be at the other end.

The importance of exposure has been amply demonstrated and also its connections with other factors. Exposure and age seem to be particularly related, in that most authors agree that the combination of high quality and extensive exposure together with early starting age is a good predictor (although not a determiner) of native or near-native FL acquisition (Asher & Garcia, 1969; Flege *et al.*, 1995, 1997b; Singleton, 1989; Thompson, 1991).

We can but agree with authors such as Singleton (1989, 1995) and Ellis (1994), who question the applicability of the CPH to formal instruction contexts. The argument is that native-like acquisition of the phonetic component of an FL may only be attained if a child receives the extensive input and exposure characteristics of language learning in a natural context, similar to the one experienced in NL acquisition, whereas adults rarely attain native competence even if subject to such exposure (Oyama, 1976; Tahta *et al.*, 1981). Singleton (1989) proposes that in the case of non-naturalistic instructed learning, it would take around 18 years of instruction for the advantage shown by young learners over older ones to be neutralised.

Another issue which has deserved researchers' attention in L2 phonological acquisition concerns differences in the behaviour of various phonological components, especially in view of previously mentioned factors such as onset age, exposure and rate of acquisition. L2 learners themselves appear to be aware of these differences since they have reported varying degrees of difficulty for TL vowels, consonants, stress or intonation (Cenoz & García Lecumberri, 1999a). According to some experiments in naturalistic situations (Flege *et al.*, 1997a), age of L2 learning initiation does not seem to play an equal role in L2 consonant acquisition and L2 vowel acquisition. Specifically, while the perception and production of consonant sounds are not especially affected by the age at which L2 learning begins, vowel proficiency turns out to be related to an early onset age in a much more crucial way since it is aided by young starters' facility for L2 category formation.

Some recent perception studies in formal instruction environments have also found differences in the behaviour of different phonological components with regard to exposure, age and rate of acquisition. Contrary to Flege *et al.*'s (1997a) assertion, Fullana & Muñoz (1999) pointed out the resistance of vowel and consonant segments to the facilitating effects of an early onset age and a longer time of exposure. However, the degree of vowel resistance turned out to be different from that of consonants: although in all cases older learners performed better than younger learners, vowel superiority was statistically significant at two different times in the acquisition process, while consonant superiority did not turn out to be significant at Time 2. This was interpreted as younger ones 'catching-up' with older learners, at least for consonant perception. Likewise, an investigation with three different age groups in which subjects' biological age and their time-span of TL learning could not be separated (Lengyel, 1995) discovered that (1) younger subjects were better at recognising segment-level differences, (2) intermediate learners were better at perceiving feature level differences between consonants and suprasegmental differences and (3) older children were better at recognizing feature level differences between vowels. Nevertheless, the differences were not found to be statistically significant.

The present chapter is part of a research project[2] which employs age as one of its main research variables. One of its aims is to find age-related differences in linguistic development for children starting FL instruction at three different ages or school grades. The research is being conducted in an attempt to test the validity of the CPH in formal language instruction and to determine other factors which may influence linguistic development amongst language learners. Our chapter reports on FL English phonetic and phonological acquisition by Basque–Spanish bilingual children learning English as a third language.

Our research aimed to answer the following questions:

(1) What are the differences in English sound perception and pronunciation by groups of children who started formal English learning at three different ages?
(2) Do perception differences support early starting age as a positive factor?
(3) Are there age-related differences between vowel and consonant perception abilities?
(4) Are foreign accent and intelligibility related to starting age?
(5) What other factors can explain learner group differences?

Methods

Our data emerge from a longitudinal study which is being conducted in the English Department of the University of the Basque Country. The data we analyse here corresponds to the third year of the study in which we compare the development of English in children who had started learning this language at school at three different ages: 4, 8 and 11 years of age (see

Table 1 Sample distribution

	Age of first exposure	Mean time-span of exposure (yr)	Age at the time of testing (mean age)
Age group1	4	6	9–11 (9.75)
Age group 2	8	6	13–15 (13.80)
Age group 3	11	6	16–18 (16.75)

Table 1). Twenty children were studied in each of the groups, with a total of 60 subjects.

Participants belonged to three age groups, since they had started learning English at three different ages. Groups were selected so that children had the same average number of years of instruction (they were either in their sixth and seventh year) in English at the same school. Within each age group half of the subjects were in their sixth year of English instruction while the other half were in their seventh year. Therefore, there were no significant differences among the three age groups with regard to the time-span of L3 English learning. None of the children had had extra-curricular tuition in English so their knowledge of the English language came exclusively from their exposure in the classroom context.

The period of instruction at which we analysed our students could be considered to be a 'mid term' or 'short-mid term', as opposed to short term (weeks, months) or 'long-term' (probably the 18 years suggested by Singleton [1989]).

All the subjects were Basque–Spanish bilinguals, differing in whether Basque or Spanish were their NL. Basque is the minority language in the community but it is the instruction language at school. Spanish, however, is the dominant language in the Basque Country but just one of the subjects in the school curriculum. English has FL status in the community and it fills up no more than three hours per week in the school curriculum. Therefore, students were learning English as a third language (L3).

Amongst the instruments used for elicitation of oral data, we analysed their telling of a story common to all of them (*Frog, Where Are You* by Mercer Mayer, 1969) which was presented as an unscripted cartoon with 24 scenes, and the re-telling of a known story (different for each group). Students completed the task individually in the presence of the interviewer and their production was recorded on audio-tape.

Three minute production excerpts were prepared and randomised so that a native English speaker with no specific training in linguistics or phonetics, that is, a 'blind judge' assessed them for degree of foreign accent and intelligibility. Two nine-point Likert scales were used for the two measurements. These scales have previously been found to be appropriate for the task (Munro & Derwing, 1999). Higher scores on each scale corresponded to more 'native-likeness' – that is, lower degree of foreign accent – and to higher intelligibility respectively. Learners' productions were also analysed auditorily and a description of each group's pronunciation was elaborated.

In addition, specific sound perception tests were given to the children. Tests consisted of two similar minimal pair discrimination tasks – one for consonant sounds and one for vowel sounds. Altogether, aural stimuli amounted to 45 English minimal pairs, 23 of them for consonants and 22 for vowels. In order to draw students' attention to the target phoneme oppositions, all stimuli consisted of monosyllable words.

Target consonant sounds were selected on the basis of previous research on consonant difficulties for the three languages considered (García Lecumberri & Elorduy, 1994; Quilis & Fernández, 1996) and on our own acquisition and teaching experience. Some of the contrasts presented in the minimal pair monosyllables referred to problematic initial positions (*goat–coat*), while in other contrasts it was the final consonant that was tested (*bag–back*).

As for vowel sounds, all the R.P.[3] monophthongs were included except for the weak vowel 'schwa'.[4] Those target vowel minimal oppositions which caused the greatest confusion in a previous investigation on EFL vowel perception conducted in the Basque Country (García Lecumberri & Cenoz, 1997) were selectively chosen to be part of the vowel contrasts in our test. Vowel sounds appeared in monosyllable words with a CVC structure, since consonant onsets and especially consonant codas have been found to favour English vowel identification (Strange *et al.*, 1979). In addition, given that not all consonants seem to have the same effect on vowel identification (García Lecumberri & Cenoz, 2003; House & Fairbanks, 1953; Jenkins *et al.*, 1999; Strange *et al.*, 2001), we selected the codas which have been shown to create the most favourable phonetic context for English vowel discrimination, i.e. the alveolar stops /d/ and /n/ (García Lecumberri & Cenoz, 1997; Stevens & House, 1963), as we see, for instance, in the minimal pairs '*good–god*' or '*ban–barn*'.

Stimuli words were recorded, produced by a British female speaker with no particularly marked regional accent. Stimuli were randomised before presenting them to the students. Three months before students took the test, teachers were provided with a list of the words which were to appear in the tests. In this way, they could include them in their English lessons so that students were acquainted with the vocabulary at the time they took part in the experiment. Teaching staff were never informed about the specific aim of the tasks, i.e. that the tests were specifically designed for pronunciation. This was done so as to avoid teachers insisting on the phonetic characteristics of the words when teaching them in the classroom. With this very same purpose, words in the vocabulary list given to the teachers were grouped in semantic fields, i.e. they were not arranged according to their pronunciation but by meaning.

Perception tests were administered individually. Stimuli were presented aurally from an audio-tape and no training was provided beforehand. Each oral stimulus was presented simultaneously with a card where the two possible answers appeared both as printed words and as drawings. Drawings representing words' meanings were much larger than the corresponding orthographic representations and students were urged to point to the drawing and not to the letters, all of which was designed to minimise the possible influence of spelling on children's perceptions.

Data Description

The following tables display perception test results (Tables 2–4) and native judge ratings (Tables 5 and 6). Perceptions are presented as means or percentages (as indicated in each table). Comparisons between the three groups were carried out using ANOVAS. Comparisons between any two groups were done by means of Scheffé tests. Possible correlations between results were explored using Pearson correlation coefficients. Since the consonant perception test had one more item than the vowel perception test, their mean scores were normalized by means of Z scores, which enabled us to establish comparisons. In the corresponding tables, significant differences are marked with an asterisk.

Table 2 presents mean perceptions by each student group for vowels and consonants, as well as ANOVA comparisons of the results for the three groups (*F*). Mean discriminations for both vowels and consonants can be seen to increase proportionally with age so that the youngest students (Group 1) show the worst results, the eldest learners (Group 3) had the best

Table 2 Mean scores, standard deviations and Anova comparisons of correct vowel and consonant discriminations in the three age groups

	Age group 1		Age group 2		Age group 3		Anova	
	x	*SD*	*x*	*SD*	*x*	*SD*	*F*	*p*
Vowels (max = 22)	14.80	2.48	15.80	2.57	17.10	2.02	4.73	0.01*
Consonants (max = 23)	15.20	3.29	16.55	2.50	18.95	2.04	10.20	0.00*

Table 3 Probability in Scheffé two-way listener group comparisons of mean scores

	Age groups 1–2	Age groups 2–3	Age groups 1–3
Vowels	0.41	0.23	0.01*
Consonants	0.28	0.02*	0.00*

Table 4 Right discrimination percentages and Z score t-test comparison probabilities for sound discrimination in all groups and in each of them

	All groups	Age group 1	Age group 2	Age group 3
Vowels	72.2%	67.2%	71.8%	77.7%
Consonants	73.4%	66.0%	71.9%	82.3%
Probability	1.00	0.65	0.75	0.33

discriminations and the performance of the intermediate age group (Group 2) lay in between. Differences among the three groups were significant.

Table 3 presents two-way comparisons of discrimination results. In the case of vowel discriminations, the eldest subjects' discriminations were significantly better ($p < 0.01$) than the youngest group, whereas differences between the intermediate group and the youngest group ($p < 0.41$), and between the intermediate group and the oldest group ($p < 0.23$) were not statistically significant. As for consonant discriminations, group comparisons show that the eldest subjects discriminated significantly better than either of the other groups (versus group 1 $p < 0.00$, versus group 2 $p < 0.02$), whereas the difference between Groups 1 and 2 ($p < 0.28$) is not statistically significant.

Discrimination results are presented as percentages in Table 4 in order to compare vowel and consonant perceptions. Overall, consonants display better discrimination scores than vowels. We can see that the bias in favour of consonant discrimination also increases linearly as a factor of age. Thus in the youngest students the opposite is true, intermediate students favour consonants but only slightly and the eldest do so more noticeably. However, differences do not reach significance levels in any case.

The following tables (5 and 6) display native-speaker judgements on students' productions. The judgements of learners' DFA (degree of foreign accent) and general intelligibility are presented as mean scores and standard deviations. Judgements assigned a score on a scale from 1 to 9 in which 1 represented 'heavy accent' and 'difficult to understand' respectively and at the other end 9 stood for 'slight accent' and 'easy to

Table 5 Mean scores, standard deviations and Anova comparisons of learner Intelligibility and DFA (degree of foreign accent) judgements for the three listener groups

	Age group 1		Age group 2		Age group 3		Anova	
	x	*SD*	*x*	*SD*	*x*	*SD*	*F*	*p*
Foreign accent (min = 1; max = 9)	2.25	0.97	2.20	1.01	3.20	1.47	4.63	0.01*
Intelligibility (min = 1; max = 9)	2.00	1.30	2.95	1.99	4.70	2.13	11.07	0.00*

Table 6 Probability in Scheffé two-way comparisons of mean scores for learner Intelligibility & DFA judgements

	Age groups 1–2	Age groups 2–3	Age groups 1–3
Foreign accent	0.99	0.04*	0.03*
Intelligibility	0.27	0.00*	0.01*

understand'. Thus the higher the scores the lesser the accent and the more intelligible students are considered to be.

As can be seen, in the case of DFA, the two younger groups receive nearly equal scores (with the intermediate group displaying slightly worse FA score) whereas the eldest learners are considered to have less marked foreign accents. In Table 6 we can see that indeed, the difference between Groups 1 and 2 is not significant, whereas Group 3 differs significantly from the other two in this respect.

In contrast, and considering intelligibility, we once more see that this variable increases linearly with age so that the older they are, the more intelligible students are considered to be. This difference is again non-significant when comparing the two younger groups but it is significant when comparing the eldest learners with the others.

Results indicate that overall DFA and intelligibility are directly correlated (Pearson $r = 0.563$; $p = 0.0001$) so that higher intelligibility scores are accompanied by better FA judgements, as would be expected (Munro & Derwing, 1999). Individual group correlations reach significance for Groups 1 and 2 (Group 1, Pearson $r = 0.671$, $p = 0.001$; Group 2, Pearson $r = 0.664$, $p = 0.001$). For Group 3 the correlation does not reach significance level (Pearson $r = 0.305$, $p = 0.190$), probably because of its high standard deviation given the number of participants.

Auditory analyses of each of the student's connected speech production were also performed (see previous section). Descriptions were elaborated for each student. Subsequently, a joint characterisation was produced for each of the three groups and finally groups' characteristics were compared. Auditory analyses indicate that all three groups predominantly use the NL vowel and consonant systems as well as NL phonotactics,[5] that is, students in all three groups employ transfer as their main TL pronunciation strategy. However, lexical transfer with anglisisation, which is more frequent in the two older groups, is effected mainly by stress placement and final syllable vowel deletion: /'pingwin'/ (Spanish 'pin'guino', English 'penguin'; /bosk/ (Spanish 'bosque', English 'forest').

Reading pronunciation is a strategy which shows linear progression with age. In Group 1 many speakers do not show any traces of it at all, and others show only a few instances. In Group 2 all speakers show a few instances and this frequency increases in Group 3. A similar trend was also found by other researchers working with the same population sample (Lasagabaster & Doiz, this volume, Chapter 7). Overall, we found more intra-group differences than inter-group differences with some students standing out from the rest at both ends of the pronunciation scale.

Discussion

In the light of these data, we will now try to answer some of the research questions mentioned in section 1 above.

(1) What are the differences in English sound perception and pronunciation by groups of children who started formal English learning at three different ages?

The results presented here show that, although auditory analyses of student productions do not evince considerable differences (more in point 5 later), the three experimental groups differ from each other both as far as sound discrimination is concerned and also in the judge's estimation of their pronunciations. However, it is worth pointing out that for most variables observed, the eldest learners (Group 3) differ significantly from the other two groups whereas differences between the youngest and intermediate students are found to be non-significant in all cases.

There are considerable inter-group differences for most variables and, in all cases, differences favour older students. As far as sound-type perception is concerned, both vowels and consonants are discriminated better by older students.

Regarding estimations of students' pronunciations, we find that, on the one hand, differences between the two youngest groups are quite small: in particular, DFA is nearly the same for these two groups. On the other hand, and once more, the eldest group (Group 3) differs significantly on both judgement scores from the other two groups so that they are considered both more intelligible and as having a weaker foreign accent. Overall, these two variables are directly correlated so that higher intelligibility ratings correspond to more TL-like accent judgements. These findings agree with a previous study by Munro and Derwing (1999)[6] but not with research on long-term FL learners in native contexts (Flege *et al.*, 1995; Munro *et al.*, 1996), which again highlights the essential differences between the two types of learning situations.

(2) Do perception differences support early starting age as a favouring factor?

It seems quite clear that our results do not support the CPH nor early starting age as a favourable factor, which is not surprising given the context of FL acquisition of our learners and the evidence already mentioned in this respect – Singleton (1995) for example.

The perception results actually indicate that sound discrimination is directly correlated with starting age, so that the older the starting age the better the discrimination results that are obtained. The difference is statistically significant both for vowel ($p < 0.01$) and for consonant ($p < 0.001$) discrimination. Therefore, we see that after an average of 6 years' formal instruction, students who began English instruction at the age of 11 showed significantly better sound discrimination than those who started earlier (age 8 and 4), and that, in turn, those who started at age 8 discriminate better than those who started at age 4. These results agree with previous studies which support the advantage of older learners over younger ones in formal instruction contexts, even for pronunciation skills (Burstall, 1975; Olson & Samuels, 1973). Therefore, in a formal setting and in the mid-term, early starting age does not show any advantage in the perception assessments carried out.

(3) Are there age-related differences between vowel and consonant perception abilities?

There are few differences between vowel and consonant discrimination, which is contrary to previous studies of FL acquisition in natural and formal contexts (Flege *et al.*, 1997a; Fullana & Muñoz, 1999) which argue that different phonological components, specifically vowels and consonants, behave differently depending on age of initiation. The results are also unexpected in the light of the differences between the three languages' vowel and consonant systems and previous research on students' difficulty rating for the two types of sound (Cenoz & García Lecumberri, 1999a), considering which we would have expected consonants to be more accurately perceived by all groups. However, we found that the older the students are, the better they perform on consonant discrimination. Although there are no significant differences, the gap between vowel and consonant discrimination abilities appears to widen as a factor of age which is the opposite to what was found in naturalistic contexts by Flege *et al.* (1997a). In our case English vowel discrimination has not been found to be easier for younger learners and we also found that consonant acquisition is facilitated by late starting age. Our results agree partially with Fullana and Muñoz (1999) in that vowels are not favoured by early starting age, but we disagree as far as consonants are concerned since our younger learners have not caught up with older ones. In fact, we found that both vowel and consonant perception skills are always significantly better for late starters, who are, contrary to Fullana and Muñoz´s (1999) findings, even better at consonant discrimination.

(4) Are foreign accent and intelligibility related to starting age?

In this respect, if early starting age is a favourable factor for FL pronunciation acquisition, we would expect that (1) the degree of foreign accent would be proportional to starting age, so that the older they are, the stronger DFA[7] they would possess; and (2) that intelligibility would be inversely proportional to starting age, such that older students would be less intelligible.

As far as (1) is concerned, we found the opposite to be true since DFA is stronger with younger and intermediate students. However, there are no significant differences between these two groups, so that starting English instruction at age 4 or at age 8 does not seem to matter for DFA, whereas starting at age 11 seems to be relevant since these students obtain significantly better DFA estimations. As for intelligibility, it seems clear that hypothesis (2) is not supported by the data either. Again, the opposite is true: older students are considered significantly more intelligible than younger ones. Consequently, intelligibility is not favoured by early starting age but we find that it is related to age since it increases linearly with age. As would be expected, DFA and intelligibility are statistically correlated and they present the same trends as perception tests results, as discussed earlier. These results would suggest that late starting age is an advantage for our variables, DFA and intelligibility. However, we must bear in mind that none of the students is anywhere near acquiring a native-like pronunciation and that there are other influential factors at work. Still, we could say that results seem to indicate that students starting instruction around age 8 or before are more subject to NL interference as far as a global native judgements of their production are concerned. The caution with which this statement is made is not casual: our own analysis of student productions (see previous section) do not quite agree with the judge's appreciation of DFA, which we consider to be very similar in all groups - with some trends favouring youngest learners- but the consistency of the judge's assessments[8] renders them worthy of consideration. As Munro and Derwing (1999) and Markham (1997) point out, judgements of DFA may be considerably influenced by factors other than phonetic and phonological ones.

(5) What other factors can explain learner group differences?

Auditory analysis of the participants' oral productions shows that NLs' interference is a powerful influence in all three groups, with few differences amongst their pronunciations, although some features indicate more frequent TL realisations amongst the youngest learners. Nevertheless, vowel, consonant and phonotactic components are, overall, very much like the learners' NLs.

NL interference has also been seen as related to the so called 'age factor' by Singleton (1989) in as much as older learners already possess a sound knowledge of their first language which is not the case in very young learners (below school age) which may account for different degrees of interference. However, in our study, since all the participants started learning English after their NLs' were almost totally established (minimum age was 4), at least as far as their phonological systems are concerned, we should not expect the weight of NL interference to be less for the younger participants. Indeed, NL influence is pervasive in all three age groups and the main strategy for all the participants independent of age.

One of the age-varying elements we found between groups is an increase in reading pronunciation proportional to age. This is probably related to teaching methods, since the youngest learners started instruction without written materials and thus during their instruction period they had less exposure to spelling.[9] However, reading pronunciation may also be a type of NL influence since in both their NLs, orthography and pronunciation bear a strong correspondence and, clearly, in the older groups this correspondence has a stronger establishment since the creation of orthographic images for pronunciation increases with children's age (Harris & Coltheart, 1986; Singleton, 1989: 74). This would be NL influence in the wider sense of the term as well as a cognitive maturation effect.

To be sure, the varying ages of our students with correspondingly differing cognitive maturation levels must have exerted considerable influence on some of the tasks performed in the perception tests and particularly in the narratives where age-varying communication strategies reflect on their global effect and intelligibility. Although it is generally accepted, following Cummins,[10] that cognitive maturity benefits are usually associated with syntax and morphology rather than with pronunciation, in fact Cummins

(1981) himself finds that some sound discrimination tests may involve cognitive abilities which favour older students. Moreover, in our data, intelligibility and foreign accent are also directly correlated with starting age since late starters are significantly better than early ones in both accounts. As we have stated, auditory analyses suggest that pronunciations display quite similar characteristics in all groups but older students' communication strategies may have influenced the judge's appreciations, particularly as far as intelligibility is concerned. The productions of the eldest group may not actually be better as far as DFA is concerned but they may seem to be and they may be more intelligible because of their cognitive maturation which allows them to use other communication strategies and a more fluent delivery, which compensate for their accent and make them easier to understand.

In addition, there are some pronunciation characteristics which differ amongst the groups and which have more to do with the strategies employed by students when faced with the FL system because of their cognitive maturation, rather than with instruction starting age. Thus, intermediate and older students show more cases of over-generalisation, reading pronunciation, pronunciation guessing/re-interpretation etc. which the younger children do to a lesser extent. Younger children seem more prone to displaying fixed word pronunciations, whereas older children, even in the words they know well, vary between a learnt pronunciation (which may be more or less TL-like) and the pronunciations that result as outputs of their various strategies. These findings support what has been suggested by other researchers (Lengyel, 1995; Pennington, 1998), namely that individual learning strategies and training methods may have an important bearing in FL pronunciation results.

Finally, results must also be partly due to the type of input, since instructors were non-native English speakers. In order to ascertain the relative weight of teachers' influence compared with other factors such as spelling, cognitive strategies, NL influence etc., the English which our subjects are receiving as input needs to be analysed. However, for obvious reasons, this can be quite a sensitive issue, which we have not been able to address yet.

Conclusions

Our results agree with other studies (Cummins, 1981; Fullana & Muñoz, 1999; Olson & Samuels, 1973) in finding a direct relationship between age and perception skills. Our oldest subjects obtained better scores than the two younger groups, with the youngest learners, who had received a slightly inferior amount of exposure, performing least well. However, both vowel and consonant perception were very similar within each group, contradicting both Flege *et al.*'s (1997a) and Fullana & Muñoz's (1999) findings.

Intelligibility and degree of foreign accent judgements follow the same direction as perception results: older students are considered to have more TL-like accents and to be more intelligible. However, judgements, particularly those of intelligibility, must be treated with some caution since communicative skills associated with cognitive development play an important part in students' productions. Other age-varying factors such as instruction methods and number of pronunciation strategies have been found to be responsible for several students' speech characteristics. Nevertheless, NL influence is the strongest and prevailing factor.

We can conclude that early starting age is not a factor which facilitates FL sound acquisition in the case of formal non-natural exposure to the FL in the medium term. This conclusion corroborates similar findings by other researchers (Krashen *et al.*, 1982; Patkowski, 1980; Singleton, 1989, 1995). It may be that in formal settings, early starting advantage requires much longer exposure than in natural contexts (Singleton, 1989, 1995) and that six to seven years has not been sufficient time for the youngest children either to catch up or overtake older learners.

It is to be hoped that subsequent data and analyses may help confirm and expand these conclusions. We also hope to be able to isolate some of the variables, such as teachers' input, in order to refine the analyses and investigate our data further.

Acknowledgements

This study was supported by a grant from the Spanish Ministry of Education (PS95–0025) and by a grant from the Basque Government (PI–1998–96). We would like to thank staff and students at the school where the data were obtained. I would like to thank Duncan Markham for comments on an earlier version of this paper.

Notes

1. In all these models the NL sound system is considered to be a reference point for the interpretation of FL sounds. Although this is reminiscent of traditional transfer-based theories who propose that the L1 sound system acts as a 'sieve' through which L2 sounds are perceived (Stockwell & Bowen, 1965), these current models go deeper in the analyisis of NL interference.
2. A description of this project can be found within the present volume in Cenoz's chapter (4).
3. R.P. (Received Pronunciation) is the non-regional prestige accent in England.
4. Since stimuli were monosyllables produced in isolation, they would be stressed and 'schwa' cannot appear as the nucleus of a stressed syllable (see also García Lecumberri & Cenoz, 1997).
5. For reasons of space it is not possible to include the descriptions elaborated for

each group but they may be obtained from the first author. We simply point out here some of the pronunciation strategies observed.

6. Our use of the term 'intelligibility' is equivalent to 'perceived comprehensibility' in Munro and Derwing's study (1999) whilst they employ 'intelligibility' for a separate dimension.

7. As previously mentioned, in our experiment DFA was judged using a scale which where low scores (minimum = 1) are given to strong foreign accents and high scores (maximum = 9) correspond to weak foreign accents, that is to say, a high DFA score actually means more TL-like.

8. The judge's scores presented here reflect the first round of his listening analysis. He listened to the same productions a second time showing strong consistency. Equally, these judgements are quite consistent with his assessment of the same learners on other aural production tasks, such as imitation, reading etc. (see Gallardo forthcoming).

9. The youngest learners only started doing some reading/writing in English in their fourth year of instruction (at age 7–8), and more in their fifth year. The intermediate group, who started learning English at age 8–9, did a little reading/writing at the beginning and it increased progressively in the following years. The eldest group started learning English at age 11–12 and from the beginning their instruction involved reading and writing to a considerable extent.

10. Cummins' known distinction between Basic Interpersonal Communication Skills (BICS) and Cognitive Academic Language Proficiency (CALP) (see, for instance Cummins & Swain, 1986).

References

Altenberg, E.P. and Vago, R.M. (1983) Theoretical implications of an error analysis of second language phonology production. _Language Learning_ 33, 427–47.

Asher, J. and García, R. (1969) The optimal age to learn a foreign language. _Modern Language Journal_ 53, 334–41.

Best, C.T. (1994) The emergence of native-language phonological influences in infants: A perceptual assimilation model. In J.C. Goodman and H.C. Nusbaum (eds) _The Development of Speech Perception_ (pp. 167–224). Cambridge, MA: MIT Press.

Blanco, M., Gayoso, E. and Carrillo, M. (1997) Phonological and metaphonological training and its influence on the learning of pronunciation, reading and writing of English as a second language. In K. Karavas-Doukas and P. Rea-Dickins (eds) _Proceedings of the Teaching of Foreign Languages in European Primary Schools Conference_ (pp. 81–94). Warwick: University of Warwick Print Services.

Bohn O.S. and Flege, J.E. (1992) The production of new and similar vowels by adult German learners of English. _Studies in Second Language Acquisition_ 14, 131–58.

Bongaerts, T. (1999) Ultimate attainment in L2 Pronunciation: The case of very advanced late L2 learners. In D. Birdsong (ed.) _Second Language Acquisition and the Critical Period Hypothesis_ (pp. 133–60). New Jersey: Lawrence Erlbaum.

Bongaerts, T., Planken, B. and Schils, E. (1995) Can late learners attain a native accent in a foreign language? A test of the Critical Period Hypothesis. In D. Singleton and Z. Lengyel (eds) _The Age Factor in Second Language Acquisition_ (pp. 30–50). Clevedon: Multilingual Matters.

Bongaerts, T., van Summeren, C., Planken, B. and Schils, E. (1997) Age and ultimate attainment in the pronunciation of a foreign language. _Studies in Second Language Acquisition_ 19: 447–65.

Burstall, C. (1975) Factors affecting foreign-language learning: A consideration of some recent search findings. *Language Teaching and Linguistics Abstracts* 8, 5–25.

Carlisle, R.S. (1994) Markedness and environment as internal constraints on the variability of interlanguage phonology. In M. Yavas (ed.) *First and Second Language Phonology*. San Diego: Singular Publishing Group.

Cenoz, J. and García Lecumberri, M. L. (1999a) The acquisition of English pronunciation: Learners' views. *International Journal of Applied Linguistics* 9, 3–17.

Cenoz, J. and García Lecumberri, M. L. (1999b) The effect of training on the discrimination of English vowels. *International Review of Applied Linguistics* 37(4), 261–75.

Cook, V. (1991) *Second Language Learning and Languge Teaching*. London: Edward Arnold.

Cook, V. (1995) Multicompetence and effects of age. In D.Singleton and Z. Lengyel (eds) *The Age Factor in Second Language Acquisition* (pp. 51–66). Clevedon: Multilingual Matters.

Cummins, J. (1981) Age on arrival and immigrant second language learning in Canada: A reassessment. *Applied Linguistics* 11, 132–49.

Cummins, J. and Swain, M. (1986) *Bilingualism in Education*. London: Longman.

Eckman, F. R. (1977) Markedness and the contrastive analysis hypothesis. *Language Learning* 27, 315–30.

Ellis, R. (1994) *The Study of Second Language Acquisition*. Oxford: Oxford University Press.

Flege, J.E. (1992) Speech learning in a second language. In C. Ferguson, L. Menn and C. Stool-Gammon (eds) *Phonological Development: Models. Research and Applications* (pp. 565–604). York: York Press.

Flege, J.E. (1999) Age of learning and second language speech. In D. Birdsong (ed.) *Second Language Acquisition and the Critical Period Hypothesis* (pp. 101–32). New Jersey: Lawrence Erlbaum.

Flege, J.E., Bohn, O.S., and Jang, S. (1997a) Effects of experience on non-native speakers´ production and perception of English vowels. *Journal of Phonetics* 25, 437–70.

Flege, J.E., Frieda, E.M. and Nozawa, T. (1997b) Amount of native language use affects the pronunciation of an L2. *Journal of Phonetics* 25, 169–86.

Flege, J.E., Munro M.J. and MacKay, I.R. (1995) Effects of age of second language learning on the production of English consonants. *Speech Communication* 16, 1–26.

Fox, R.A., Flege, J.E. and Munro, M.J. (1995) The perception of English and Spanish vowels by native English and Spanish listeners: A multidimensional scaling analysis. *Journal of the Acoustic Society of America* 97, 2540–551.

Fullana, N. and Muñoz, C. (1999) The development of auditory discrimination skills in EFL learners of different ages. Paper presented at the XXIII AEDEAN Conference, León.

Gallardo, F. (forthcoming) La Adquisición de la Pronunciación del Inglés como Tercera Lengua. PhD thesis, Universidad del País Vasco.

García Lecumberri, M.L. and Cenoz, J. (1997) Identification by L2 learners of English vowels in different phonetic contexts. In J. Leather and A. James (eds) *New Sounds 97: Proceedings of the 1997 Klagenfurt Symposium on the Acquisition of Second-Language Speech* (pp. 196–205). Klagenfurt: University of Klagenfurt.

García Lecumberri, M.L. and Cenoz, J. (2003) Phonetic context variation vs. vowel perception in a foreign language. In A. Braun and H.R. Masthoff (eds.) *Festschrift for Professor Koester*. Marlborg: Universität Trier.

García Lecumberri, M.L. and Elorduy, A. (1994) Sistema fonológico de la lengua inglesa: I, II y III. *Temario de Inglés para Profesores de Secundaria*. Madrid: C.E.N.

Guiora, A., Acton, W., Erard, R. and Strickland, F. (1980) The effects of benzodiazepine (valium) on permeability of ego boundaries. *Language Learning* 30, 351–63.

Hammarberg, B. (1990) Conditions on transfer in second language phonology acquisition. In J. Leather and A. James (eds) *New Sounds 90: Proceedings of the 1990 Amsterdam Symposium on the Acquisition of Second-Language Speech* (pp. 198–215). Amsterdam: University of Amsterdam.

Harris, M. and Coltheart, M. (1986) *Language Processing in Children and Adults: An Introduction.* London: Routledge & Kegan Paul.

House, A.S. and Fairbanks, G. (1953) The influence of consonant environment upon the secondary acoustical characteristics of vowels. *Journal of the Acoustic Society of America* 25, 105–113.

Ioup, G. (1984) Is there a structural foreign accent? A comparison of syntactic and phonological errors in second language acquisition. *Language Learning* 34, 1–17.

Ioup, G. (1995) Evaluating the need for input enhancement in post-critical period language acquisition. In D. Singleton and Z. Lengyel (eds) *The Age Factor in Second Language Acquisition* (pp. 95–123). Clevedon: Multilingual Matters.

Jenkins, J.J., Strange, W. and Trent, S.A. (1999): Context-independent dynamic information for the perception of coarticulated vowels. *Journal of the Acoustic Society of America* 106, 438–48.

Klein, W. (1986) *Second Language Acquisition.* Cambridge: Cambridge University Press

Krashen, S., Scarcella R. and Long, M. (eds) (1982) *Child–Adult Differences in Second Language Acquisition.* Rowley, MA: Newbury House.

Kuhl, P.K. (1993) Early linguistic experience and phonetic perception: Implications for theories of developmental speech production. *Journal of Phonetics* 21, 125–39.

Leather, J. and James, A. (1991) The acquisition of second language speech. *Studies in Second Language Acquisition* 13, 305–41.

Lengyel, Z. (1995) Some critical remarks on the phonological component. In D. Singleton, and Z. Lengyel (eds) *The Age Factor in Second Language Acquisition* (pp. 124–134). Clevedon: Multilingual Matters.

Long, M. (1990) Maturational constraints on language development. *Studies in Second Language Acquisition* 12, 251–85.

Major, R.C. (1987a) Foreign accent: Recent research and theory. *International Review of Applied Linguistics* 15, 185–202.

Major, R.C. (1987b) Phonological similarity, markedness, and rate of L2 acquisition. *Studies in Second Language Acquisition* 9, 63–82.

Major, R.C. (2001) *Foreign Accent: The Ontogeny and Philogeny of Second Language Phonology.* Mahwah, New Jersey: Lawrence Erlbaum Associates.

Markham, D. (1997) *Phonetic Imitation, Accent and the Learner.* Lund: Lund University Press.

Mayer, M. (1969) *Frog, Where are You?* New York: Dial Press.

Munro, M.J. and Derwing, T.M. (1999) Foreign accent, comprehensibility and intelligibility in the speech of second language learners. In J. Leather (ed.) *Phonological Issues in Language Learning* (pp. 285–310). Oxford: Blackwell.

Munro, M.J., Flege, J.E. and MacKay, I.R. (1996) The effects of age of second learning on the production of English vowels. *Applied Psycholinguistics* 17, 313–34.

Muñoz, C. (2000) Bilingualism and trilingualism in school students in Catalonia. In J. Cenoz and U. Jessner (eds) *English in Europe: The Acquisition of a Third Language* (pp. 157–178). Clevedon: Multilingual Matters.

Neufeld, G. (1979) Towards a theory of language learning ability. *Language Learning* 29, 227–41.

Odlin, T. (1989) *Language Transfer*. Cambridge: Cambridge University Press.

Olson, L. and Samuels, S. (1973) The relationship between accuracy of foreign language pronunciation. *Journal of Educational Research* 66, 263–7. Reprinted in S.D. Krashen, R.C. Scarcella and M.H. Long (1982) (eds) *Child–Adult Differences in Second Language Acquisition* (pp. 67–75). Rowley, MA: Newbury House.

Oyama, S. (1976) A sensitive period in the acquisition of a non-native phonological system. *Journal of Psycholinguistic Research* 5, 261–85.

Patkowski, M.S. (1980) The sensitive period for the acquisition of syntax in a second language. *Language Learning* 30, 449–72.

Patkowski, M.S. (1990) Age and accent in a second language: A reply to James Emil Flege. *Applied Linguistics* 11, 73–89.

Pennington, M.C. (1998) The teachability of phonology in adulthood: A re-examination. *International Review of Applied Linguistics* 36 (4), 323–41.

Purcell, E.T. and Suter, R.W. (1980) Predictors of pronunciation accuracy: A reexamination. *Language Learning* 30, 271–87.

Quilis, A and Fernández, J.A. (1996) *Curso de Fonética y Fonología Españolas para Estudiantes Angloamericanos*. Madrid: Consejo Superior de Investigaciones Científicas.

Scholes, R.J. (1986) Phonemic interference as a perceptual phenomenon. *Language and Speech* 11, 86–103.

Scovel, T. (1988) *A Time to Speak: A Psycholinguistic Enquiry into the Critical Period for Human Speech*. Rowley, MA: Newbury House.

Singleton, D. (1989) *Language Acquisition: The Age Factor*. Clevedon: Multilingual Matters.

Singleton, D. (1995) A critical look at the Critical Period Hypothesis in second language acquisition research. In D. Singleton and Z. Lengyel (eds) *The Age Factor in Second Language Acquisition* (pp. 1–29). Clevedon: Multilingual Matters.

Snow, C. and Hoefnagel-Höhle, M. (1977) Age differences in the pronunciation of foreign sounds. *Language and Speech* 20, 357–365. Reprinted in S.D. Krashen, R.C. Scarcella and M.H. Long (1982) (eds) *Child–Adult Differences in Second Language Acquisition* (pp. 84–92). Rowley, MA: Newbury House.

Snow, C. and Hoefnagel-Höhle, M. (1978) Age differences in second language acquisition. In G. Nickel (ed.) *Applied Linguistics: Psycholinguistics*. Stuttgart: Hochschulverlag.

Stevens, K.N. and House, A.S. (1963) Perturbations of vowel articulations by consonantal context: An acoustical study. *Journal of Speech and Hearing Research* 6, 11–128.

Stockwell, R.P. and Bowen, J.D. (1965) *The Sounds of English and Spanish*. Chicago: University of Chicago Press.

Strozer, J.S. (1994) *Language Acquisition after Puberty*. Washington: Georgetown University Press.

Strange, W., Akahane-Yamada, R., Kubo, R., Trent, S.A. and Nishi, K. (2001) Effects of consonantal context on perceptual assimilation of American English vowels by Japanese listeners. *Journal of the Acoustic Society of America* 109, 1691–704.

Strange, W., Edman, T.R. and Jenkins, J.J. (1979) Acoustic and phonological factors in vowel identification. *Journal of Experimental Psychology, Human Perception and Performance* 5, 643–56.

Tahta, S., Wood, M. and Loewenthal, K. (1981) Age changes in the ability to replicate foreign pronunciation and intonation. *Language and Speech* 24, 363–72.

Thogmartin, C. (1982) Age, individual differences in musical and verbal aptitude, and pronunciation achievement by elementary school children learning a foreign language. *International Review of Applied Linguistics* 20 (1), 66–72.

Thompson, I. (1991) Foreign accents revisited: the English pronunciation of Russian immigrants. *Language Learning* 41, 177–204.

Wenk, B. (1986) Crosslinguistic influence in second language phonology. In E. Kellerman and M. Sharwood Smith (eds) *Crosslinguistic Influence in Second Language Acquisition*. Oxford: Pergamon.

Wode, H. (1980) Phonology in L2 acquisition. In S. W. Felix (ed.) *Second Language Development*. Tübingen: Gunter Narr.

Chapter 7

Maturational Constraints on Foreign-language Written Production

DAVID LASAGABASTER and AINTZANE DOIZ

Introduction

The relationship between the age of initiation of the process of learning a foreign language and the level of proficiency attained is a crucial issue in current research. Two are the main reasons for this interest. First, there is a widespread desire for new generations to reach a high level of proficiency, at least, in one foreign language. Second, the majority of people feel entitled to take a position on this issue and it may be stated that, for the most part, there is a generalised tendency to favour the earliest possible start on foreign-language (FL) learning. In fact, in a study conducted in 1997, Torras *et al.* (cited in Muñoz, 1999) showed that a group of parents of children between 2 and 6 years of age who had started learning English in nursery school firmly believed that these children were better learners than adults. They believed that the main advantages would affect pronunciation and vocabulary acquisition and, in spite of the fact that positive results were scarce during the initial stage of acquisition, they set their hopes in the future where the advantages of the early start would be more evident. The results of this study correspond with the *consensus view* proposed by Singleton (1995), according to which the sooner the exposure to the L2 is, the better the results are in the long term. Among the theoretical reasons considered by Segalowitz (1997) (based on Ellis, 1994) to facilitate the language-learning process by younger learners, we select the following:

> First, the capacity to perceive and segment sounds may become progressively impaired as a function of age. Second, there may be a loss of neurological plasticity after some critical period that inhibits an adult's ability to acquire certain aspects of new linguistics skills (e.g. phonology, grammar). Third, the older one is, the less motivated one may become to communicate with native speakers of another language or

integrate into their community. Also, the older one is, the more self-conscious and anxious one may be when communicating in the L2. . . . Fifth, younger learners may receive superior language input compared to what adults receive for language learning purposes. (Segalowitz, 1997: 87)

However, a broader review of the studies on the subject shows that the aforementioned results and ideas are not conclusive, as revealed by the fact that the hypothesis on the existence of a critical period during which L2 acquisition is facilitated is still very much at the centre of the debate among researchers of the field (see Singleton, Chapter 1, this volume). One of the main reasons for the non-resolution of the debate is the fact that it is very difficult to isolate the age factor from the numerous variables (sociological, emotional, etc.) which interact with it.

The goal of this chapter is to show that the controversy surrounding the influence of the age factor in the acquisition of foreign languages is also determined by a number of factors which are external to the students, as for example the nature and properties of the particular aspect of the linguistic competence under study. Noteworthy in this respect is the study by Sasaki and Hirose (1996) of written production by non-native speakers, which revealed that adult learners attained a higher level of proficiency than younger students.

Whatever the case may be, the issue regarding the influence of the age factor over L2 acquisition (Singleton, 1997), the subject matter of this book, has consequences both at the theoretical level (whether the innate capacity to learn languages functions beyond a certain age) and at the practical level (what the age of initiation of the teaching of the L2 in the schooling system should be). Furthermore, the increasing interest in the study of local languages as well as foreign languages necessitates a search for more or less definite answers regarding the degree of efficiency of early L2 learning with respect to specific communicative aspects.

The Age Factor and Written Production

In spite of the fact that research on written production in L2 includes research carried out on any language which differs from L1, the majority of studies take English as the object language (Reichelt, 1999). In addition, a study of the 233 projects on written production in a foreign language in the United States by Reichelt (1999) revealed that the great majority of these studies were carried out at college level, some at secondary school level and a very small percentage at primary school. This tendency is also found in the Basque Autonomous Community, where studies on written production are based on samples of college students or adult students.

Consequently, one of our objectives is to analyse and compare the results at the pre-college level, an issue which has not received much attention in current research.

It should be borne in mind that we concentrate on a formal learning context, namely, the school, where written-language competence is as important as oral competence, as reflected by the fact that university entrance exams evaluate written production exclusively. It follows from these observations that the subject-matter of this chapter is of much interest and applicability.

Celaya *et al.* (1998a) classify the existing studies of the field into two groups. One group includes research designed to revise the measures used by investigators to evaluate written production in the L2. The other group includes discussions of the data considered in the light of a number of criteria and measures. Our study belongs in the latter group, since it takes the measures and criteria used in Doiz and Lasagabaster (2001) as working tools and deals with the analysis of written production in English by students of three different age groups.

Research on written production in the L1 and the L2 has concluded that students of an L2 resort to the same strategies and follow the same guidelines whether they are writing in their L1 or in the L2. In relation to this issue, Zamel (1983) stated that students characterised by a higher level of written competence have more developed and effective strategies than their fellow students, as a result of which, it is concluded that the role of the linguistic competence is not a decisive factor for written production. By contrast, Cumming (1989) showed that the greater the linguistic competence is, the better the quality of the written production in the L2. Likewise, Pennington and So (1993), who designed a study to clarify whether the level of linguistic competence or the processing capacity is the relevant factor in the attainment of written proficiency, concluded that the former played a greater role on the quality of the compositions.

Sasaki and Hirose (1996) considered the influence of factors of a different kind on written production. In particular, they analysed the role of written practice metaknowledge in the L2, which included such notions as coherence, cohesion, topic, conclusion, thematic organisation and the practice of writing compositions in class. The results of the study undertaken by these researchers was translated into the following hierarchy of factors responsible for variation in the degree of L2 written attainment: the level of competence in the L2 was found to be the most relevant factor for differences in L2 written attainment (52%), next was the skill in the writing of compositions in the L1 (18%) and, in the third place, was the factor associated with metaknowledge which is responsible for 11% of the variation. Finally, from a different perspective Smith (1994) considered the cognitive style used by each individual in the process of text production, text evaluation as well as the cognitive effort required by the task as the factors which determine the level of influence of the L1 and the level of written competence achieved in the L2.

The Analysis of Written Texts: The Errors

The degree of attainment in written production competence in the L2 has traditionally been determined by the study of the errors made by the language learners in the assigned written tasks. However, the interpretation and relevance of the study of systematic errors have undergone variations within the field of language acquisition with time. Thus, at first, the occurrence of systematic errors in the written texts was invariably interpreted as the result of defective knowledge of the L2 and the absence of adequate acquisition of the rules in the L2. This approach has progressively been replaced by the view that errors represent a stage of the interlanguage (Selinker, 1972), a temporal/transitional stage in the development of competence in the L2 and in the acquisition of writing abilities (Horning, 1987). Recently, errors in written production made by L2 learners have been characterised as evidence of progress in composition writing, where the criteria for language accuracy and language competence are defined in terms of the communicative and functional adequacy of the text to the assigned task. Thus, within this new perspective the appropriateness of the written language is analysed in relation to the communicative purpose of the written task, as opposed to being a product unrelated to the applicability and context of the task.

The change in the role of the study of errors as well as the change in the nature of the errors to be considered have affected the importance of the role assigned to the learner in the acquisitional process of the L2. Within this new frame, the learner is no longer a passive receptor of structures whose only task is to repeat a set of exercises but rather becomes an active agent in the learning process (Péry-Woodley, 1991).

Evaluation Procedure of the Written Production of the Study

There are two main approaches in the evaluation of written production: the holistic evaluation and frequency count. Under the holistic approach, the scores assigned to the compositions are based on the general impression that the evaluator has of the text. Under the frequency count approach, the score is determined by the presence or absence of certain elements (e.g. number of subordinators, number of grammatical errors, number of lexical errors, etc.). In this study, we take both approaches.

We followed the scale proposed by Jacobs *et al.* (1981) for the holistic evaluation of the compositions. This scale considers the communicative effect of the speaker's linguistic production on the receptor and, therefore, comes close to the main objective of the process of language acquisition, namely, interpersonal communication. This evaluation scale has already been used in other studies and doctoral theses (Cenoz, 1991; Lasagabaster, 1998; Pennington & So, 1993; Sagasta, 2000).

Within the quantitative analysis we considered several measures classified into three groups: fluency, complexity and accuracy. In order to obtain a higher degree of reliability we followed the results obtained by Wolfe-Quintero *et al.* (1998), who examined the degree of reliability of over 100 measures used in 39 different studies on written production, and selected the measures which obtained better results in reliability and were judged to be of greater significance.

Finally, the evaluation of written production is complemented by a description of the different kinds of errors made by the three different age groups which participated in our study. We would like to point out that the errors which have been studied are a representative sample of the most frequently made errors. As in prior studies (Celaya *et al.*, 1999), the nature of the assignment entails the absence of a specific type of errors which may have been more frequent in a different kind of assignment. For example, in our study there were hardly any negative or interrogative sentences but this was a consequence of the kind of task they were assigned (i.e. writing a letter) rather than the reflection of their lack of familiarity with these structures.

Hypothesis

Previous analyses carried out in Cataluña (Celaya *et al.*, 1998b; Muñoz, 1999) as well as in the Basque Autonomous Community (Cenoz, 1999, Doiz & Lasagabaster, 2001) have revealed that students at a higher cognitive stage obtained better results in some aspects of the acquisition of English than students of a younger age. Based on these results, we propose the following three hypotheses:

Hypothesis 1:
The age factor will determine the degree of competence achieved as revealed by the holistic evaluation of the participants' written production.

Hypothesis 2:
The older the students are, the better the results obtained in fluency, complexity and accuracy will be.

Hypothesis 3:
The age of the students will influence the kind of errors made by the participants.

Our Study

The sample

In his study on the relationship between competence in the L2 and written production, Cumming (1994) concludes that the time spent learning the L2 is a decisive factor in the level of competence attained. Accordingly, our sample consists of students with a similar amount of time exposure to the foreign language thereby allowing us to isolate the influence of the age factor in the level of foreign language written competence attained.

The students who took part in our study belonged in three age groups. The first group was made up of 31 students of sixth grade of primary school (11–12 year-olds) who had started their English lessons when they were 4/5 years old; at the time in which the study was conducted, they had had a total of 704 hours of tuition in English. The second group had 18 fourth graders of secondary education (15–16 year olds) and had received their first English lessons at the age of 8/9 with a total of 792 hours. The third group, 13 students of second grade in high school (17–18 years olds) had started learning English at the age of 11/12 with a total of 693 hours of tuition in English. While there is a 101-hour difference between the groups of second graders and fourth graders, the difference is not significant since it involves an eight-year time span, that is, the older group had an extra 12 hours per year as compared to the other group. It should be stated that the decrease in the number of subjects in each group results from the exclusion of students who had had extra-curricular English lessons or some kind of external tuition in English.

The age of initiation in the foreign language tuition which characterises each of the groups is of the outmost importance for the purpose of this study: students in the sixth grade of primary school started their English classes at the age of 4/5, students in the fourth grade of secondary school were 8/9 years old when they first started learning English and students in 2nd grade of high school were 11/12 years old. That is, we intend to study the influence that the starting age of L2 learning has on their written production in three groups of students with a similar time of exposure to the L2.

The 62 participants of the study are Spanish–Basque bilinguals and participate in the D-model schooling system, i.e. a linguistic model where all curriculum instruction is conducted entirely in Basque with the exception of Spanish and Spanish literature (see Lasagabaster [2001] for further details on the Basque Educational System). Basque is the native language of 36% of the students in the sample, Spanish 18% and both languages of 45.9% of the students. Table 1 identifies the native language/s of the

Table 1 L1 of the students in each group

	Sixth graders in primary school (%)	*Fourth graders in secondary school (%)*	*Second graders in high school (%)*
Basque	38.7	29.4	38.5
Spanish	12.9	29.4	15.4
Both	48.4	41.2	46.2

students for each group and provides the percentages for each of the groups.

Instruments

In order to avoid any influence over the results particularly in the case of the younger students, the topic of the assignment was very general in nature and did not pose a problem for any of the groups. The students were given the following instructions:

> This year you are going to spend a month in England with an English family, the Edwards. Mr and Mrs Edwards have two children, Peter and Helen, who live in Oxford. Write a letter of introduction to them and tell them about yourself, your family, your school, your hobbies and any other fact that you think might be of interest to them.

The task was carried out in class, and no time limit was given. Each of the letters was analysed according to the holistic, quantitative and descriptive evaluating systems which are discussed next.

First evaluation: the holistic analysis

The application of the holistic analysis requires two evaluators who are familiar with the grading scales. Each evaluator assigns a grade to each of the letters, so that each letter receives two independent grades guaranteeing the reliability of the results. Jacobs *et al.* (1981) have demonstrated that as long as certain conditions are followed, the reliability of this evaluating system is guaranteed. The evaluating system consists of five criteria which measure different aspects of written production:

(1) Content (30 points): this category considers the development and comprehension of the topic as well as the adequacy of the content of the text.
(2) Organisation (20 points): several factors are considered here, namely, the organisation of ideas, the structure and cohesion of the paragraphs and the clarity of exposition of the main and secondary ideas.
(3) Vocabulary (20 points): this category deals with the selection of words,

expressions and their usage. The appropriateness of the register used is also taken into account.

(4) Language usage (25 points): the use of grammar categories is taken into account, e.g. tense, number, subject–verb agreement in addition to word order and the use of complex syntactic structures.

(5) Mechanics (5 points): this criterion includes the evaluation of spelling, punctuation or the use of capitalisation.

The results for each of the criteria are added such that the total score will be somewhere between a minimum of 34 points and a maximum of 100. The final score is the average of the total points assigned by each of the two evaluators.

Second evaluation: the quantitative analysis
Our quantitative analysis is based on an elaboration of the model used in Wolfe-Quintero *et al.* (1998). The main criteria we considered belong in the following three groups: fluency, complexity and accuracy.

Fluency: The following items were taken into account for the analysis of fluency in the production of written texts: total number of sentences (TNS), total number of subordinate clauses (TNSC), total number of words (TNW) and total number of words per sentence (TNWS).

Complexity: The degree of complexity of the compositions was measured according to the following criteria:

- Total number of non-finite verbs (TNNFV): non-finite verbs do not carry information on person, number or tense, e.g. infinitives and participles.
- Total number of different kinds of subordinate clauses (TNDKSC): since Celaya and Tragant (1997: 241) argued that coordination is more frequently used than subordination at lower levels of acquisition, it follows that the number of different kinds of subordinate clauses is indicative of the degree of complexity of the texts.
- Types of connectors (TC): the total number of the different kinds of connectors including subordinators (*that, when*, etc.) and coordinators (*but, and*, etc.) is considered. Since we are interested in the number of different kinds of connectors used, multiple occurrences of the same kind of connector are counted as one instance of that particular kind of connector.
- Types of nouns (TS): Drawing from the topic of the written task, we consider substantives referring to nine categories: substantives refer-

ring to pet animals, school, home town, family, hobbies, personal description, the trip, the Basque Country and plans for the future.
- The types of adjectives (Tadj): Six main categories are considered: comparatives, superlatives, attributives, demonstratives, quantifiers and ordinal numbers.
- The types of adverbs (Tadv): three categories are considered: temporal adverbs, adverbs of place and manner.
- Types of verbs/predicates (TVP): following Vendler's (1967) classification, we consider four main categories: states (predicates which do not designate change, such as *to be, to like*), activities (predicates designating change; e.g. *to read, to write*), accomplishments (predicates indicating an inherently bounded change, e.g. *to write a letter, to draw a house, to sing a song*) and achievements (predicates which designate a change of state, e.g. *to win, to die, to reach the summit of a mountain*).
- The types of auxiliary verbs (TAV): auxiliary verbs are divided into five types: to be, to do, to have, modals and future auxiliaries.
- The use of different types of verb tenses (DTVT): a bigger number of different verb tenses is indicative of a greater degree of complexity (Arnold, 1991).

Accuracy: The last value to be measured is accuracy, which includes the following criteria:

- Percentage of error-free sentences (PEFS): this number is the result of the multiplication by 100 of the number of error-free sentences and by dividing the resulting number by the total number of sentences.
- Percentage of spelling mistakes (PSM): the percentage is obtained from the multiplication by 100 of the number of spelling mistakes and by dividing the number by the total number of words.
- Percentage of errors (PE): The percentage is the result of multiplying by 100 the number of errors (spelling mistakes are not included here) and dividing the result by the total number of words. We make a distinction between spelling mistakes and other kinds of errors, since the latter hinder comprehension to a greater extent than the more frequent spelling mistakes.

Third evaluation: the descriptive analysis of errors

The nature of the errors included appeals to two considerations: the level of the language the error belongs at, and the nature of the cognitive process the occurrence of the error is associated with. We consider these two issues next.

Locating errors in the language: The errors that we studied were located in two levels of the language primarily: the substance level and the text level. A third level was left aside, the discourse level (James, 1998: 129) since it was taken into account by the aforementioned holistic analysis.

Errors at the level of substance: Spelling mistakes belong at this level. James and Klein (1994) note that the origin of spelling mistakes is multiple and combines one or various of the following strategies undertaken by the students: the application of phonological rules of the L1, the application of phonological rules of the L2, the graphology of the L1 and L2.

Given the nature of the present study, we have been unable to conduct a detailed analysis of the origin of the spelling mistakes characterising the different age groups; however, we will make a number of observations in this regard in the discussion section.

The text level: This level includes errors in lexicon, grammar and syntax. In relation to lexical errors (James, 1998), we take into account errors in the formal appearance of the word such as change in the code – the use of Basque or Spanish for an English word – and the occurrence of errors such as the choice of an inappropriate word from a semantic point of view. Secondly, at the grammar level are errors in the use of articles, determiners, possessive pronouns, the use of gender and number morphemes; the choice of the verb tense, the presence or absence of grammatical elements such as the infinitive particle 'to' and the presence/absence of the main/auxiliary verb. Finally, the syntactic level includes the study of the order of the sentence constituents.

Description of the errors in terms of the cognitive processes involved: In addition to the classification of the errors in terms of the levels of the language they are part of, we also consider a taxonomy which groups the errors according to the ways in which a certain linguistic item deviates from the L2. In order to do so, we follow the proposal put forward by James (1998: 106), which in turn is based on Dulay *et al.* (1982: 150). The latter highlights the difference between the students' L2 written productions and the correct versions with regard to the following criteria: omission, addition, misformation and misorderings. James (1998) adds a fifth criterion: blends. These five criteria are explained here.

Omission: This cognitive process refers to the absence of an element, as a result of which the outcome is not grammatical. According to the results obtained by James (1998), the omission of function words in the early stages of the L2 language acquisition process is more habitual than that of content words. The following elements are included within the category of function words: omission of the article, possessive pronouns, the infinitive grammatical particle 'to' and the omission of the auxiliary. The most characteristic omission of content elements is that of the main verb. All these different omissions have been observed in our students´ written products. Our aim is to try to find out whether the age factor has some sort of influence on the type of omission produced.

Addition: Following James´s proposal, the example of oversuppliance of double marking could be regarded as a representative example of this category. Thus, this group would encompass the juxtaposition of two prepositions (*with to*) or the presence of a second plural morpheme in a word which is already plural (*childrens*). Nevertheless, and due to the limited number of examples of addition found in our students´ written texts, this category was not taken into account.

Misformation: This criterion has to do with the ungrammatical use of a morpheme or structure, which comprises errors such as selecting the wrong gender, number or verb tense.

Misorderings: In this category we will only focus on the deviations associated with the order of the constituents of the sentence, such as the alteration of the sequence 'subject + verb + object' or the position of the auxiliary verb in interrogative sentences. The phrase internal deviations, such as the postposition of the adjective with respect to the noun (*house red*), were not taken into consideration because the results obtained were not statistically significant.

Blends: James added this fifth criterion to the aforementioned four. This category includes those instances in which students produce a wrong form which is influenced by the existence of two correct ones. For instance, the ungrammatical form *according to Erica´s opinion* is a blend of two forms: *according to Erica* and *in Erica´s opinion* (James, 1998: 111). However, and due to the small number of blends in our sample´s writing, this category has been excluded from our analysis.

The errors that we examined within the descriptive analysis were the following: omission of articles and possessive pronouns, omission of main/ auxiliary verb, omission of the infinitive preposition 'to', misformation of number and gender, misformation of verb tense, misformation of the word at the semantic level, misordering of the constituents within the sentence, spelling mistakes, code-switching: Spanish, code-switching: Basque. The marking of the written compositions was carried out according to the previously described parameters for each of the three types of evaluation, with the results obtained being subsequently codified. This process ended with the analysis of the results via the SPSS (Statistical Package for Social Sciences) statistical programme.

Results

Regarding the holistic approach

With a view to corroborating our first hypothesis, *The age factor will crucially determine the degree of competence achieved as revealed by the holistic evaluation of the participants´ written production*, one-way Anova analyses were performed to compare the mean scores obtained by the three different age groups. The results are exhibited in Table 2.

Table 2 Results concerning the holistic approach

	11/12 year olds		15/16 year olds		17/18 year olds		F
	Mean	SD	Mean	SD	Mean	SD	
Overall	49.43	10.24	81.13	8.74	90.80	6.78	121.113[b]
Content (30)	17.40	2.47	25.11	2.48	27.65	2.15	106.304[b]
Organization(20)	10.40	2.17	16.33	2.19	18.38	1.50	87.804[b]
Vocabulary (20)	9.80	2.09	16.27	2.02	17.96	1.34	108.61[b]
Language use (25)	9.41	3.26	19.11	2.11	21.80	2.00	124.104[b]
Mechanics (5)	2.40	0.61	4.30	0.45	5.00	0.00	156.133[b]

[a] $p < 0.05$; [b] $p < 0.001$.

There is a clear-cut trend as regards both the five scales and the overall score; the 17/18-year-old students achieved the highest scores in all cases, whereas the 11/12-year-old students obtained the lowest scores. The differences between the 17/18 year olds and the 11/12 year olds, as well as those between the 15/16 year olds and the 11/12 year olds, turned out to be statistically significant in every single case ($p < 0.000$). Similarly the differences between the 17/18 year olds and the 15/16 year olds were significant in the scales of content ($p < 0.020$), organization ($p < 0.030$), use of language ($p < 0.032$), mechanics ($p < 0.002$) and the overall score ($p < 0.020$), while being marginally significant as regards the scale of vocabulary ($p < 0.067$).

Regarding the quantitative approach

With regard to the second hypothesis, *The older the students are, the better the results obtained in fluency, complexity and accuracy will be*, the results are shown in Tables 3, 5 and 7:

Except for the variable total number of sentences (TNS), in which the 15/16 year olds outperformed the rest (16.55), in all the other variables the 17/18

Table 3 Results in fluency

	11/12 year olds		15/16 year olds		17/18 year olds		
	Mean	*SD*	*Mean*	*SD*	*Mean*	*SD*	*F*
TNS	8.00	3.62	16.55	6.26	11.61	2.69	21.488[b]
NTSC	0.29	0.64	2.33	2.84	4.07	2.66	17.832[b]
TNW	86.90	44.59	163.94	53.46	167.46	38.88	22.324[b]
TNWS	10.95	3.39	10.26	2.05	14.58	2.69	9.386[b]

[a] $p < 0.05$; [b] $p < 0.001$.

Table 4 Significant differences in fluency

	Significant differences between groups
TNS	2 > 1 > 3
NTSC	1 > 2 > 3
TNW	1 > 3; 2 > 3;
TNWS	1 > 2; 1 > 3;

1, 17/18 year olds; 2, 15/16 year olds; 3, 11/12 year olds.

year olds did better than the other two age groups, the lowest scores being achieved by the younger students (11/12 year olds). Despite the fact that the 15/16 year old students´ written output had a higher total number of sentences (TNS = 16.55), the 17/18 year olds produced longer sentences, that is to say, sentences with a higher number of words (TNWS = 14.58). The differences which appeared to be significant between the different age groups are given in Table 4.

All these differences were statistically significant except in the case of total number of words (TNW) between Groups 2 and 1 and, in the case of total number of word per sentence (TNWS), between Groups 3 and 2.

The mean scores obtained by the three age groups in connection with the measures of complexity are given in Table 5.

As in the case of fluency, in this case the scores were closely related to the age of the participants, as the older the students were, the higher scores they obtained. The statistical significance of these differences can be seen in Table 6.

Out of the seven measures under study, four (TNNFV, TNDKSC, TC and Tadv) showed significant differences between the age groups, always in favour of the older students. Similarly, and as far as the Tadj and DTVT variables were concerned, the existing differences between groups happened to be significant, except in the case of the differences between the

Table 5 Results in complexity

	11/12 year olds		15/16 year olds		17/18 year olds		
	Mean	*SD*	*Mean*	*SD*	*Mean*	*SD*	*F*
TNNFV	1.00	1.67	2.16	2.09	4.46	2.43	14.127[b]
TNDKSC	0.22	0.49	1.44	1.58	2.84	1.57	24.255[b]
TC	1.25	0.63	2.38	1.61	4.15	1.99	22.080[b]
TS	4.32	1.30	4.77	0.80	5.07	0.95	2.391
Tadj	1.67	1.10	2.77	1.35	3.23	1.58	8.218[b]
Tadv	0.12	0.34	0.83	0.92	1.92	1.03	28.508[b]
TVP	1.80	0.79	2.55	0.98	3.46	0.51	19.880[b]
TAV	0.25	0.44	1.61	1.28	2.92	1.25	38.384[b]
DTVT	1.51	0.88	2.22	1.51	4.23	1.48	22.371[b]

[a] $p < 0.05$; [b] $p < 0.001$.

Table 6 Significant differences in complexity

	Significant differences between age groups
TNNFV	$1 > 2 > 3$
TNDKSC	$1 > 2 > 3$
TC	$1 > 2 > 3$
TS	The differences were not significant
Tadj	$1 > 3$; $2 > 3$;
Tadv	$1 > 2 > 3$
DTVT	$1 > 2$; $1 > 3$;

1, 17/18 year olds; 2, 15/16 year olds; 3, 11/12 year olds.

Table 7 Results in accuracy

	11/12 year olds		15/16 year olds		17/18 year olds		
	Mean	*SD*	*Mean*	*SD*	*Mean*	*SD*	*F*
PEFS	8.43	13.49	26.36	10.79	39.98	17.26	29.923[b]
PSM	16.94	11.49	2.98	2.42	1.15	0.83	24.556[b]
PE	22.41	10.13	16.23	7.26	13.30	8.63	5.544[a]

[a] $p < 0.05$; [b] $p < 0.001$.

Table 8 Significant differences in accuracy

	Significant differences between groups
PEFS	1 > 2 > 3
PSM	1 < 2 < 3
PE	1 < 3; 2 < 3;

1, 17/18 year olds; 2, 15/16 year olds; 3, 11/12 year olds.

Groups 2 and 1, and 3 and 2. Concerning the variable Types of Nouns (TN), there was no significant difference, as the vast majority of the students dealt with each of the aspects concerned in the task, which was directly reflected in the type of nouns chosen.

As regards the accuracy measures, the results obtained can be seen in Table 7. This table clearly demonstrates that the age factor plays a paramount role in the results, as the older the students were, the better the results they obtained. Likewise, the differences between groups turned out to be significant in all cases except for the variable percentage of error (PE) when Groups 2 and 1 were compared, as can be appreciated in Table 8.

Regarding the error analysis

The last results under scrutiny are the ones related to the different error categories proposed in our study with a view to testing our third hypothesis: *The age of the students will influence the kind of errors made by the participants.* Tables 9 and 10 reflect the different category of errors and the existence (or not) of significant differences between the three age groups, which we will now examine in more detail.

The study of these results leads us to conclude that there exist three different types of trends. In the first of these trends (Figure 1), the 11/12-year-old students made more errors than the other two groups (number of spelling mistakes, misformation of number and gender, omission of main or auxiliary verb). The origin of this can be traced back both to the students´ lack of written competence in the L2 (as revealed, for example, by the lack of main verb) and to the lack of linguistic competence, that is to say, the learners did not know or had not assimilated the linguistic rules and the vocabulary they needed.

In the second trend (Figure 2), the 17/18-year-old participants were the ones who made more errors (misformation of the word at the semantic level, misordering of the constituents within the sentence or omission of 'to'). However, these results have to be interpreted together with the ones obtained in the measures of fluency, complexity and accuracy: the older

Table 9 Results in the different error categories

	11/12 year olds		15/16 year olds		17/18 year olds		
	Mean	SD	Mean	SD	Mean	SD	F
1	0.45	0.96	1.33	1.23	0.30	0.48	5.802[a]
2	0.90	1.19	0.55	0.85	0.15	0.37	2.775[c]
3	0.00	0.00	0.16	0.51	0.46	0.51	7.490[b]
4	1.35	1.60	0.88	1.77	0.38	0.65	1.960
5	0.77	1.45	1.44	1.82	1.23	0.83	1.282
6	1.77	2.02	3.00	2.14	3.61	2.53	3.918[a]
7	0.09	0.39	0.66	1.08	0.84	1.21	4.658[a]
8	12.64	6.92	4.83	3.65	1.92	1.32	23.264[b]
9	1.35	1.88	1.72	1.90	0.46	1.19	1.967
10	4.54	5.88	1.33	2.19	0.15	0.37	5.877[a]

[a] $p < 0.05$; [b] $p < 0.001$; [c] $p < 0.09$.
1, Omission of articles/possessive pronouns; 2, Omission of main/auxiliary verb; 3, Omission of the infinitive preposition 'to'; 4, Misformation of number and gender; 5, Misformation of verb tense; 6, Misformation of the word at the semantic level; 7, Misordering of the constituents within the sentence; 8, Spelling mistakes; 9, Code-switching: Spanish; 10, Code-switching: Basque.

Table 10 Significant differences in errors

	Significant differences between age groups
Omission	$1 < 2$; $3 < 2$
Misformation of number/gender	$1 < 3$;
Omission of main/auxiliary verb	$1 < 3$;
Misformation of verb tense	$3 < 1$;
Omission of 'to'	$3 < 1$;
Misordering of constituents within the sentence	$3 < 2$; $3 < 1$
Misformation of word at semantic level	$3 < 2$; $3 < 1$
Code-switching: Spanish	$1 < 3$; $1 < 2$
Code-switching: Basque	$1 < 2 < 3$
Spelling mistakes	$1 < 2 < 3$

1, 17/18 year olds; 2, 15/16 year olds; 3, 11/12 year olds.

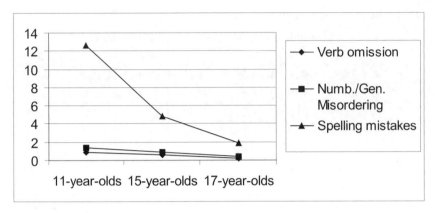

Figure 1 Trend 1 in errors

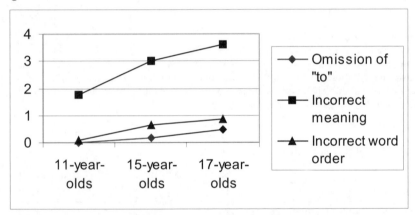

Figure 2 Trend 2 in errors

students produced texts of greater length and complexity, as a result of which the number of errors in the following categories was higher.

Concerning the third trend (Figure 3), the intermediate age group (15/16 year olds) made more mistakes than the other two groups (omission of the article and misformation of the verb tense). In the 'omission of the article' category, two points are worthy of mention: (1) the 15/16-year-old students made more mistakes than the 11/12 year olds because the former made more use of articles; and (2) the 15/16 year olds omitted the article more habitually than the 17/18 year olds, because the former had not yet assimilated the rules related to the use of the article. In the case of the 'misformation of the verb tense' category, the 15/16-year-old students were again the subjects of our sample who made the most errors, although

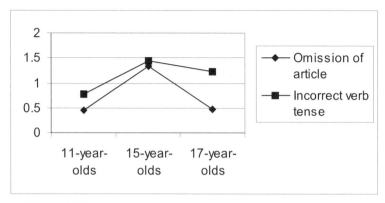

Figure 3 Trend 3 in errors

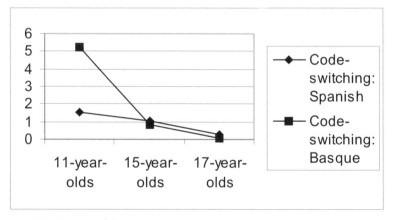

Figure 4 Code-switching

this time followed by the 17/18 year olds, who, despite using a wider range of verb tenses, utilised them more correctly. Grade 6 primary students (11/ 12 year olds) made the fewest errors, yet this was due to the fact that the vast majority of their writings were circumscribed to the use of only two verb tenses (present simple and present continuous).

The code-switching results merit further consideration. In the case of the younger students, the two official languages (Basque and Spanish) exerted greater influence on their work than in the other two age groups. Curiously enough, the youngest age group showed a clear preference for Basque when code-switching took place (for instance, among the 11/12 year olds the percentage of code-switching into Spanish amounted to 1.55%, whereas this percentage was much higher – 5.22% – when it came to Basque). Nevertheless, this trend reversed in the case of the oldest students, who fell back more on Spanish (0.27%) than on Basque (0.08). The explanation of these results could be that the older students were more aware of the existing typological relatedness between English and Spanish and also of the typological distance between English and Basque, the latter being a non-Indoeuropean language (these results coincide with those of other studies undertaken in the Basque context: [Lasagabaster, 1999]). This would mean that when students faced a lexical gap, the primary education students resorted to the vehicle language (Basque), whereas the older high school students (more aware of the differences/similarities between the three languages in contact) resorted more to Spanish. The intermediate age group (16/17 year olds) followed the pattern of the 17/18 year olds (their percentage of Spanish code-switching was 1.04% and 0.81% that of Basque), the influence of both languages being higher in their written output. This trend is clearly depicted in Figure 4.

The following are typical examples of code-switching into Basque among the 11/12-year-old participants: 'Only is 250 in this town and *gehiena* (*most of it*) is *baserriak* (*rural houses*)'; 'This town is in the *iparraldean* (*north*) of Espain, in the *euskal autonomi elkartea* (*Basque Autonomous Community*)'; 'My teacher is Gema and is *txintxoa* (*nice*)'. In the case of the older students, code-switching is basically into Spanish, while they endeavour to give the Spanish word an English appearance: 'he works in an *officine* (*oficina* is Spanish for office)'; 'to *pass* one month (*pasar un mes* is Spanish for "to spend a month")'; 'My family *composse* (*está compuesta* is Spanish for "consists of")'.

Conclusions

The main conclusion to be drawn from this study has to do with the ineluctable influence exerted by the age factor on a particular aspect of the individual´s linguistic development, namely the written production. It can be stated that those students who are at a more advanced cognitive stage take advantage of the school learning experience in general, and the writing experience in particular, as reflected in their written production in the foreign language. In fact, we could speak of the existence of maturational constraints concerning writing, since the effect of age turned out to be evident and unquestionable when considering the three different perspectives taken into account at the time of evaluating the written texts. These results bear out those of previous studies (Celaya *et al.*, 1998a and 1998b; Doiz & Lasagabaster, 2001; Muñoz, 1999).

In the first type of analysis, the so-called holistic approach, the effect of the age factor becomes evident. The older the students are, the more developed communicative ability is displayed in their texts, so much so that the differences between the three age groups happen to be significant as regards both the five scales (content, organisation, vocabulary, use of language and mechanics) and the overall score, always in favour of the older group.

The results obtained in the second type of analysis lead us to the same conclusion, since the older the students are: (1) the more extended their texts are, made up of longer sentences (fluency); (2) the greater lexical, syntactical and discoursal complexity is shown in their texts; and (3) the lower the number of errors encountered by the evaluators is, as the older students' texts are more accurate. Therefore we can assume that these three characteristics of the linguistic development evolve simultaneously, as the more competent students produce longer, more complex and more accurate texts than those students with a lower degree of competence (Wolfe-Quintero *et al.*, 1998). In this sense it should be remembered that in the early stages of the learning process, older students learn the lexical and morphosintactic aspects of the L2 faster than their younger counterparts (Harley & Wang, 1997).

The last type of evaluation focused on the variability of the nature of the errors depending on the students' age. As pointed out in the results section, three main trends stood out. In the first trend the younger students (11/12 year olds) made a higher number of what we could define as basic errors such as spelling mistakes, omission of the verb or misformation of number and/or gender. The origin of this type of errors is clear-cut: poor linguistic competence and lack of experience in foreign-language writing. However, in the second trend it is the older students (17/18 year olds) who committed the largest number of errors, with the omission of the infinitive particle 'to' (which is not present in the 11/12-year-old students' texts), misordering of the constituents within the sentence and misformation of the word at the semantic level, errors whose origin seems also to be unequivocal: since their texts are more complex and longer, they are more liable to commit errors of this nature. Finally, in the third trend it is the intermediate group (16/17 year olds) who made more errors such as the omission of the article or the incorrect use of a particular verb tense, which, on the one hand, stem from their poorer linguistic competence when compared with the oldest students and, on the other hand, from the inexistence of this kind of errors among the youngest students due to their lack of linguistic competence. Consequently, these three trends are based on two basic parameters: degree of competence and complexity of the utilised structures, parameters on which the age factor has once again a great impact.

Hence, the three hypotheses put forward in this study have been borne out. But what conclusions can be reached with these results in mind? First of all, it seems clear that the youngest students in our sample need to practice and improve their writing skills. This could be the effect of the methodology currently implemented in the Basque Autonomous Community, where little heed is paid to the writing skill until the beginning of secondary education (from the age of 13/14 onwards). Although the distinction between written and the oral production is not so evident as some authors pretend, the former is characterised by the presence of several factors which help to distinguish them, such as a greater structurisation of written language or the need for an editing and correcting process (Horning, 1987).

Second, a greater influence of the L1 (Basque and/or Spanish) was observed among the 11/12-year-old students. Thus, their writings were highly influenced by the L1 pronunciation and spelling (*I* ⇒ 'ai'; *tall* ⇒ 'toll'; *mother* ⇒ 'mader'; *very, very beautiful* ⇒ 'bery, bery biutifol'; *my house* ⇒ 'mai jaus'; *English* ⇒ 'Inglish'), whereas its influence on the older students´ writing was much less. Similarly, the younger group showed a high percentage of code-switching into Basque and Spanish (the former above all), whereas the older students tend to use Spanish words as the basis for their *English-ized* or *anglicized* words, as they seem to be more aware of the typological relatedness issue. Identification of this type of error allows us to discover which aspects of the L2 happen to be more difficult to assimilate by students in each group age, and will help the teacher to focus on and pay attention to them in everyday teaching practice.

It would be very interesting to determine whether or not the inclusion of translation and contrastive linguistic tasks in the foreign-language classroom could be beneficial when dealing with the errors observed in this study (Hawkins, 1999; James, 1999). This tendency seems to strike back into L2 methodology, as there is a need to talk about language more than has been the case in the last few decades as a result of certain misconceptions linked to the development of the communicative approach (Lasagabaster & Sierra, 2001). There are ever more authors (Duff, 1994; James, 1996; Mott, 1996; Uzawa, 1996) who consider that translation activities can be very beneficial as a means of overcoming hurdles such as the ones depicted in our study. These activities enable the student to set out and organise their ideas both in the L1 and L2, allowing the differences and similarities between all the languages in contact to be compared, resulting in an improvement in their writing skill. In this way the benefits are linked not only to the foreign language but also to Basque and Spanish, while the risk of having the languages appear as linguistic islands with little or no relation to the neighbouring islands is avoided.

Despite the fact that the final conclusion of this study is that the older the students are, the better their written competence, is, this is the result not only of a higher degree of competence but also of a higher writing competence in general, as a result of a longer exposure to formal education. It is important to point out that the age factor cannot be isolated from a series of factors that interact with it, such as the influence of experience and the level of competence achieved in the L1 and L2 (Lasagabaster, 2000), affective factors like attitudes and motivation and the students´ cognitive style or personality, to name but a few.

Last but not least, there are a few points we would like the reader to bear in mind. First, it is necessary to complete a comparative study of the students´ written competence in the three languages, which would allow us to analyse the similarities and differences between their two other languages (Basque and Spanish) and the foreign language. Second, it has to be underlined that the present study is part of a longitudinal one, and therefore definitive conclusions can only be drawn once all the students have reached the age of 17/18 (the oldest group in our sample). Only then will we be able to consider whether the economic, human and institutional efforts required by the early introduction of a foreign language are worthwhile and do really bear the expected fruit.

It is, therefore, necessary to clearly establish from the very beginning exactly which objectives need to be achieved in each linguistic skill in the foreign language, as these objectives will mark the strategies to be followed. Common-sense tells us that 11/12-year-old students cannot be expected to achieve the same written performance as their 17/18-year-old counterparts but nor can we forget that it is fundamental to establish realistic objectives so that false expectations are not created. We would like to draw the reader´s attention to the results obtained by the older two age groups. The 16/17-year-old students, albeit only two years younger, achieved significantly lower results when compared with the older group, which leads us to conclude that, when the time of exposure has been similar, the age factor becomes determinant as regards the writing skill.

Even so, and as Baker (1997) points out, the early teaching of a foreign language in a formal context entails a series of advantages: it is an intellectual stimulus, apart from the added value it represents for the curriculum; it encourages acquaintance with a new culture; it yields benefits as a result of learning an L2 throughout a longer period of time in contrast with a shorter and more intensive exposure. It is also important to emphasise that from a theoretical point of view these early teaching experimental programmes derive their impetus from the positive attitudes of learners, teachers and parents, the existence of adequate didactic materials and the need to turn learning into an alluring, enjoyable and enriching experience, unlike in subsequent school years where the motivation of the learners becomes a much more arduous question to tackle.

There is still much to do in the study of the influence of the age factor on the learning of a foreign language in a formal setting (the school), but in our opinion research is needed not only from an empirical perspective, but also from a social viewpoint. Although research studies do not usually have much social echo, due to the widespread social interest in this all too real issue, it is important that the results should reach the largest possible numbers of readers, despite the fact that for the time being the conclusions are not as conclusive as we would like them to be. We believe the need for further studies as regards this matter is evident.

Acknowledgements

This article came into being thanks to the financial patronage awarded by the Spanish Ministery of Education and Culture (DGICYT PB97–0611), the Basque Government (PI98/96) and the University of the Basque Country (UPV 103.130-HA 084/99).

References

Arnold, R. (1991) *Writing Development*. Philadelphia: Open University Press.

Baker, C. (1997) *Foundations of Bilingual Education and Bilingualism* (2nd edn). Clevedon: Multilingual Matters.

Celaya, M. L. and Tragant, E. (1997) Adquisición de lengua: código escrito. In R. Ribé (ed.) *Tramas creativas y aprendizaje de lenguas. Prototipos de tareas de tercera generación* (pp. 237–52). Barcelona: Universitat de Barcelona.

Celaya, M. L., Pérez, C. and Torras, M. R. (1998a) Matriu de criteris de medició per la determinació del perfil de competència lingüística escrita en anglès d´alumnes bilingües. Unpublished manuscript, Universitat de Barcelona i Universitat Pompeu Fabra.

Celaya, M. L., Pérez, C. and Torras, M. R. (1998b) Written performance by young bilingual learners of English as an L3. Paper presented at Eurosla 9, Paris.

Celaya, M. L., Navés, T. and Pérez, C. (1999) Perfil de competencia óptima no-nativa en la producción escrita en inglés. In F. Toda Iglesia, M. J. Mora, J. A. Prieto Pablos and T. López Soto (eds) *Actas del XXI Congreso Internacional de AEDEAN* (pp. 559–65). Sevilla: Universidad de Sevilla.

Cenoz, J. (1991) *Enseñanza-aprendizaje del inglés como L2 o L3*. Leioa: Euskal Herriko Unibertsitatea, Universidad del País Vasco.

Cenoz, J. (1999) Towards trilingualism: The introduction of a third language in bilingual education. Paper presented at the Second International Symposium on Bilingualism, University of Newcastle, Newcastle, UK.

Cumming, A. (1989) Writing expertise and second language proficiency. *Language Learning* 39, 81–141.

Cumming, A. (1994) Writing expertise and second-language learning proficiency. In A. Cumming (ed.) *Bilingual Performance in Reading and Writing* (pp. 173–221). Chicago: John Benjamins.

Doiz, A. and Lasagabaster, D. (2001) El efecto del factor edad en la producción escrita en inglés. In I. de la Cruz, C. Santamaría, C. Tejedor and C. Valero (eds) *La lingüística aplicada a finales del siglo XX. Ensayos y propuestas* (Vol. 1) (pp. 63–8). Alcalá: Universidad de Alcalá.

Duff, A. (1994) [1984] *Translation*. Oxford: Oxford University Press.

Dulay, H., Burt, M. and Krashen, S. (1982) *Language 2*. Oxford: Oxford University Press.

Ellis, R. (1994) *The Study of Second Language Acquisition*. Oxford: Oxford University Press.

Harley, B. and Wang, W. (1997) The critical period hypothesis: Where are we now? In M.B. de Groot and J.F. Kroll (eds) *Tutorials in Bilingualism. Psycholinguistic Perspectives* (pp. 19–51). Mahwah, NJ: Lawrence Erlbaum Associates.

Hawkins, E.W. (1999) Foreign language study and language awareness. *Language Awareness* 8, 124–42.

Horning, A. (1987) *Teaching Writing as a Second Language*. Published for the Conference on College Composition and Communication. Carbondale and Edwardswile: Southern Illinois University Press.

Jacobs, J.L., Zinkgraf, S.A., Wormuth, D.R., Hartfiel, V.F. and Hughey, J.B. (1981) *Testing ESL Composition*. Newbury: Rowley.

James, C. (1996) A cross-linguistic approach to language awareness. *Language Awareness* 5, 138–48.

James, C. (1998) *Errors in Language Learning and Use. Exploring Error Analysis*. London: Longman.

James, C. (1999) Language awareness: Implications for the language curriculum. *Language, Culture and Curriculum* 12, 94–115.

James, C. and Klein, K. (1994) Foreign language learners' spelling and proof-reading strategies. *Papers and Studies in Contrastive Linguistics* 29, 31–46.

Lasagabaster, D. (1998) *Creatividad y conciencia metalingüística: Incidencia en el aprendizaje del inglés como L3*. Leioa: University of the Basque Country.

Lasagabaster, D. (1999) Typological relatedness, age and the learning of English as an L3. *Interface, Journal of Applied Linguistics* 14, 35–52.

Lasagabaster, D. (2000) Three languages and three linguistic models in the Basque educational system. In J. Cenoz and U. Jessner (eds) *English in Europe: The Acquisition of a Third Language* (pp. 179–97). Clevedon: Multilingual Matters.

Lasagabaster, D. (2001) Bilingualism, immersion programmes and language learning in the Basque Country. *Journal of Multilingual and Multicultural Development* 22, 401–25.

Lasagabaster, D. and Sierra, J.M. (eds) (2001) *Language Awareness in the Foreign Language Classroom*. Leioa: University of the Basque Country.

Mott, B. (1996) *A Course in Semantics and Translation for Spanish Learners of English*. Barcelona: Ediciones Universitarias de Barcelona.

Muñoz, C. (1999) The effects of age on instructed foreign language acquisition. In S. González, R.A. Valdeón, D. García, A. Ojanguren, M. Urdiales and A. Antón (eds) *Essays in English Language Teaching. A Review of the Communicative Approach* (pp. 1–22). Oviedo: Universidad de Oviedo.

Pennington, M. C. and So, S. (1993) Comparing writing process and product across two languages: A study of 6 Singaporean university student writers. *Journal of Second Language Writing* 2, 41–63.

Péry-Woodley, M-P. (1991) Writing in L1 and L2: analysing and evaluating learners' texts. *Language Teaching* 2, 69–83.

Reichelt, M. (1999) Toward a more comprehensive view of L2 writing: Foreign language writing in the U.S. *Journal of Second Language Writing* 8, 181–204.

Sagasta, P. (2000) La producción escrita en euskara, castellano e inglés en el modelo D y en el modelo de immersión. Unpublished PhD thesis. Vitoria-Gasteiz: University of the Basque Country.

Sasaki, M. and Hirose, K. (1996) Explanatory variables for EFL students' expository writing. *Language Learning*, 46, 137–174.

Segalowitz, N. (1997) Individual differences in second language acquisition. In M.B. de Groot and J.F. Kroll (eds) *Tutorials in Bilingualism. Psycholinguistic Perspectives* (pp. 85–112). Mahwah, NJ: Lawrence Erlbaum Associates.

Selinker, L. (1972) Interlanguage. *International Review of Applied Linguistics* 10, 209–31.

Singleton, D. (1995) A critical look at the critical period hypothesis in second language acquisition research. In D. Singleton and Z. Lengyel (eds) *The Age Factor in Second Language Acquisition* (pp. 1–29). Clevedon: Multilingual Matters.

Singleton, D. (1997) Age and second language learning. In G.R. Tucker and D. Corson (eds) *Encyclopedia of Language and Education, Volume 4: Second Language Education* (pp. 43–50). Dordrecht: Kluwer.

Smith, V. (1994) *Thinking in a Foreign Language. An Investigation into Essay Writing and Translation by L2 Learners*. Tübingen: Gunter Narr.

Uzawa, K. (1996) Second language learners´ processes of L1 writing, L2 writing, and translation from L1 into L2. *Journal of Second Language Writing* 5, 271–94.

Vendler, Z. (1967). *Linguistics in Philosophy*. Ithaca, NY: Cornell University Press.

Wolfe-Quintero, K., Inagaki, S. and Kim H.-Y. (1998) *Second Language Development in Writing: Measures of Fluency, Accuracy and Complexity*. Hawai´i: University of Hawai´i.

Zamel, V. (1983) The composing of advanced ESL writers: Six case studies. *TESOL Quarterly* 17, 165–87.

Chapter 8

Variation in Oral Skills Development and Age of Onset

CARMEN MUÑOZ

Age Differences on Second Language Acquisition

Previous findings

Two important distinctions have been proposed in connection with the effects of age on the acquisition of a a second language (L2) by two different lines of research. First, it has been concluded, on the basis of a significant body of research findings, that the effects of age on rate of acquisition must be distinguished from the effects of age on the level of ultimate attainment. Second, it has been claimed that the effects of age on literacy-related L2 skills are different from the effects of age on interpersonal communicative L2 skills. The first distinction allows us to separate older and younger learners' respective advantages: older learners have been found to have a superior rate of acquisition, particularly in the acquisition of morphosyntactic aspects. Younger learners, however, have shown a higher level of ultimate attainment in the long term and have also been observed to catch up and eventually outperform older learners (Krashen *et al.*, 1979). Such rate differences contribute to explaining the apparent contradiction between studies which claim advantages for one or the other group.

In general, studies which focus on subjects whose length of exposure (or residence) was relatively short claim an advantage on the part of older learners. Snow (1983) suggests that data for studies in which adults show superior results were collected during the first two years of residence. Slavoff and Johnson (1995), however, fail to establish differences in learning rate subsequent to three years of residence between two groups of children having arrived in the United States between the ages of 7–9 and 10–12, respectively. However, those studies which focus on subjects whose length of residence extends longer than 2 years show that the younger starters are favoured. Nevertheless, it has been suggested that a minimum of 5 years (Snow, 1983) and, more recently, ten (De Keyser, 2000) is required in order to methodologically insure measurement of ultimate attainment and not rate. Similarly, length of residence has been considered to affect the accent of subjects whose stay in the host country has been relatively short (for example, from 1 to 8 years; see Asher & García, [1969[) but not that of subjects whose stay in the target language community has been for longer periods of time (from 5 to 15 years; see Oyama, [1978]).

The second distinction differentiates between the effects of age on literacy-related L2 skills and the effects on interpersonal communicative L2 skills. Cummins has argued that older learners show higher mastery of L2 syntax, morphology and other literacy-related skills, such as vocabulary and reading comprehension, due to their greater cognitive maturity. However, they do not show an advantage in the areas of pronunciation and oral fluency because these appear to be among the least cognitively demanding aspects of both L1 and L2 proficiency (Cummins, 1980: 180; Cummins & Swain, 1986: 88). According to Cummins (1981: 133), measures of syntax, morphology and literacy-related skills assess a cognitive dimension of language proficiency, while measures of basic interpersonal communicative skills may be less sensitive to individual cognitive differences and to academic development. Additionally, L2 face-to-face communicative skills may be more dependent on personality and motivational factors (Cummins, 1983).

Nevertheless, other studies seem to show that with short-term experience older learners also have rate advantages in the previously mentioned aspects. For example, Ervin-Tripp (1974) reported that after 9 months of instruction in French, a group of 7–9 year olds performed better than a group of 4–6 year olds in the areas of comprehension, imitation and conversation. Similarly, Asher and Price (1967) found adults to perform better on listening comprehension tasks than 7-, 9- and 13 year-old children in an experimental language learning technique, which included a very short-term exposure, and for which, therefore, the results could be interpreted as an effect of the adults' superior learning rate. In other short-term studies (Ekstrand, 1976; Grinder *et al.*, 1962) older learners also performed better than younger ones on listening comprehension tests . Florander and Jansen (1969, cited in Ekstrand, 1976) compared students from Grades 4 and 6 (that is, 9 and 11 year olds) after 80 hours and 320 hours and established that the difference in favour of the older students decreased after 320 hours. Fathman (1975) found 11–15 year olds to score higher in pronunciation than 6–10 year olds in the first year of study but after three years the latter group overtook the former. In Snow and Hoefnagel-Höhle's (1978) study in a naturalistic situation, results of the older learners were superior to those of the younger learners on comprehension and pronunciation tests but the younger learners caught up with the older learners within 12 months. Therefore, in these studies the findings could be ascribed to the older starters' initial quicker rate of learning.

However, with greater amounts of exposure, learners with an earlier onset age seem to attain higher results in communicative skills. For example, in Ekstrand's (1977) study it was found that oral production was the only variable on which older immigrant learners did not perform significantly better than younger learners. Furthermore, Oyama (1976) observed that the younger immigrant learners (6–10 year olds on arrival) obtained higher scores on productive phonology than the older and, in a later study, also reported that younger immigrant learners obtained higher scores than older learners on listening comprehension tests (Oyama, 1978). Likewise, the youngest immigrants in Asher and García's (1969) study had the highest probability of attaining near-native English pronunciation and even more so if combined with a longer stay (5–8 years *versus* 1–5 years).

Furthermore, there could also be significant differences in the early acquisition of the various communicative skills. In particular, listening comprehension may be the skill at which gains obtained through early exposure in a formal context are more easily maintained after a number of years. For example, a study contrasting performance in French of early and late immersion students in Canada found the former group to outperform the latter solely in listening comprehension, while the late immersion group perfomed better on reading comprehension and there were no group differences on a cloze test. The authors interpreted these results in terms of the interdependence of academic skills across languages, that is, older learners come to the acquisition task equipped with L1 reading and writing skills, lexical and grammatical knowledge (Lapkin *et al.*, 1980: 124–5). However, no such transfer of listening comprehension skills appears to help older learners in L2 acquisition.

Moreover, in the study conducted by the National Foundation for Educational Research in Britain with learners of French of different starting ages, listening comprehension was the only skill at which the early starters outperformed the late starters after a few years (Burstall, 1975). It is important to note that this study differs from the majority of the studies previously described by the fact that acquisition of French occurred in England in a foreign-language context. Findings from this study should be more directly generalisable to the foreign-language teaching situation commonly found in, for example, European countries. However, the study has been severely criticised on methodological grounds, one of the flaws being that early starters were, at some point, mixed in with late starters in the same class. Nevertheless, the fact remains that the early starters could retain a certain level of superiority, in spite of the greater number of accumulated hours, only in the area of listening comprehension.

Finally, listening comprehension skills have been shown not to be generally related to IQ scores (Ekstrand, 1977), while the acquisition of literacy-related skills has (Genesee, 1976; Swain, 1984). Moreover, in a study which investigated the relationship between different aptitude measures and proficiency in early and late immersion students, listening comprehension appeared only related to memory and analytical abilitites among early immersion students but not among late immersion students (Harley & Hart, 1997).

In sum, the first distinction, between rate of acquisition and ultimate attainment, has been generally supported by research findings. The second distinction, however, between the effects of age on literacy-related skills and on communicative skills, seems to be also mediated by rate of acquisition and, ultimately, by length of exposure to the target language. On the basis of these findings the present study sets out to explore the effects of age on the acquisition of communicative skills in a foreign-language situation.

Age effects and communicative skills acquisition in a foreign-language context

Foreign-language acquisition differs from immersion (or partial immersion) acquisition in two main aspects. First, the amount and intensity of exposure to the target language in a foreign-language learning setting is much lower and so is the acquisition rate. Second, the opportunities for engaging in authentic and meaningful interaction in the target-language range from minimal to non-existent in a foreign language situation in which the target language is not used as the vehicle of instruction.

Despite the wealth of studies on the effects of the age factor on a naturalistic learning context, relatively little is known about the development over an extended period of time of communicative oral and auditory skills in a foreign-language learning situation. As the area is relatively undemanding in a cognitive sense, it seems that in an instructed situation older children may not show an advantage over younger children. Nevertheless, reported evidence has shown conflicting results, which furthermore may have been affected by length of exposure. As Krashen (1982: 219) argues, it remains to be demonstrated that the older–younger difference in rate holds only for aspects of L2 related to cognitive-academic proficiency. Consequently, this study assumes as a first general research question whether or not early starters in a foreign language situation show a similar, poorer or higher performance than late starters on oral and aural communicative skills.

In a similar fashion, while researchers in previous studies set in a naturalistic acquisition situation have been able to estimate the length of time

needed for younger starters to catch up and overtake the older starters –
twelve months, for example, in Snow and Hoefnagel-Höhle's (1978) study
– parallel estimates of the time needed for early starters to show their long-
term advantage are harder to obtain and require a more extensive period of
study time (Singleton, 1995). With the aim of providing relevant evidence
concerning this issue, our second research question examines the relation
between length of instruction and language development in students with
different onset ages (different ages at beginning of instruction in this case)
and, specifically, the length of time required for younger starters to catch
up with or overtake late starters if these show an initial superiority.

Method

Subjects
The subjects in the study are bilingual Catalan–Spanish learners of
English in a foreign language context. The schools they attend are all
Catalan-medium state-funded schools but they vary in the degree to which
Catalan is used as the language of instruction and communication, with
Spanish having a lower presence at primary than at secondary levels. Fur-
thermore, students show different degrees of dominance in one or the other
language depending mainly on their family linguistic background.

The students of this study are comprised of a subset of subjects from a
much more extensive research project on the effects of age on foreign-
language acquisition which includes several groups with different starting
ages. The present subset includes learners who began formal instruction of
English at the age of 8 (grade 3) and learners who began at the age of 11
(grade 6). The former follow the current curriculum which imposes a
younger starting age and will be referred to as early starters (ES) and the
latter the previous curriculum and will be referred to as late starters (LS).
During some academic years both curricula coexisted and the data in
question here were collected at that time.

Three different data collection times were established in order to assess
acquisition during both primary- and secondary-school periods, as well as
the ultimate attainment reached by both groups of students. The first test
was administered after 200 hours of English instruction. The ES1 group, 10, 9
year olds on average, had had at that point 3 years of instruction of 120
minutes per week and the LS1, 2 years at a higher intensity of 180 minutes
per week.

The second data collection took place 216 hours later, that is, after a total
of 416 instructional hours. The ES2 were then 12,9 year olds and the LS2
14,9. In this study a comparative analysis of the results at the first and the
second administration time will be presented.[1] Table 1 shows information

Table 1 Subjects in the study

	ES (OA = 8)	*LS (OA = 11)*
Time 1 = 200 hr	ES1 (AT = 10,9)	LS1 (AT = 12,9)
Time 2 = 416 hr	ES2 (AT = 12,9)	LS2 (AT = 14,9)

OA, Onset age; AT, Age at testing

about the subjects: age, accumulated hours of instruction, and time of test administration.

L2 Proficiency measures and procedures

In addition to a series of tests subjects completed a written questionnaire which requested information about the learners' uses of the three languages (Catalan, Spanish and English), their extracurricular exposure to English, if any, and biographical data. The tests administered can be largely divided into two groups: first, the academically oriented and literacy related tests, and second, the communicatively oriented tests.

The tests oriented towards the measurement of communicative skills relevant to the two major research questions are the oral interview and the listening comprehension tests. The oral interview was administered to a randomly selected sample of those students who had not had any type of extracurricular exposure to English according to their answers in the questionnaire mentioned earlier. The interview began with a warming-up phase which helped students to feel more at ease, since for many of them, especially the younger and less proficient learners, it may have been the first time they were asked to use the target language productively and spontaneously for longer than a controlled response in a typical teaching exchange.

This semi-guided interview began as most oral interviews do (for example, the LS Oral Proficiency Test) with a series of questions about the subject's family, daily life and hobbies, questions considered not to be cognitively demanding for learners of any age. Not all learners performed in the same way, however. Proficiency level and personality characteristics (of both interviewer and interviewee) provided for wide variation. In general, interviewers attempted to elicit as many responses as possible from the learners and accepted learner-initiated topics in order to create as natural and interactive a situation as possible. However, the questions previously established were, for the most part, all posed by the (seven) interviewers to guarantee the comparability of interviews across learners and groups (Muñoz & Cortés, 2001).

Learners' performance was assessed by means of two scales, one for production and one for comprehension. The same procedures were followed in the construction, piloting and assessing phases. The scales were piloted with three different raters until the level of inter-rater agreement was found to be satisfactory. This inevitably entailed a decrease in the number of levels until a balance was established between accuracy and reliability. In the end, a seven-level scale satisfied accuracy and reliability requirements for both production and reception skills. The final evaluation was conducted by three raters and each interview was independently assessed for production and reception by two of them. The Pearson product–moment correlation coefficient between the judgements of the two raters for oral production was very high: 0.96 ($p = 0.000$) for groups ES1 and LS1, and 0.93 ($p = 0.000$) for groups ES2 and LS2, and the correlation coefficients for the assessment of reception skills was also high: 0.81($p = 0.000$) for groups ES1 and LS1, and 0.83 ($p = 0.000$) for groups ES2 and LS2 .

The listening comprehension test was conducted in class with intact groups and only later limited to a sub-set including only those tests of students who had not had any type of extracurricular exposure. The test consisted of 25 items in an increasing order of difficulty. The first three items requested the learners to identify the drawing (out of three) that corresponded to the word they heard. In the remaining 22 items learners were asked to select the picture (also out of three) that reflected the meaning of the sentence they had heard. Learners were asked to listen to each stimulus twice and then tick the drawing that corresponded to the oral stimulus. The stimuli had been audio-recorded by a native speaker of British English, since this model was thought to be the most common among their non-native-speaking teachers.

Learners were informed of the increasing order of difficulty of the items, and of the proportion of answers that were expected from their grade group, given the high degree of difficulty of the last items for the lower proficiency groups. Finally, it should be noted that for the sake of comparability all proficiency groups in the three administration times completed the same tests (or different forms of the same tests).

Comparison of Results

Previous analyses of the same subsets of learners' scores on the literacy related tests had confirmed an advantage of the LS groups over the ES groups. At both administration Times 1 and 2 the LS groups had significantly higher scores on the cloze, dictation and grammar test (Muñoz, 1999), as well as on the composition test (Celaya *et al.*, 2001; Pérez-Vidal *et al.*, 2000). These results thus confirmed the superior rate of acquisition of the older learners already established in previous studies. Furthermore,

Muñoz (2001) shows that the variables 'proficiency in L1' and 'grade' have the greatest influence on the scores on these tests.[2]

The purpose of this section is to compare the scores obtained by the different groups on the communicatively oriented tests, first, the measures of productive skills, and second, the measures of receptive skills.

Oral productive skills

Oral productive skills of the ES and LS learners were measured through their performance on the oral interview as assessed by the production scale. Each student was given a score based on the stage at which s/he was assigned. Thus, a student performing at stage 1 was given one point, while a student performing at stage 7 was given seven points (the maximum score). The scores obtained by each group in the oral production scale are presented in Tables 2 and 3.

Table 2 displays the results obtained by the two groups, ES and LS, after 200 hours of instruction. A t-test performed on these data revealed that the LS's mean is significantly higher than the ES's mean at the first measurement time ($t = 3.813$; $p = 0.000$; a Levene test showed that the variances of the two groups were not significantly different). Thus, the analysis reveals that those learners who began instruction in English at the age of 11 scored significantly higher in this task than those who began at the age of 8.

Table 2 Scores on oral productive skills: time 1

Groups	N	Mean[a]	SD
ES1	46	2.50	0.68
LS1	34	3.13	0.83

[a]Maximum score = 7

The means obtained by each group show their position in the production scale. Group ES1, with a mean score of 2.5, appears to be half way between stage 2 and 3. The following example from an interview with one of the students in that group also serves to illustrate one of the descriptors that characterizes stage 2:

> Example 1 The learner can take words/one word from the interviewer's utterance for his/her answer
> **Interviewer:** your bedroom, is it big or small?
> **Learner:** ai!

Interviewer: your bedroom
Learner: *una mica* small (Mixed / Cat.: *a bit* small)

Example 2 from an interview with a student from group LS1 illustrates an exchange at stage 3:

> Example 2 Learner can produce a mixed phrase or phrasal chunks in the target language
> **I:** what's your name?
> **L:** it is Alan
> **I:** okey, Alan, how old are you?
> **L:** *it is* ten

The scores obtained by the ES2 and LS2 on the identical interview after 216 additional instructional hours reveal the progress attained. The difference between the means shown in Table 3 is statistically significant ($t = -6.531; p = 0.000$) according to a two-tailed t-test (preceded by a Levene test to ensure homogeneity of variances).

Table 3 Scores on oral productive skills: time 2

Groups	N	Mean[a]	SD
ES2	54	3.60	0.69
LS2	29	4.82	1.01

*Maximum score = 7

The data demonstrate that a certain number of the learners in group ES2 could be identified with the descriptors from stage 3 (as in Example 2, and others with the descriptors from stage 4. One descriptor from stage 4 is illustrated in the following example taken from an interview with a student in the ES2 group:

> Example 3 *Learner can produce simple sentences with grammatical errors, but they do not hamper communication*
> **I:** in your free time what do you do?
> **L:** I like play play basketball.

Finally, a high number of learners in group LS2 performed at stage 5. A descriptor from this stage is illustrated in the following example:

> Example 4 *Past or future reference may be marked lexically or grammatically but not consistently*
> **I:** you played basketball but that was Sunday morning, and then on Saturday?

L: on Saturday I stay at home and Saturday I will I will I went to to a friend's.

The data analysed reveal the higher productive abilities at the oral interview of late starters, both after 200 instructional hours and after 416 hours. These results confirm the tendency already attested in the case of the more cognitively or academically oriented tests.

A stepwise regression analysis was conducted in order to observe the relative influence of different factors on the English scores. The results indicated that at Time 1 the variable 'proficiency in L1' was the strongest predictor variable, entering the equation at Step 1; 'school' was also a significant predictor and entered the equation at Step 2, increasing the adjusted square R from 0.18 at Step 1 to 0.27 at Step 2. At Time 2 also 'proficiency in L1' was the strongest predictor, and the variable 'grade' entered the equation at Step 2 increasing the adjusted square *R* from 0.36 to 0.45.

Auditory receptive skills

The project design allowed measurement of reception skills through two distinct sources: the first, the learners' performance on a listening comprehension test and the second, the learners' performance on the oral interview described earlier. These two related measures differ in an important aspect. The interview occurred in an interactive situation, in which comprehension of the interlocutor's utterance allows the continuation of the exchange or elicits conversational adjustments. The interviewee in such a situation may benefit from the interlocutor's verbal and non-verbal cues as well as influence the interlocutor's interactional performance. The listening comprehension test, in contrast, requires only identification of the visual stimuli that correspond to the auditory stimuli provided, with no interaction, possibility of repair or benefit from interactional aids or contextual clues.

Receptive skills in the listening comprehension test

Tables 4 and 5 reveal that more subjects participated in the listening comprehension test than in the oral interview, because the former was suited to administration to intact groups, whereas the latter only to randomly selected groups within the specific subset of learners lacking extracurricular contact with the target language.

Table 4 contains the scores obtained at the first measurement time. A *t*-test conducted subsequent to checking homogeneity of variances through a Levene test, showed the scores between the two groups not to be statistically different ($t = -0.063$; $p = 0.950$), although the LS1 group had a slightly higher mean.

Table 4 Scores on the listening comprehension test: time 1

Groups	N	Mean*	SD
ES1	163	9.28	3.28
LS1	104	9.31	3.10

ᵃMaximum score = 25

Table 5 Scores on the listening comprehension test: Time 2

Groups	N	Mean[a]	SD
ES2	138	12.88	9.21
LS2	95	14.25	3.07

ᵃmaximum score = 25

The same test was administered to the ES2 and LS2 groups after 416 instructional hours, and this time the results did not reveal a statistically significant difference either ($t = -1.403$; $p = 0.162$) (see Table 5).

The results discussed to this point demonstrate the less extensive advantage of the LS groups on these tests as compared to the other tests (those literacy-related previously mentioned and the oral productive scale presented here). As before, a stepwise regression analysis was conducted and the results reveal that none of the factors examined appears to explain a high enough proportion of the variance.

Receptive skills in the interview

The scale used to measure the learners' receptive skills was also divided into seven stages. Three raters assessed all the interviews independently following the previously mentioned procedures. Two-tailed *t*-tests performed on these data, subsequent to a Levene test that showed the variances of the two groups were not significantly different, revealed that group LS1 scored significantly higher than group ES1 ($t = -2.413$; significant at 0.018). That is, after 200 hours of instruction the late starters' receptive skills were higher (see Table 6).

Example 5, corresponding to Stage 3 on the reception scale, illustrates the receptive skills of learners in the ES1 group:

> Example 5 Learner often needs reassurance and uses clarification requests in L1
> **I:** and what did you do last week-end?

Table 6 Scores on the receptive scale. First administration time

Groups	N	Mean[a]	SD
ES1	46	3.24	0.97
LS1	34	3.78	1.02

[a]Maximum score = 7

I: what did you do?
L: no t'entenc (Cat.: I don't understand you)
I: aquest cap de setmana? (Cat.: last week-end)
I: espera (Cat.: wait)
   okey, my question is what did you do last week-end?
   (silence)
I: el cap de setmana passat (Cat: last week-end)
L: sí (Cat.: yes)
I: what did you do?
L: on vaig anar? (Cat.: where did I go?)
I: no, what did you do?
L: mm Calafell (a near-by beach resort)

However, some learners in the LS1 group performed at stage 4, illustrated by the following example:

Example 6 Learner can understand (more than 6) questions on some basic topics (daily life and family) without prompting
I: and do you like this school?
L: mm, yes
I: well, mm, let's talk about your family, your family. How many broth ers and sisters have you got?
L: mm one
I: brother or sister?
I: sister

After 416 hours, the LS appear to perform better than the ES again. Similarly, a Levene test and a two-tailed t-test were conducted and the difference was found to be significant ($t = -4.178$; $p = 0.000$) (see Table 7).

The relative position of each group in the reception scale is indicated by the means obtained in each case after 416 instructional hours. Group ES2 appears closer to the lower extreme of stage 4, while many learners in group LS2 perform at stage 5. Example 7 illustrates an exchange at stage 4

Table 7 Scores on the receptive scale. Second administration time

Groups	N	Mean[a]	SD
ES2	54	4.29	0.63
LS2	28	4.96	0.80

[a]Maximum score = 7

of an ES2 learner, while example 8 is an illustration of an exchange at stage 5 of another ES2 learner:

> Example 7 Learner cannot follow conversation on open questions. S/he performs better with follow-up questions of the closed type
> **I:** and what will you do?
> **L:** quan de temps? (Cat.: for how long?)
> **I:** no, no, what will you do?
>   will you watch TV, will you eat?
> **L:** ah! watch TV

> Example 8 Can follow limited conversation with open and closed questions on all basic topics, although there may appear a few errors, misunderstandings, and questions unanswered
> **I:** and what will you do when you finish today?
> **L:** I go to to my house
> **I:** aha
> **L:** and I listen music

Again, a stepwise regression analysis was conducted and the results revealed that the factor 'proficiency in L1' seemed to exert some influence on the variance of the dependent variable, scores on the reception scale, entering the equation at Step 1 at both measurement times. The variable 'school' added 0.08 at Time 1, increasing the adjusted square R from 0.13 at Step 1 to 0.21 at Step 2. At time 2 the variable 'grade' added 0.04 to the adjusted square R from 0.24 at Step 1 to 0.28 at Step 2.

Summarising, the comparison of the results on the listening comprehension test and the reception scale from the oral interview test indicates that the LS groups obtain higher scores on both tests and at both the first and second administration times. The difference, however, is only significant on the interview reception scores but not on the listening comprehension test scores. It, therefore, seems clear that the younger learners' lower receptive performance on the interview than on the listening comprehension test deserves further exploration, and thus in the next section, our learners' global performance on the oral interview will be analysed from a qualitative perspective. By considering their responses, silences included, and their recourse to their better known languages, a more complete picture of their oral communicative skills can be outlined.

An analysis of the different groups' performance on the interview

In order to assess in greater depth our learners' performance on the oral interview, the responses to the interviewer's questions of a subset of ten learners from each group, five with Spanish as their dominant language and five with Catalan were analysed. Subjects were randomly chosen from among those who fulfilled the language dominance condition. Different patterns of responses could be expected for different age groups, mainly in terms of the use of the target language and recourse to L1–L2.[3] Responses were categorised as follows.

(1) Use of the target language: all turns uttered in English, language to be referred to as L3.
(2) Mixed utterances: includes all utterances in which the L3 is mixed with the L1–L2.
(3) Learner-initiated code-switching: includes all turns in which the learner chooses to answer in Spanish or Catalan, his/her dominant language (L1) or not (L2).
(4) Interviewer-initiated code-switching: learner's use of his/her L1 or L2 following the interviewer's previous code-switch behaviour, categorised as code-switching since in theory the interviewee could have chosen to answer in the interview target language (English).
(5) No answer: the learners' complete lack of verbal (or non-verbal) response.

In Table 8 the respective percentages of each group's responses appear. The groups are categorised by increasing level of proficiency and age at testing.

The last column in Table 8 illustrates the high variability of the length of the interviews of the different groups. Although the interview was semi-structured and organised around a fixed set of topics, the proficiency level

Table 8 Percentage of response types by different groups

Groups (AT)	Use of L3	Mixed U	L-I C-S	I-I C-S	No Answer	Turns Total
ES1 (10,9)	44.53	4.37	16.39	5.74	26.23	366
LS1 (12,9)	43.51	4.91	35.96	3.68	13.28	570
ES2 (12,9)	57.47	5.64	15.55	6.25	13.87	656
LS2 (14,9)	67.23	8.12	15.16	0.92	7.35	653

AT; age-at-testing

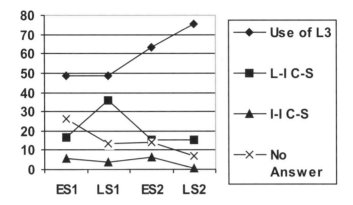

Figure 1 Response types

and the age of the interviewees seem clearly to have affected the interviewers' attempts to continue the interview or not. It can also be observed that the
progression shown in Table 8 reflects only partially the different groups'
proficiency in English. First, the use of L3 after 200 hours of instruction
appears to be a consequence of the learners' experience with the target
language, since both groups ES1 and LS1 show a very similar percentage. Yet
with more instructional hours progression is not similar, and LS2 – the more
proficient of the two – shows a higher frequency of use of the target language
than ES2 does.[4] Mixed utterances also seem to increase generally with L2
proficiency. In Figure 1 both Use of L3 and Mixed Utterances have been col-
lapsed into a single measurement.

The frequency of responses in which learners code-switch or choose not to
answer seems to be an effect of the factors age-at-testing and proficiency. A
comparison of groups ES1 and LS1 reveals a pattern of (learner-initiated)
code-switching (L-I C-S) that seems a mirror image of the pattern of No
Answer. That is, the 10 year olds (ES1) tend to remain silent when unable to
answer in the L3 or to understand the interviewer's question, while the 12
year olds (LS1) tend to code-switch into L1 or L2. At measurement time 2, 12
year olds (ES2) share a similar percentage of No Answer with the less proficient 12-year olds (LS1) but fewer instances of code-switch since their use of
L3 is greatly increased. As can be seen in Figure 1, the frequency of No
Answer shows a clear tendency to diminish with higher proficiency and age.
Finally, the use of L1–L2 in response to the interviewer's previous code-

switch (I-I C-S) corresponds to the frequency of this behaviour on the part of the interviewers for each group.

In sum, starting age appears not to affect the type of responses made by learners to the questions posed by the interviewers. Instead, the factors which do influence the learners' reactions are proficiency level and age-at-testing. In this last respect, it is interesting to compare the two 12-year-old groups, LS1 and ES2, because even with different proficiency levels, the two groups show a strong similarity in the frequency of interactional attempts. That is, on slightly more than 13% of occasions only do they choose to remain silent, resulting in half the frequency of the silences of 10 year olds.[5] Yet the distribution of their active responses vary in accordance with their proficiency level in L3: the more proficient group uses L3 more often while the less proficient group code-switches into L1–L2. This finding is in the line of previous findings by Scarcella and Higa (1982), who reported adolescents (14.5–16.5) to carry out more negotiation work than younger L2 learners (8.5–9.5). Although a more detailed study of our subjects' negotiation work is needed in order to examine the differences due to age, our analysis indicates a more active role on the part of the older L2 learners, a fact which may explain why the younger learners do not benefit more from the context-embeddedness of the task. It may also be argued that this finding results from the very low level of proficiency of the ES1 group, a characteristic which prevented them from adopting an active role in the interview despite the communicative nature of the task and the lower level of inhibition thought to correspond to their younger age.[6] However, use of similar strategies by both groups of 12 year olds, despite their differing proficiency levels, suggests an explanation based on age differences rather than proficiency differences.

General Discussion and Conclusions

With respect to oral productive skills, analysis of the interview scores reveals that at the productive level the LS reached a higher level than the ES. With respect to auditory receptive skills, comparative analysis of the interview and listening comprehension scores reveals a contrast in the measurement of reception skills. Although the LS (also older at time of testing) perform better on both tests, the difference is only statistically significant for the interview, not for the listening comprehension test. Based on these results, an important difference surfaces between the two types of reception skills being assessed, the interactive skills elicited in the interview and the recognition or identification skills in the listening comprehension test.

These findings generalise the superior rate of the older learners, attested for the more academically oriented tests (Muñoz, 1999; Pérez-Vidal *et al.*, 2000), to non-literacy related skills, with the exception of those required for listening comprehension (recognition). Therefore, the answer to the first research question, with respect to the acquisition of oral and aural skills, must include the previous distinction: whereas late starters perform better than early starters with the same number of hours of instruction in both the productive and receptive skills employed during an interview, no significant differences are found between late and early starters in the receptive skills in aural recognition.

Furthermore, and in line with the results of the more literacy-related tests, the factor that appears to explain the higher percentage of variance of productive and receptive scores on the interview is 'proficiency in L1', which seems more a reflection of cognitive maturity and perhaps of general language aptitude. Differences between schools appear also to account for some of the variation in students' scores at Time 1, while curriculum differences represented by the factor 'grade' account for some additional variation at Time 2. In that respect, the most important distinctive characteristic of the two different curricula may be that the ES2 students belong to the new compulsory secondary education period, while the LS2 students belong to the former non-compulsory secondary education period. In other words, an academic filter, of both a scholastic and attitudinal nature, has selected learners into the LS2 group but not into the ES2 group.

The analysis of the more frequent types of responses to the interview questions shows effects of both proficiency in L3 and age-at-testing. Interestingly, the 12 year olds exert a more active role in the interview than the 10 year olds, confirming previous findings of the effects of age differences on the amount of negotiation work carried out by L2 learners (Scarcella & Higa, 1982). This finding may help to explain the older children's reported superior learning rate of communicative skills, at least in certain contexts. Furthermore, the minimal participation required on the listening comprehension test compared to the interview may be a factor that explains the different results of these two tests. Further research should confirm that listening comprehension skills benefit from an early exposure more than other types of skills, a fact not evident in the interview results due to the requirement of active involvement, more difficult for the younger learners to fulfill.

The observation of the learners' evolution from the point referred to as 'short term', after 200 accumulated hours, to a point after 416 accumulated hours referred to as 'mid-term' provides an answer to the second research question, that of how much time is required for early starters in a foreign-language situation to catch up with and outperform late starters whose rate of success is higher at short term. Contrary to the findings reported by

Florander and Jansen (1979), according to which the advantage of the older students decreased after 320 hours, in our results no differences in productive and receptive skills at the interview are attested with time in that direction. In fact, the tendency observed in the listening comprehension scores is just the opposite, since the difference, without reaching significance, increases from measurement time 1 to 2. The persistence of the older learners' superiority may also be partly explained through other factors. First, the accumulation of exposure hours could have benefitted the older learners simply in terms of general test-wiseness ability. Second, the superiority of the older learners could be an effect of school and curriculum differences, as pointed out before.

The design of our study allows a third comparison to be made (ES3 and LS3) after 726 hours (very near the end of the previous curriculum) and even a fourth one when the new curriculum students reach the end of secondary education (ES4 and LS3) after 800 hours. This number of instructional hours is still quite distant from the estimated 2.600 hours of Snow and Hoefnagel-Höhle's (1978) study, where younger learners were observed to take a minimum of 12 months in a natural situation to catch up with older learners. If no change in trend is observed at the end of secondary education, it should then be concluded that the current system of formal education does not provide enough exposure to students in order for the early starters to outperform the late starters eventually, a conclusion which has obvious consequences from both a pedagogical and a language-in-education policy viewpoint, in this and similar foreign language situations.

It has been stated that native-like levels can be attained through acquiring a second language at a young age because of the use of implicit language-learning mechanisms. But these mechanisms require massive exposure to the language, the level of exposure that children learning their mother tongue have (De Keyser, 2000). If schools do not provide this level of exposure, young children may be deprived of this natural advantage. However, older children, more cognitively mature, benefit from explicit language-learning mechanisms which do not require a high level of exposure. In other words, older children are less affected by the fact that the school does not provide enough exposure to the foreign-language while they benefit to a higher degree from the explicit teaching common to a formal setting (Muñoz, 2001). In conclusion, in order to enhance foreign language learning in a school setting, changes that guarantee sufficient exposure to and meaningful interaction in the target language have to be implemented.

A final word seems to be in order on the trilingual condition of these learners for which the school system has to provide enough time to reach native levels both in their L1 and their L2. In such a tight schedule the only programmes that guarantee a greater amount of exposure without lengthening school hours are those in which the target language is used as the language of instruction of other content-subjects. In fact, the minority language, Catalan, is already introduced for non-Catalan speakers through immersion at school. The implementation of partial immersion for the L3 may indeed be a feasible way of providing young children with enough exposure and opportunities to engage in communicative interaction. In such a case, immediate gains, particularly at communicative and non-literacy related skills, should naturally be observed. Further research should provide information about whether younger learners' long-term advantage in terms of higher ultimate attainment will eventually be revealed within the school period in such conditions.

Acknowledgements

The research reported on here has received financial support from the Spanish Ministry of Education through research project PB97-0901.

Notes

1. The third data collection, after 726 hours, has not yet been undertaken with one of the groups due to the longitudinal nature of some of the data.
2. The following variables were introduced in the step-by step regression analysis: 'proficiency in L1', 'grade', 'school' and 'sociocultural background'; others such as 'attitude towards English' did not correlate highly enough. The values for the first variable, 'proficiency in L1' were obtained through the tests in Catalan and Spanish that the students answered together with the English tests: a dictation and a cloze test in each of these two languages. The scores came from the two tests in Catalan when this was the learner's dominant language, the two tests in Spanish when this was the dominant language or the four tests when the learner seemed to show a balanced use of both languages, according to their answers in a written questionnaire. The values for all the other variables were also drawn from the background questionnaire.
3. L1–L2 stands for any or both of the two languages of these bilingual learners when there is no need or convenience of further specification. English will be referred to as L3 in this section.
4. Although data are not yet available from group ES3 to make the comparison after 726 hours (third test administration time), the analysis of group LS3 from which data are already available, shows an important increase in the use of L3, in accordance with their higher proficiency level (Muñoz, in preparation).
5. This higher frequency of interactional attempts is matched with a clear increase of interactional adjustments by the interviewers with these two groups. See Muñoz (in preparation).
6. But then this becomes circular since with the same time and exposure they achieve lower levels and these lower levels prevent them from taking a more active role at the interview, a fact which could benefit their language learning.

References

Asher, J. and García, R. (1969) The optimal age to learn a foreign language. *Modern Language Journal* 53, 334–42. Reprinted in S.D. Krashen, R.C. Scarcella and M.H. Long (eds) (1982) *Child–Adult Differences in Second Language Acquisition* (pp. 3–12). Rowley, Mass.: Newbury House Publishers.

Asher, J. and Price, B. (1967) The learning strategy of the total physical response: Some age differences. *Child Development*, 38 (4), 1219–27.

Burstall, C. (1975) Primary French in the balance. *Foreign Language Annals* 10 (3), 245–52.

Celaya, M.L., Torras, M.R., and Pérez-Vidal, C. (2001) Short and mid-term effects of an earlier start: An analysis of EFL written production. In S. Foster-Cohen and A. Nizegorodcew (eds) *Eurosla Yearbook.* Volume 1 (pp. 195–209). Amsterdam: John Benjamins.

Cummins, J. (1980) The cross-lingual dimensions of language proficiency: Implications for bilingual education and the optimal age issue. *TESOL Quarterly* 14 (2), 175–87.

Cummins, J. (1981) Age on arrival and immigrant second language learning in Canada. A reassessment. *Applied Linguistics* 11 (2), 132–49.

Cummins, J. (1983) Language proficiency, biliteracy and French immersion. *Canadian Journal of Education* 8 (2), 117–38.

Cummins, J. and Swain, M. (1986) *Bilingualism in Education*. London: Longman.

De Keyser, R. (2000) The robustness of critical period effects in second language acquisition. *Studies in Second Language Acquisition* 22 (4), 499–533.

Ekstrand, L.H. (1976) Age and length of residence as variables related to the adjustment of migrant children, with special reference to second language learning. In G. Nickel (ed.) *Proceedings of the Fourth International Congress of Applied Linguistics*. Stuttgart Hochshul. Reprinted in S.D. Krashen, R.C. Scarcella and M.H. Long (eds) (1982) *Child–Adult Differences in Second Language Acquisition* (pp. 123–35). Rowley, MA: Newbury House.

Ekstrand, L.H. (1977) Social and individual frame factors in L2 learning comparative aspects. In T. Skutnabb-Kangas (ed.) *Papers from the First Nordic Conference on Bilingualism* (pp. 41–60). Helsingfors: Universitetet.

Ervin-Tripp, S.M. (1974) Is second language learning like the first? *TESOL Quarterly* 8, 111–27.

Fathman, A. (1975) The relationship between age and second language productive ability. *Language Learning* 25, 245–53.

Genesee, F. (1976) The role of intelligence in second language learning. *Language Learning* 26, 267–80.

Grinder, R., Otomo, A. and Toyota, W. (1962) Comparisons between second, third, and fourth grade children in the audio-lingual learning of Japanese as a second language. *The Journal of Educational Research* 56 (4), 463–9.

Harley, B. and Hart, D. (1997) Language aptitude and second language proficiency in classroom learners of different starting ages. *Studies in Second Language Acquisition* 19 (3), 379–400.

Krashen, S. D. (1982) Accounting for child–adult differences in second language rate and attainment. In S.D. Krashen, R.C. Scarcella and M.H. Long (eds) (1982) *Child-Adult Differences in Second Language Acquisition* (pp. 202–26). Rowley, Mass.: Newbury House Publishers.

Krashen, S., Long, M., and Scarcella, R. (1979) Age, rate and eventual attainment in second language acquisition. *TESOL Quarterly* 9, 573–582. Reprinted in S.D. Krashen, R.C. Scarcella and M.H. Long (eds) 1982. *Child–Adult Differences in Second Language Acquisition* (pp. 161–72). Rowley, Mass.: Newbury House.

Lapkin, S., Swain, M., Kamin, J. and Hanna, G. (1980) Report on the 1979 evaluation of the Peel County late French immersion program, grades 8, 10, 11 and 12. Unpublished report, University of Toronto, OISE.

Muñoz, C. (1999) The effects of age on instructed foreign language acquisition. In S. Fernández, R. Valdeón, D. García, A. Ojanguren, M. Urdiales, A. Antón (eds) *Essays in English Language Teaching. A Review of the Communicative Approach* (pp. 1–22). Oviedo: Servicio de Publicaciones de la Universidad de Oviedo.

Muñoz, C. (2001) Factores escolares e individuales en el aprendizaje formal de un idioma extranjero. In S. Pastor and V. Salazar (eds) *Tendencias y líneas de investigación en adquisición de segundas lenguas* (pp. 247–68). Monograph *Estudios de Lingüística* Universidad de Alicante.

Muñoz, C. (in preparation) Codeswitching and interactional modifications in L3 interviews. The role of age and proficiency.

Muñoz, C. and Cortés, C. (2001) El uso de escalas para medir la proficiencia oral en inglés. In I. de la Cruz, C. Santamaría, C. Tejedor and C. Valero (eds) *La lingüística aplicada a finales del siglo XX. Ensayos y propuestas* (Vol. 1) (pp. 113–18). Alcalá: Universidad de Alcalá.

Oyama, S. (1976) A sensitive period for the acquisition of a nonnative phonological system. *Journal of Psycholinguistic Research* 5, 261–85. Reprinted in S.D. Krashen, R.C. Scarcella and M.H. Long (eds) (1982) *Child–Adult Differences in Second Language Acquisition* (pp. 20–38). Rowley, MA: Newbury House.

Oyama, S. (1978) The sensitive period and comprehension of speech. *Working Papers on Bilingualism* 16, 1–17. Reprinted in S.D. Krashen, R.C. Scarcella and M.H. Long (eds) (1982) *Child–Adult Differences in Second Language Acquisition* (pp. 39–51). Rowley, MA: Newbury House.

Pérez-Vidal, C., Celaya, Mª L. and Torras, Mª R. (2000) Age and EFL Written Performance by Catalan/Spanish Bilinguals. *Spanish Applied Linguistics* 4 (2), 267–90.

Scarcella, R. and Higa, C. (1982) Input and age differences in second language acquisition. In S.D. Krashen, R. C. Scarcella and M.H. Long (eds) *Child-Adult Differences in Second Language Acquisition* (pp. 175–201). Rowley, MA: Newbury House.

Singleton, D. (1995) A critical look at the Critical Period Hypothesis in second language acquisition research. In D. Singleton and Z. Lengyel (eds) *The Age Factor in Second Language Acquisition* (pp. 1–29). Clevedon: Multilingual Matters.

Slavoff, G.R. and Johnson, J.S. (1995) The effects of age on the rate of learning a second language. *Studies in Second Language Acquisition* 17 (1), 1–16.

Snow, C. (1983) Age differences in second language acquisition: Research findings and folk psychology. In K.M. Bailey, M.H. Long, and S. Peck (eds) *Second Language Acquisition Studies* (pp. 141–50). Rowley, MA: Newbury House.

Snow, C. and Hoefnagel-Höhle, M. (1978) The critical period for language acquisition: Evidence from second language learning. *Child Development* 49, 1114–28.

Swain, M. (1984) A review of immersion education in Canada: Research and evaluation studies. In B. Honig (ed.) *Studies on Immersion Education: A Collection for United States Educators* (pp. 87–112). Sacramento, CA: California State Department of Education.

Chapter 9

Learner Strategies: A Cross-sectional and Longitudinal Study of Primary and High-school EFL Learners

MIA VICTORI and ELSA TRAGANT

Introduction

Learner strategies have been defined as the mental operations that we deploy when we acquire, store, retrieve and use information (Rigney, 1978; Wenden, 1991); or, to put it simply, they are the behaviours or steps that we take to aid the acquisition of a language. Learner strategies have such an important impact on the learning of a language that, within the area of SLA, they have become the focus of a large number of studies, from those that have endeavoured to define and classify them (Faerch & Kasper, 1984; O'Malley & Chamot, 1990; Oxford, 1990; Rubin, 1975; Stern, 1975; Tarone, 1981; Wenden & Rubin, 1987) to those that have examined their applications in the classroom (Cohen, 1990, 1998; Ellis & Sinclair, 1989; Rubin & Thompson, 1982; Wenden, 1991).

There is a general consensus among researchers that all language learners use strategies of some type, yet the range of strategies as well as the frequency with which they are deployed varies among learners (Chamot & Küpper, 1989). It is precisely those differences that have led some studies to analyse the variance in strategy use among learners of different characteristics, such as proficiency level, sex, cognitive style, motivation, personality or context, with the aim of identifying different learner profiles based on their strategic behaviour.

Certainly, the most fruitful studies have been those that have compared the strategies used by successful and less successful learners. Findings derived from these studies show that the most effective learners have a very active approach and a responsible learning behaviour, with a wide repertoire of task-based strategies which they deploy effectively and with flexibility (Cohen, 1998; Chamot & Beard El-Dinary, 1999; Lawson &

182

Hogben, 1996; Naiman *et al.*, 1978; O'Malley & Chamot, 1990; Oxford & Nyikos, 1989; Oxford & Burry-Stock, 1995; Rubin, 1975; Stern, 1975), just the opposite of what has been observed with less successful learners. These results, nevertheless, have not been supported by the work of other scholars (Lahuerta, 1998; Naiman *et al.*, 1978; Porte, 1988; Vann & Abraham, 1990) who have observed unsuccessful learners using strategies typically associated with successful learners.

The same discrepancies can be found with the research that has been undertaken comparing strategies used by learners with different proficiency levels. The review of studies done by Oxford and Crookall (1989) suggests that as the learner's proficiency level increases so does his or her repertoire as well as the complexity and frequency of strategy use. In addition to metacognitive and social strategies, some studies have pointed out specific cognitive strategies that are associated with higher levels of language proficiency, such as contextual guessing and encoding (Gu & Johnson, 1996), practising with rules and forms (Bialystok, 1981; Rossie-Le (1989) cited in Oxford & Burry-Stock, 1995), note taking and word analysis (Takeuchi, 1993), paraphrasing and avoidance of verbatim translation (Philips, 1991) and compensation strategies (Green & Oxford, 1993). Other research, however, has come up with mixed results. For example, in the findings reported by Bremner (1999) and Politzer & McGroarty (1985), 22% and 20% respectively of the variance in strategy use observed is explained by differences in the subjects' language proficiency; yet the remaining strategies are deployed by students of different levels indistinctly. Less positive are the results reported by Sanaqui (1995) who did not find differences at all between the strategies used by learners of different proficiency levels. Hence, the discrepancies in the findings obtained in those different studies suggest that the use of strategies is not clearly related to learners' proficiency level but it seems to be mediated by other influencing variables.

The learners' cultural background as well as their educational context are two of the factors that have been frequently associated with certain strategic behaviours (Dickinson, 1996; Parry, 1993; Politzer & McGroarty, 1985). For example, contrary to the preferences of Hispanic language learners, Asian learners are said to prefer the use of memorisation and linguistic analysis to communicative strategies (Politzer & McGroarty, 1985; Tyacke & Mendelsohn, 1986). Likewise, there is evidence pointing to a direct relationship between strategy use and learning context, particularly, the kind of instruction received (Leeke & Shaw, 2000; de Prada, 1993; Purdie & Oliver, 1999). In her study with secondary education learners, de Prada (1993) quantified a larger number of vocabulary and grammar strategies than communicative ones, including listening and speaking. In her conclusions, de Prada attributes the different use of strategies to the type of instruction received and to the objectives of the school curriculum whereby the teaching of linguistic elements is emphasised at the expense of communicative skills. Similarly, Purdie and Oliver (1999) attributed their subjects' little use of social strategies to the educational context, whose methodology does not enhance the development of this type of strategies.

Whereas sociocultural and educational factors appear to be decisive in the learners' strategic preferences, according to Willing (1988), individual variables exert a far greater influence. Several studies have found strong links between the use of effective strategies and positive motivation (Oxford & Nyikos, 1989), attitude (Bialystok, 1981; Chamot & Küpper, 1989), and self-esteem (Oxford & Burry-Stock, 1995). Likewise, certain personality profiles (Ehrman & Oxford, 1989; Wakamoto, 2000) as well as learning styles (Witkin *et al.*, 1979) have been directly associated with specific strategy preferences, for instance, attributing a greater use of social and communicative strategies to extroverted learners. More recently, research done in the area of learners' beliefs (Horowitz, 1988; Mori, 1999; Victori, 1992, 1999; Victori & Lockhart, 1995; Wenden, 1987, 1991) has shown how learners can adopt or avoid certain types of strategies, based on the beliefs they hold about their usefulness and appropriateness.

We can see, therefore, that learner strategies do not operate alone; their use is tied to a number of mediating factors which range from sociocultural to personal differences. There are some variables, nevertheless, whose relationship with learners' strategy use has barely been explored, one of them being learner's age.

The extensive literature that exists in the area of learner strategies is usually based on studies that have been done in tertiary education (see, for example, Bremner, 1999; Ghadessy, 1998; Lawson & Hogben, 1996; Leeke & Shaw; 2000; Oxford & Nyikos, 1989; Palacios Martínez, 1995; Wakamoto, 2000) and, to a lesser degree, secondary education (Bialystok, 1981; García López, 2000; Naiman *et al.*, 1978; O'Malley & Chamot, 1990; de Prada, 1993; Rubin, 1981). However, we know very little about the strategies used by younger learners. The only research involving students of primary education has been done in contexts of first (Pressley & El-Dinary, 1993; Pressley *et al.*, 1992; Zimmerman & Martínez-Pons, 1990) and second language acquisition with bilingual learners (Chesterfield & Chesterfield, 1985; Padrón & Waxman, 1988; Purdie & Oliver, 1999; Wong-Fillmore, 1976). According to these studies, learners start using very rudimentary strategies from a very early age, which, quoting Chesterfield and Chesterfield (1985: 47), 'can play an important part in the schooling experience'. However, because most of these studies have been carried out in the contexts of L1 and L2 acquisition, and because most of them have focused on analysing learners' strategy use in their interaction with other native and non-native classmates,[1] they have revealed relatively little about the strategies used by children in the context of learning a foreign language.

Neither are there many studies that offer a comparison of strategy use among learners of different age groups. There are a few notable exceptions to this trend. Zimmerman and Martinez-Pons (1990) analysed, among other aspects, the use of self-regulating learning strategies of fifth-, eighth- and eleventh-grade learners. On some of the measures of self-regulated learning, they found that eleventh-grade students surpassed eighth graders, who in turn surpassed fifth graders. However, this increasing developmental pattern was not observed across subjects in all of their behaviours, and hence, their findings cannot always be related to differences in students' age and grade level. Similarly, Grenfell and Harris' (1999) case studies of three British adolescents aged 12, 15 and 17, attributed students' variation in strategy use not only to differences in the developmental stages of their subjects but also to variations in students' competence, learning style, nature of the task and motivation. Hence, how differences in age specifically relate to the use of strategies remains a question that needs to be explored.

Finally, the longitudinal research in this field examining the developmental use of strategies over time is scarce and contradictory. In his study, Nyikos (1987) (cited in Oxford & Crookall, 1989) observed a different strategic behaviour as his subjects progressed from semester to semester. Similar results were reported in Chesterfield and Chesterfield's (1985) work, which pointed at a consistent progression and developmental sequence in the range of strategies used by pre-school and first-grade bilingual students. Nevertheless, O'Malley & Chamot (1990) did not find any clear pattern of strategy change with the learners that were interviewed in the period of 1 year, with the exception of certain changes at an individual level.

It was precisely this scarcity of studies on age differences that partly prompted a recent study by Purdie and Oliver (1999) involving bilingual school-aged children. Nevertheless, in the conclusion to their work these authors make an open call to the research community to further explore the differences in language learning strategy use of primary, secondary, and tertiary students. The current study aims to partially answer this question and to some extent fill the gap in this field. Its purpose is, then, to examine the relationship between age and strategies of school-aged learners of English as a foreign language and to look at the development of those strategies over a period of time. Specifically, the following research questions are addressed in this study: (1) are there significant differences between the strategies used by EFL learners of different age groups?; (2) is there a developmental trend of strategy use as students' grow older? If the answers to these questions are positive, (3) do these changes occur progressively as the learner's age increases or are there specific age periods at which strategic changes can be observed?

Method

The present study, which is part of a larger project that examines the age factor in the acquisition of English as a foreign language,[2] focuses on the study of learning strategies as reported by learners of English in Spain. These learners come from several state schools (six primary schools and seven high schools) located in the centre of Barcelona in fairly homogeneous neighbourhoods. Our study includes cross-sectional as well as longitudinal data. The cross-sectional data involved 766 students from three age groups (10, 14 and 18 year olds), whereas the longitudinal data involved 38 students over a two-year period (from 12 to 14 years old).

Preliminary studies

A preliminary study was initially undertaken by comparing two groups of subjects with the same age (12 years old) who had received different amounts of instruction at school [200 hours [n = 83] and 416 hours [n = 185]).[3] Results showed neither significant differences in the total number of strategies mentioned by each group nor in the reported strategy use of three out of the four areas under study, thus pointing at an apparently little interaction between hours of instruction received and learner strategy use.

A second preliminary study followed in order to compare groups of subjects that had received the same amount of instruction and which were only two years apart in age. The first comparison was made between 10 year olds (n = 284) and 12 year-olds (n = 286) after 200 hours of instruction. The second comparison was made between 12 year-olds (n = 277) and 14 year olds (n = 236), after 416 hours of instruction. Results showed no significant differences in the reported strategy use of either the groups of students aged 10 and 12 or the groups aged 12 and 14.

Results from these two preliminary studies seem to show that differences in reported strategy use are more likely to occur due to differences in the age of the learners rather than in the amount of instruction received. The results also seem to indicate that with only a difference of two years no significant changes in strategy use could be observed; at least not with a quantitative analysis. We, thus, decided to compare groups with a wider age difference, although this would not allow us to keep the number of hours of instruction received constant. The subjects that took part in this study are described later.

Subjects

The cross-sectional data comes from intact groups and is comprised of 766 subjects from three age groups: 10, 14 and 17 year olds.[4] The three age groups differ in the number of hours of instruction received at school and the grade they are in, as shown in Table 1. The youngest group included 284 primary school students who had started learning English at school at the age of 8,[5] and who had a mean age of 10 (grade = 5 EP[6]). The next group included 186 high school students who had started learning English at the age of 10 and had a mean age of 14 (grade = 1 BUP). The oldest group included 296 high-school students who had also started learning English at school at the age of 10 and had a mean age of 18.5[7] (grade = COU).

Table 1 Cross-sectional subjects

Age groups	Hours of instruction	Grade
10 year-olds (n = 284)	200	5 EP
14 year-olds (n = 186)	416	1 BUP
17 year-olds (n = 296)	726	COU

The proportion of male and female students in the sample was 46–54% and the sociocultural level of their families was distributed as follows: upper (28%), upper-middle (21.7%), middle (13.6%), lower-middle and lower (20.1%). A remaining 16.4% did not answer or mentioned one of the parents being unemployed. Students reported using Catalan and Spanish, the two official languages of the community, to different extents: 28% used Catalan mainly, 25% used Spanish mainly and 40% used both languages equally.[8] As regards exposure to English, most of them had had little exposure to English outside the school system, while some (over one-quarter) had made short stays in an English-speaking country or were attending or had attended after-class instruction in English.

The longitudinal data comes from a subsample of 38 students who were 12 years old (grade = 7 EGB) at Time 1 and 14 years old (grade = 1 BUP) at Time 2. They had received 200 hours of instruction at Time 1 (T1) and 416 hours at Time 2 (T2).

Instruments and analysis

A questionnaire, written in Catalan, was used to obtain information on the strategies students employed to learn English, a foreign language to them. The questionnaire included five open-ended questions which aimed at eliciting the subjects' use of learner strategies when learning vocabulary, pronunciation, spelling, reading and writing (at the sentence level). The

Table 2 The questionnaire

Question	Variable
Do you have any method to remember the meaning of English words? Which one(s)?	Vocabulary
Do you have any method to learn the pronunciation of English words? Which one(s)?	Pronunciation
Do you have any method to know how to spell new words in English? Which one(s)?	Spelling
Do you have any method to read in English? Which one(s)?	Reading
Do you have any method to write correct English sentences? Which one(s)?	Writing

actual questions, which students answered in their L1, have been translated and are reproduced in Table 2. In addition to these, the questionnaire also comprised biographical questions about our subjects' use of Catalan and Spanish, their exposure to English outside school, information about their parents' jobs, their use of communication strategies as well as their attitude and orientations towards English learning. All in all the instrument included 26 questions which students were to answer in about 20 minutes during classtime. After completing the questionnaire, students were asked to do a number of proficiency tests (cloze, dictation, short essay, etc.) which are core data in the larger project, even though they are not part of this study.

The process of development of a classification to code students' answers was mainly data-based, even though Oxford's (1990) as well as O'Malley and Chamot's (1990) inventories of strategies were used as a starting point. Preliminary codes were developed and refined in the process of analysis of a sample of the questionnaires. This process of refinement of the coding system was time-consuming given that some students' answers were open to interpretation and what they meant was not always expressed clearly enough. Once this process was finished, two independent raters applied the final coding system to a number of questionnaires with a resulting inter-rater reliability of coding of 80.5%. Given the difficulty of interpreting some students' answers, coders followed a procedure for the coding of the remaining questionnaires by which they always double checked ambiguous answers with each other and reached an agreement.

The final classification system (see Table 3) includes the most frequently mentioned strategies. Most of the strategies in this classification are applicable to any of the five questions in the questionnaire (for example, the

Table 3 Classification of learning strategies

Strategy	Examples
Copying words	*I write them several times* (meaning)
Other methods of memorisation of words: oral, visual, auditory and kinesthetic	*I say the words to myself* (pronunciation) *I spell out the word* (spelling)
Study of grammar and memorisation of sentences	*I learn the sentences by heart* (writing) *I study orally* (writing)
Classification	*I have a notebook for vocabulary* (meaning)
Annotation of pronunciation	*I write the words the way they sound* (pronunciation)
Mnemotechniques: Auditory, visual and semantic associations	*I play with words to memorize them* (meaning) *I learn the word in a context so that I can remember it* (meaning) *I make personal connections* (meaning)
Imagery	*I memorize the words as images* (spelling)
Analysis/deduction: Drawing relationships with L1, English and other languages and using context	*I seek similarities with other words* (spelling). *I try to find the logic by thinking of words that I already know* (meaning)
Intuition	*I focus on the words that I know and the ones I don't, I try to imagine what they mean* (reading) *I am guided by what sounds better* (pronunciation)
Practice: Self-initiated controlled and extended (non-interactive) practice	*I try to write sentences with the new words* (meaning) *I speak to myself at home* (pronunciation) *I write lots of compositions* (writing)
Exposure to the L2: Listening (songs, films, TV, etc.), reading (books, storybooks etc.), paying selective attention to input (teacher, native speakers, etc.)	*I watch films in the original version* (meaning). *In class I pay attention to how the teacher pronounces new words* (pronunciation) *As I read in English, I gradually learn to write them* (words) (spelling).
Reference materials: Looking up meaning, spelling and pronunciation.	*I look up my classnotes* (reading) *I use the dictionary* (meaning)
Imitation of pronunciation	*I imagine I am a native speaker of English* (pronunciation) *I imitate the teacher* (pronunciation)

Table 3 (*contd*)

Use of **model sentences** and grammar books and application of rules	*I try to follow this structure S + V + O* (writing) *I look up other sentences* (writing) *I have a look at the textbook* (writing) *I try to remember the structures we have learnt* (writing)
Social strategy: practising with someone outside the classroom and getting help from the teacher, etc.	*I practice them (the words) with someone who knows a lot of English* (pronunciation)
Translation	*I make the sentences in Catalan and then I translate them* (writing) *I need to know the translation* (meaning)

strategy of 'practice') while others are specific to one or more questions (for example, 'annotation of pronunciation').

In the analysis of the cross-sectional data, χ^2 tests were used to measure significant differences across the reported strategy use of the three age groups under study.[9] In the analysis of the longitudinal data, four stages of development were defined and the results are reported in terms of frequencies.

Methodological caveats

A preliminary observation that needs to be mentioned before presenting the results of the study is the relatively high number of students from the three age groups for whom no information could be retrieved about their use of learning strategies in one or more questions. These were cases where students reported using no strategy whatsoever[10] as well as others where they left a question unanswered[11]. This was most evident in the question about reading, where a good proportion of the youngest subjects either failed to answer it or interpreted it as a question of reading out loud. Because of this, we decided to discard this question from the cross-sectional study.

In order to further explore these cases, a random sample of subjects were contacted again. Consequently, it was found that some students had interpreted the word 'method' in the questions as 'a formal and systematic technique' rather than as a more general reference to 'any type of personal way to make learning more effective'. However, other students had actually interpreted the question well and confirmed that they had not provided any information in some questions because they did not do anything special or use any method to learn English.

Other studies have also reported obtaining few responses from their school subjects (Low *et al.*, 1993). This, together with the results of our study, led us to question whether these students did not actually have any strategy when they reported none or rather they had not stopped to think about how they go about learning English. If we turn to the literature on this topic (Flavell, 1979; Piaget, 1976), one would think that the latter may have well been the case. Brown (1978) suggests that young children have a limited knowledge of their learning processes and are deficient in self-questioning skills that would enhance their metacognitive knowledge. This knowledge appears relatively late and is often less than well developed even in college populations. The literature also reports different degrees of difficulty for reflection for different areas of language learning. Kellerman (1991) states that the language learner is more able to develop a capacity for reflection over the learning of lexis than over the learning of other areas of the language, and de Prada (1993) attributes this fact to the learners' familiarity with the type of instruction, that gives a primary role to vocabulary learning at the expense of other skills. These two factors would also help to explain why in our data it was the questions on writing and reading, rather than those on meaning, pronunciation and spelling, which got more negative or blank answers.

Cross-sectional Study

Results

A preliminary look at the data suggests that our subjects vary in the number of strategies reported, with some learners showing a narrow range of strategy type (up to 2) while others displaying a wider range (up to six different strategies). To see if there were any significant differences across the three groups, an analysis of variance (ANOVA) was undertaken (see Tables 4 and 5), and the *post hoc* Scheffé test was subsequently run (see Table 6) to see where those differences lay. The tests showed that the mean obtained by the youngest group of students (10 year olds) varied significantly from that of the other two groups, who comparatively reported a

Table 4 Mean strategy use for each of the three age groups

Age groups	N	Mean	Standard deviation
10	284	1.07	1.34
14	186	1.96	1.57
17	296	2.01	1.64
Total	766	1.65	1.58

Table 5 Analysis of variance

	Sum of squares (SS)	Degrees of freedom (df)	Mean squares (MS)	F	Sig.
Inter-groups	151.219	2	75.610	32.680	0.000
Intra-groups	1765.315	763	2.314		
Total	1916.534	765			

Table 6 Post hoc Scheffé test

(I) Age group (years)	(J) Age group (years)	Mean difference	Typical error	Signif.
10	15	−0.89*	0.143	0.000
	18	−0.94*	0.126	0.000
14	11	0.89*	0.143	0.000
	18	−4.44E−02	0.142	0.953
17	15	4.44E−02	0.142	0.953
	11	0.94*	0.126	0.000

greater number of strategies. No differences were found between the mean strategy use of 14 and 17 year olds.

Our next step was to look individually at each of the four questions on learning strategies included in the questionnaire for vocabulary, pronunciation, spelling and writing. After carrying out χ^2 tests, significant differences were found in each of the questions, a description of which follows.

Strategies used for vocabulary learning

A comparison of the frequencies obtained[12] by each group (see Table 7) shows that the oldest students display a more balanced distribution of reported strategy use, compared to the youngest learners, whose range of strategies is narrower, mainly limited to memorisation (52%, namely, repetition and copying) and to a lesser degree, use of reference materials (24%). A closer look at the data also suggests that as the learners' age increases so does the use of more cognitively demanding strategies such as mnemotechniques, classification and analysis which are, nevertheless, used along with other strategies. Furthermore, from the age of 14 onwards we note an outstanding decrease in those strategies that involve using reference materials to learn new words, and an increase in the overall use of 'other' strategies, such as exposure to the L2, translation and practice.

Table 7 Strategies used for vocabulary learning

Strategies	Age groups			
	10 year-olds (n = 86)	14 year-olds (n = 101)	17 year-olds (n = 159)	Total (N = 346)
Copying	18 (20.9%)	9 (8.9%)	19 (11.9%)	16 (13%)
Oral methods of memorization and other	27 (31.4%)	15 (14.9%)	29 (18.2%)	21 (21.5%)
Mnemotechniques	1 (1.2%)	5 (5%)	21 (13.2%)	27 (7.8%)
Analysis	1 (1.2%)	9 (8%)	13 (8.2%)	23 (6.6%)
Classification	1 (1.2%)	6 (5.9%)	23 (14.5%)	30 (8.7%)
Reference materials	21 (24.4%)	39 (38.6%)	10 (6.3%)	70 (20.2%)
Other strategies:[a] Practice, exposure to the L2, translation	17 (19.8%)	18 (17.8%)	44 (27.7%)	79 (22.8%)

χ^2 Pearson: 78.087; _df_, 12; _p_ = 0.000
[a] Under the category of 'Other' we grouped those reported strategies whose expected frequencies were too low (i.e. cells appeared with frequencies below 0) to allow us to undertake χ^2 tests.

Strategies used for the pronunciation of words

As shown in Table 8, at the age of 17 there is an increase in the use of strategies that involve exposure to the L2 which reflects a greater readiness to listen to songs, films, native speakers or the language teacher. Curiously, social strategies, such as asking others, asking the teacher for correction, studying with others, etc. appear slightly less frequently as the learner's age increases, with a marked decline in the older group (only 7.9%). There is also a progressive decrease (from 38.2% to 31.7%) in the use of repetition (oral memorisation) as students get older, the tendency being stronger in the oldest students (16.9%). Annotation of pronunciation, as a strategy, does not show a clear developmental trend and, comparatively, the younger students make less use of this strategy (3.9%) than the other two groups (11.9% and 8.1%). Finally, the use of 'other strategies', such as analysis, practice and intuition, is kept constant across the three groups.

Strategies used for the spelling of words

A comparison of the frequencies obtained (see Table 9) shows a progressive decline (from 31.6 to 22.9%) in the reported use of reference materials as a strategy for learning or checking the spelling of new words, with a noticeable drop in the group of older learners (7.2%). Whereas the use of copying words remains fairly constant across the three groups, the use of

Table 8 Strategies used for the pronunciation of words

Strategies	Age group			
	10 year-olds (n = 76)	14 year-olds (n = 101)	17 year-olds (n = 136)	Total (N = 313)
Exposure to the L2	9 (11.8%)	11 (10.9%)	53 (39%)	73 (23.3%)
Social strategy	16 (21.1%)	19 (18.8%)	10 (7.9%)	45 (14.4%)
Oral memorization	29 (38.2%)	32 (31.7%)	23 (16.9%)	84 (26.8%)
Annotation of pronunciation	3 (3.9%)	12 (11.9%)	11 (8.1%)	26 (26%)
Other strategies Intuition, practice, analysis	19 (25%)	27 (26.7%)	39 (28.7%)	85 (27.2%)

χ^2 Pearson, 46.728; *df*: 8; $p = 0.000$

Table 9 Strategies used for the spelling of words

Strategies	Age group			
	10 year-olds (n = 76)	14 year-olds (n = 83)	17 year-olds (n = 139)	Total (N = 298)
Reference materials	24 (31.6%)	19 (22.9%)	10 (7.2%)	53 (17.8%)
Copying	23 (30.3%)	25 (30.1%)	48 (34.5%)	96 (32.2%)
Other methods of memorization	16 (21.1%)	7 (8.4%)	19 (13.7%)	42 (14.1%)
Other strategies: Exposure to the L2, analysis	13 (17.1%)	32 (38.6%)	62 (44.6%)	107 (35.9%)

χ^2 Pearson, 33.637; *df*, 6; $p = 0.000$

other methods of memorisation, such as spelling out the words, reading them repeatedly, etc., is irregular across the three age groups, being more frequently reported by the group of younger learners. Finally, one can also note a progressive increase in the use of 'other strategies', such as intuition, exposure to the L2 and analysis, as students get older.

Learning strategies used in writing sentences

At the age of 17, our data show a decrease in the use of model sentences or basic structures to write sentences (see Table 10). Compared to the other two groups, the oldest students appear to use more creative strategies instead, such as extensive practice, which increases progressively, as well as strategies that involve the study of grammar, such as the writing of

Table 10 Strategies used in writing sentences

Strategies	Age group			
	10 year-olds (n = 77)	14 year-olds (n = 61)	17 year-olds (n = 132)	Total (N = 270)
Model sentences	35 (45.5%)	27 (44.3%)	33 (25%)	95 (35.2%)
Practice	6 (7.8%)	9 (14.8%)	25 (18.9%)	40 (14.8%)
Study of grammar	12 (15.6%)	8 (13.1%)	32 (24.2%)	52 (19.3%)
Other strategies: Exposure to the L2, analysis, intuition, translation.	24 (31.2%)	17 (27.9%)	42 (31.8 %)	83 (30.7%)

χ^2 Pearson, 15.363; *df*, 6; *p* = 0.018

outlines, the memorisation of grammatical structures or parts of speech. Finally, the use of 'other strategies', such as translation, intuition and analysis, remains constant.

Discussion of cross-sectional study

The findings obtained in the cross-sectional study show significant differences in reported strategy use across the three age groups in each of the four questions analysed. This variation, nevertheless, does not seem to follow a regular pattern of development with increasing or decreasing age but it fluctuates depending on the strategies reported. Upon considering the general tendency for each strategy analysed, as they appear in Tables 7–10, at times we observe a linear progression in the use of a specific set of strategies; other times we can see a variation between only one of the groups and the other two; and less often do we find the case of a similar frequency of strategy use reported by all three groups. These irregular patterns have also been reported in previous research, such as the work done by Zimmerman and Martínez-Pons (1990), who found different developmental trends in their fifth-, eighth- and eleventh-grade subjects' use of self-regulated learning strategies.

Of special relevance for our study is the pattern we observe in 35% of the cases, in which strategy changes occur progressively either with increasing or decreasing age as well as proficiency. Particularly, one notes with interest that as students' age increases so does the reported strategy use of more cognitively complex strategies, such as, mnemotechniques, analysis or classification (see Table 7). As a matter of fact, similar results have been reported in other studies (Kojic-sabo & Lighbown, 1999; Oxford, 1989), which suggest there is a probable link between the increased use of these strategies and a growth in cognitive maturation (Brown & Palincsar, 1982). Along the same lines, we observe a trend for older students to report a greater number of 'other strategies' (see Tables 8 and 9) such as intuition, practice or analysis. This shows that with increasing age and proficiency, learners can report – and presumably use – a wider repertoire of strategies. These findings are in line with those observed in previous research (Chesterfield & Chesterfield, 1985; Lawson & Hogben, 1996; Palacios Martínez, 1995) where more proficient or academically advanced learners have reported a larger variety of strategic use. These findings are, in turn, supported by the results we obtained with the ANOVA test that showed a greater number of different strategies reported by the older groups (see Tables 4–6).

However, an inverted pattern emerges with the reported use of social strategies, such as studying with the help of siblings, asking peers, etc., which decreases progressively as the subjects' age increases (see Table 8). Empirical support is also provided by Zimmerman and Martinez-Pons (1990) who observed a significant decline in students' reliance on adult assistance between the eighth and the eleventh grades.

The remaining cases of strategic variation do not follow a progressive decline or increase as with the strategies described earlier, but changes occur at a particular age. In 35% of the cases, the use of specific strategies is kept constant between the ages of 10 and 14 and undergoes a marked change at the age of 17. In particular, this pattern is observed with the following strategies: exposure to the L2 (see Table 8), copying words (see Table 9) and the use of model sentences and the study of grammar (both in Table 10). Where this change is most evident and systematic, however, is with strategies that involve the use of reference materials and model sentences which, at the age of 17, undergo a sudden decline in the learning of vocabulary (see Table 7), spelling (see Table 9) as well as in writing sentences (see Table 10).

Finally, a less frequent pattern of change is observed in 25% of the cases where the use of specific strategies is kept constant between the ages of 14 and 17 and it increases or decreases with the youngest learners. That is the case with the use of strategies that involve analysis of word meaning (see Table 7), as well as with some memorisation strategies (see Tables 7 and 9). Previous research (Chesterfield & Chesterfield, 1985) has suggested that memorisation strategies tend to be reported more frequently by the youngest learners and our data provide evidence to support this claim.

While we cannot offer an explanation for all of the different developmental patterns examined so far, some of them can be accounted for. The sudden or progressive decline observed with older students in strategy use may obey a shift in the subjects' approach (Zimmerman & Martinez-Pons,

1990) and/or to a widening in the repertoire of strategies. For example, even if memorisation strategies for vocabulary, spelling and pronunciation are used across all three groups, the decay we observe with older learners is probably due to the aforementioned increase in the use of more cognitively complex strategies. Another case in point is found with the writing strategies reported by our subjects. The decline we observe with our oldest subjects in their use of model sentences is accompanied by an increase in more demanding and academically oriented strategies such as extensive practice and the study of grammar. This increase may certainly result from the instructional practices offered at school which, as students' age, grade and proficiency level increases, tend not to be limited to the teaching of vocabulary and basic syntactic structures but they gradually incorporate more practice in productive and receptive skills. Similarly, a shift in the strategies deployed by the oldest group of learners for improving their pronunciation might also be an effect of instructional practices. In that case, a decline in the use of social strategies is produced at the expense of an increase in the strategies that involve getting exposed to input through audiovisual resources, such as listening to songs, watching videos, etc. Finally, the greater tendency of younger learners to use reference materials and human resources, such as parents, siblings or teachers, and the subsequent decline that is observed for both strategies as their age increases, shows a learning behaviour that is clearly more dependent on external sources and therefore, less autonomous in its approach.

Longitudinal Study

Results

In the longitudinal analysis of the data, students' answers to the questionnaire were analysed globally. That is, by considering the types of strategies mentioned by each learner in the five questions at Time 1 (T1, after 200 hours of instruction) and at Time 2 (T2, after 416 hours). A preliminary qualitative analysis involving multiple readings of the data and a comparison of individual students' answers at T1 and T2 seemed to indicate that there were observable differences over time. For example, two strategies were only mentioned at T1 (asking relatives for help or reading the spelling of words out loud), while one of them appeared for the first time at T2 (references to the concepts of 'patterns' and 'grammar' in writing). There were also more general patterns of change over time that were observable in most of the students' answers:

- Social strategies and reference materials were either not mentioned or mentioned less frequently at T2.

- Oral and written methods of memorisation were mentioned for the first time or were mentioned more frequently at T2.
- Other strategies that do not involve memorisation, the use of social strategies and reference materials were mentioned for the first time or were mentioned more frequently at T2.
- The number of questions answered increased at T2.

This qualitative analysis of the data later led us to develop a framework to trace students' changes over time in a more systematic manner. As a result, four stages of development were identified, which allowed us to distribute our subjects into fairly homogeneous groups as well as trace changes over time.

A preliminary stage (*Stage 0*) represents a *failure to answer* any of the five questions in the questionnaire. *Stage 1* includes instances where students seek to solve a problem or carry out a task exclusively by getting *external help* from people (social strategy) or from reference materials. *Stage 2* represents those students' answers that mention strategies based upon *written* or *oral repetition* to learn the meaning of words, their spelling or pronunciation. *Stage 3* includes more *elaborate memorisation techniques to learn words* (i.e. writing down the pronunciation or the translation of words, writing down a sentence, word games, testing) as well as *simple strategies for writing sentences, reading or learning grammar* (e.g. use of model sentences, translation, controlled practice, study of grammar). *Stage 4* involves strategies that imply *a higher degree of elaboration or association on the part of the learner*. These include mnemotechniques, analysis/deduction, extended practice and imitation.

Three rules were followed to place students in one of the stages described earlier. First, the criteria followed to analyse the data did not take into account the number of questions answered or strategies mentioned but their type. Secondly, one single mention of a strategy corresponding to a given higher stage sufficed to situate one student at that stage. Third, one stage could include one or more mentions of strategies corresponding to previous stages.

A first overall analysis of the number of students in each stage (see Table 11) shows that at the age of 12 (T1) almost one-third of the students fail to report any strategy (stage 0) and that a great portion of them (39.5%) make exclusive use of memorisation strategies to learn meaning, pronunciation or spelling of words (stage 2). Table 11 also shows that there is a minority of students (5.3%) who report the use of strategies requiring the highest levels of elaboration (stage 4).

If frequencies from T1 and T2 are compared, one can observe two phenomena: an overall move to higher level strategies at T2 as well as a more

Table 11 Frequencies of strategy use for each stage

Stage	Time 1 (n = 38)		Time 2 (n = 38)	
	n	%	n	%
0	12	31.6	7	18.4
1	5	13. 2	3	7.9
2	15	39.5	9	23.7
3	4	10.5	12	31.6
4	2	5.3	7	18.4

Table 12 Frequencies of moves to higher stages

Move	T1 → T2 (n = 22)	
	n	%
1-stage	7	31.8
2-stage	11	50
3-stage	3	13.6
4-stage	1	4.5

balanced distribution of subjects into the four stages, even though the number of subjects who fail to report any strategy is still quite important at that time (18.4%). At age 14 (T2) there is an overall decline in the reported use of strategies that fall in the first three stages (stages 0–2). That is, there is a decrease in exclusively using reference materials and social and memorisation strategies. At the same time, there is an important increase in the number of students who report use of complex memorisation strategies as well as other, sometimes more elaborate, strategies (stages 3 and 4).

A second analysis where the individual changes of the subjects at T1 and T2 are recorded takes us to Figure 1. There we can observe three different patterns of change, the first and most frequent one being that of 22 subjects who progress from a lower to a higher stage. Another is the case of nine subjects who show no change over time (see black dots in the figure). Perhaps more perplexing is the third pattern observed in seven subjects who undergo a move to a lower stage at T2 (see arrows pointing towards the left).

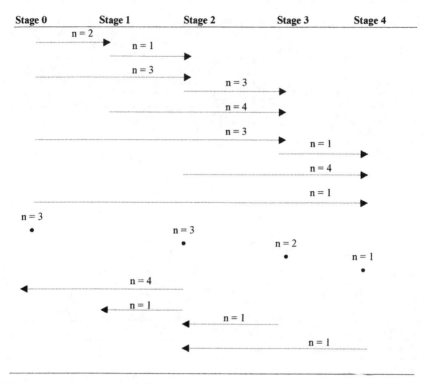

Figure 1 Frequencies of changes in reported strategy use from T1 to T2

An examination of the length of the arrows accounting for those 22 subjects who progress to a higher stage in Figure 1 makes it evident that each stage can be reached from *any* of the previous stages. This means that in the sample analysed there are learners who are in stage 2 at T2 coming from stage 0 ($n = 1$) as well as from stage 1 ($n = 3$) at T1. Similarly, there are students in stage 3 at T2 coming from stage 0 ($n = 3$), stage 1 ($n = 4$) as well as from stage 2 ($n = 3$). A similar pattern occurs with learners who are at stage 4 at T2. Nevertheless, if the length of the arrows in the figure is taken into account, it will be observed that most of them stand for one- and two-stage moves, while three- and four-stage moves are much less common as shown in Table 12.

In order to exemplify the more frequent moves from one stage to another over time, in what follows we reproduce sample answers to the questionnaire for T1 and T2. The first one (see example A, in Table 13) illustrates a one-stage move and the other two (examples B and C) are instances of two-stage moves. In example A, the student is in stage 2 at T1 because, in

Table 13 Example A: a one-stage move

Type of strategy	T1 (stage 2)	T2 (stage 3)
Word meaning	I repeat (the words) many times until I memorize them.	I repeat them several times.
Spelling	I write them (the words) several times.	I write them several times.
Pronunciation		I read them several times.
Writing	I look up English textbooks.	I pay attention and write what I know and leave blank spaces when I do not know something. Later I correct what I did not know and sometimes I make it up.
Reading		I practise by translating (the text)

Table 14 Example B: a two-stage move

Type of strategy	T1 (stage 1)	T2 (stage 3)
Word meaning		I study them and then I write a list and try to write down the meaning next to each word.
Spelling	I use my notebook or ask the teacher.	I do not have any (especial technique). I do not have many problems when writing in English.
Pronunciation	I ask the teacher.	I do not have any. I say the word the way I hear it.
Writing	I write them the way I think they should be written.	I follow the order of the different components that I have been taught at school.
Reading		

addition to reporting the use of reference materials to solve problems with writing (a strategy belonging to stage 1), he also reports repetition strategies to learn the meaning and spelling of words. This student's answers at T2 place him in stage 3 because in addition to reporting memorisation strategies, he also mentions other strategies such as translation for reading practice.

Table 15 Example C: a two-stage move

Type of strategy	T1 (stage 2)	T2 (stage 4)
Word meaning		I write them out on index cards. Then I ask someone to read the definition to me and I say the word.
Spelling	I spell them (the words) out in English.	If I do not know how to write them, when I hear them I ask the teacher.
Pronunciation	I listen closely to the teacher.	Through repetition at home.
Writing		Studying.
Reading		If there is any word that I do not understand, I try to figure it out from the context and get the main idea.

In Example B (see Table 14) the student is in stage 1 at T1 because of his exclusive references to external sources for help, the teacher or his class-notes. In contrast, at T2 this same student reports making use of testing to memorise meaning of words as well as model sentences for writing, which place him in stage 3.

The student in Example C (see Table 15) is in stage 2 at T1 because of his reported use of oral memorisation. This same student is in stage 4 at T2 because of the use of context when reading in addition to other strategies that would otherwise have placed him in stage 3 (word games and study of grammar).

Discussion of longitudinal study

The results that come out of the longitudinal data show that there is room for individual variability as well as evidence of some general trends in the reported use of learning strategies over time. With regard to the direction of the change in strategy use between T1 and T2, there are students who fail to show any type of change, others who show a regression to a lower stage and a majority of them who progress to a higher stage. The fact that most of the students in the first two groups fail to answer any of the questions at T2 could be due to actual failures to show any sort of progress over time as well as to methodological problems (see the second section). In any case, the more general trend of students moving upwards in the scale means that, as students grow older and become more proficient in English, there is a tendency not to rely exclusively on outside sources for the learning of English, such as the teacher, a relative or a dictionary. There is also a strong tendency over time not to rely exclusively on simple memorisation strategies such as reading out lists of words or copying them out several times. Likewise, as students grow older and consequently more proficient, they come to use learning strategies for purposes other than vocabulary learning, and report strategies for the skills of reading and writing. The study has also made it evident that strategies that require higher levels of elaboration both for vocabulary learning as well as for reading and writing are more frequent with older learners. These results are in line with those obtained in the cross-sectional study as well as those from a previous year-long study by Chesterfield and Chesterfield (1985) involving much younger children in an ESL bilingual primary classroom. In that longitudinal study as well as the present one, as learners grow older, and consequently more proficient, they employ or report fewer strategies belonging to the lower stages of the framework and they are also shown to have a greater variety of second language strategies.

With regard to the strength of the change in strategy use between T1 and T2, the data again suggest that even if there are students who move along the scale in a lockstep fashion, that is from a given stage to the contiguous one, there are others who do not follow this pattern. However, our results also show there is a strong tendency to undergo either one- or two-stage moves rather than changes of a longer distance. This means that, even if there is some individual variability, there is evidence of a pattern of development of strategy use between the ages of 12 and 14.

To sum up, this study has provided evidence that it is possible to trace changes over the use of learning strategies in longitudinal subjects between 12 and 14 year-olds. The fact that common trends of development were evident in the data proves that age, and possibly competence, are important explanatory factors. The fact that individual variability was also found proves that factors such as the learners' cognitive maturity, learning style or metalinguistic awareness may be other intervening factors.

Conclusions and Future Research

In the cross-sectional study differences in the reported strategy use were made evident in primary and high-school learners who were three and four years apart, whereas in the longitudinal study developmental differences could also be traced in learners over a two-year period. Results in both studies converge: as students become older, and consequently more proficient in English, they also become more resourceful language learners. This is because (1) they tend to report a wider range of learning strategies, (2) they tend to use strategies that are more complex, cognitively speaking, (3) they tend not to rely exclusively on simple memorisation strategies and, finally (4) they generally become more autonomous in their approach to language learning. This evidence confirms that age together with proficiency level are factors that cannot be overlooked in the study of learning strategies.

The fact that the groups that were compared differed in age as well as in hours of instruction received means that these two variables are confounded in the present cross-sectional and longitudinal studies. However, if we take into account the results from the first preliminary study, where no major differences were found in two groups of 12-year-old learners who had received different amounts of instruction, we are led to think that age plays a more determining role than proficiency level in the educational context under study.

Further evidence in the present study also suggests that these are probably not the only two factors at play in the study of learning strategies. The fact that the reported use of a good number of strategies in the cross-sectional study did not follow a linear progression as students grew older is a case in point. Also, the variability among learners in the longitudinal study, which did not make it possible to make reliable predictions at T2 based on strategic behaviour at T1, confirms that we are dealing with a complex phenomenon – a phenomenon that, in addition to proficiency level, probably includes other factors such as cognitive maturation, learning style or metacognitive awareness.

In spite of the fact that the present study has not taken into account these other factors, it is meant to open ground in an area that, to date, has received little attention. It is precisely due to this scarcity of previous research that the study was originally devised as an exploratory piece of research. Based on the results of this work, as well as an awareness of its methodological limitations, we would like to make a number of suggestions for further research on the relationship between age and learner strategies.

The first one concerns the age groups investigated. Given that the cross-sectional study covered learners who were three and four years apart in age, it would be interesting to investigate whether differences can likewise be traced in cross-sectional groups of learners that are just one or two years apart. Similarly, and given that our longitudinal study covered learners over a two-year period, it would be interesting to find out if differences can be traced over the course of one academic year, possibly with the use of elicitation procedures such as structured questionnaires or interviews.

The second suggestion concerns the need to further explore the interplay between age and hours of instruction received. Even though our preliminary study pointed out that age plays a major part in determining strategy use, the sample under study just included a limited number of students belonging to a specific age group who had received relatively few hours of instruction. It would be interesting to see if similar results would obtain from older learners after more hours of instruction. Perhaps with higher levels of proficiency, the hours of instruction received play as or more important a role than age.

The third suggestion is about the framework used in the longitudinal study to describe learners' stages of development. Since this was elaborated from the reported strategy use of a small sample of students of a particular age group, namely early adolescence and adolescence, the framework would need to be validated with a larger sample and with learners of a different age group, such as children and young adults.

The fourth and last suggestion for further research springs from the evidence in the cross-sectional study that the use of some strategies follows a non-linear pattern across the age groups investigated. This observation makes us think that there may be a certain age period or proficiency level when students' use of learner strategies undergoes a more noticeable development. To be able to know what this age is would be quite relevant to programs that include a strategy training component in the syllabus.

Nevertheless, the relevance of this line of research on learning strategies as it relates to school-aged students is not limited to such programmes. On the contrary, information on what students do on their own initiative to help themselves learn a foreign language should be of interest to any language instructor since results such as those obtained in this study can only contribute to a better match between what is taught and what is actually learned.

Acknowledgements
The authors acknowledge the support of the Ministerio de Educación y Cultura through project PB97–0901.

Notes
1. In their study with bilingual Mexican children, aged between 5.7 and 7.3, Wong-Fillmore (1976) concluded that social strategies were more important for these subjects than cognitive ones, as they were more interested in establishing social relationships with their native American friends than in learning the language. Chesterfield and Chesterfield's (1985) longitudinal study also focused on the verbal interactions of bilingual Mexican pre-school and first form children and found that their subjects used strategies more interactively over time.
2. See work by Muñoz (2001, this volume, Chapter 8), Pérez-Vidal *et al.* (2000), and Tragant and Muñoz (2000).
3. All the subjects in this preliminary study had had little exposure to English outside the school system according to self-reported information about stays in foreign countries and after-class instruction in English.
4. These were the ages most students had at the start of the school year.

5. The youngest group of students had started learning English earlier than the other two groups because these students followed a new educational system (LOGSE) by which foreign language instruction is introduced earlier than in the former system (EGB).
6. EP stands for primary education; BUP for secondary education and COU is the preparatory course before university.
7. The mean age of this group of students is quite high because a number of them were repeating or had repeated a grade level.
8. 7% of the students did not answer this question about language use and 3.6% of them had a different L1.
9. Because of the restrictions of this type of statistical test, only the first mention has been taken into account in those students who mention more than one strategy in a given question.
10. The mean proportions of students reporting no strategy by group are as follows: 14 year-olds 21.7%, 14 year-olds 26.8% and 17 year-olds 41.4 %.
11. The mean proportions of blank answers by group are as follows: 10 year-olds 34.8%, 14 year-olds 12.3% and 17 year-olds 4.8%.
12. The figures in Tables 7–10 are based on total number of strategies reported; missing, negative, unintelligible or ambiguous answers have not been included and so the number of subjects in each question may vary.

References

Bialystok, E. (1981) The role of conscious strategies in second language proficiency. *The Modern Language Journal* 65, 24–35.

Bremner, S. (1999) Language learning strategies and language proficiency: Investigating the relationship in Hong Kong. *The Canadian Modern Language Review* 55(4), 490–514.

Brown, A.L. (1978) Knowing when, where and how to remember: A problem of metacognition. In R. Glaser (ed.) *Advances in Instruction Psychology* (Vol. 1). Mahwah, NJ: Erlbaum.

Brown, A.L. and Palincsar, A.S. (1982) Inducing strategic learning from texts by means of informed, self-control training. In D.K. Reig and W.P. Hresko (eds) *TL & LD: Metacognition and Learning Disabilities* 2 (1), 1–18. (Rockville: Aspen.)

Cohen, A. D. (1990) *Language Learning: Insights for Learners, Teachers and Researchers.* Rowley, MA: Newbury House.

Cohen, A.D. (1998) *Strategies in Learning and Using a Second Language.* Harlow, Essex: Longman.

Chamot, A.U. and Küpper, L. (1989) Learning strategies in foreign language instruction. *Foreign Language Annals* 22, 13–24.

Chamot, A.U. and Beard El-Dinary, P.B. (1999) Children's learning strategies in language immersion classrooms. *The Modern Language Journal* 83(iii), 319–38.

Chesterfield, R. and Chesterfield K.B. (1985) Natural order in children's use of second language learning strategies. *Applied Linguistics* 6 (1), 45–59.

De Prada, E. (1993) La adquisición de la autonomía en contextos académicos: introducción a la problemática en el caso de la enseñanza secundaria. *Primeres Jornades sobre Autoaprenentatge de Llengües* (pp. 125–31). Castelló de la Plana: Publicacions de la Universitat Jaume I.

Dickinson, L. (1996) Culture, autonomy and common sense. *Proceedings of the International Conference Autonomy 2000: The Development of Learning Independence in Language Learning*. Bangkok, Thailand: King Mongkut's Institute of Technology Thonburi,

Ehrman, M. and Oxford, R. (1989) Effects of sex differences, career choice, and psychological type on adults' language learning strategies. *The Modern Language Journal* 73, 1–13.

Ellis, G. and Sinclair, B. (1989) *Learning to Learn English: A Course in Learner Training*. Cambridge: Cambridge University Press.

Faerch, C. and Kasper, G. (1984) Two ways of defining communicative strategies. *Language Learning* 34 (1), 45–63.

Flavell, J. H. (1979) Metacognition and cognitive monitoring. *American Psychologist* 34 (10), 906–11.

García López, M. (2000) Estrategias de aprendizaje de vocabulario de inglés utilizadas por los estudiantes de Secundaria. *Lenguaje y Textos* 15, 61–70.

Ghadessy, M. (1998) Language learning strategies of some university students in Hong Kong. *Estudios Ingleses de la Universidad Complutense* 6, 101–28.

Green, J. and Oxford, R. (1993) New analyses on expanded Puerto Rican strategy data. Unpublished manuscript, University of Puerto Rico and University of Alabama.

Grenfell, M. and Harris, V. (1999) *Modern Languages and Learning Strategies in Theory and Practice*. London: Routledge.

Gu,Y. and Johnson, R.K. (1996) Vocabulary learning strategies and language learning outcomes. *Language Learning* 46(4), 643–679.

Horowitz, E.K. (1988) The beliefs about language learning of beginning university foreign language students. *The Modern Language Journal* 72 (3), 283–94.

Kellerman, E. (1991) Compensatory strategies in second language research: A critique, a revision, and some (non-)implications for the classroom. In R. Phillipson, E. Kellerman, L. Selinker, M. Sharwood-Smith and M. Swain (eds) *Foreign/Second Language Pedagogy*. Clevedon: Multilingual Matters.

Kojic-sabo, I. and Lightbown, P. (1999) Students' approaches to vocabulary learning and their relationship to success. *The Modern Language Journal* 83(2), 176–92.

Lahuerta, C. (1998) Descriptive study of English as a foreign language (EFL): Students' perceptions about effective strategies and about what causes them difficulty while reading. In I. Vázquez and I. Guillén (eds) *Perspectivas Pragmáticas en Lingüística Aplicada*. Zaragoza: Anubar.

Lawson, M. J. and Hogben, D. (1996) The vocabulary-learning strategies of foreign-language students. *Language Learning* 46(1), 101–35.

Leeke, P. and Shaw, P. (2000) Learners' independent records of vocabulary. *System* 28, 271–89.

Low, L., Duffield, J., Brown, S. and Johnstone, R. (1993) *Evaluating Foreign Languages in Primary Schools*. Stirling: Scottish CILT.

Mori, Y. (1999) Epistemological beliefs and language learning beliefs: What do language learners believe about their learning? *Language Learning* 49 (3), 377–415.

Muñoz, C. (2001) Factores escolares e individuales en el aprendizaje formal de un idioma extranjero. *ELUA: Tendencias y Líneas de Investigación en ASL* (1), 249–70.

Muñoz, C. (this volume) Variation in oral skills development and age of onset.

Naiman, N., Fröhlich, M., Stern, H.H. and Todesco, A. (1978) The good language learner. *Research in Education Series 7*. Ontario Institute for Studies in Education.

Nyikos, M. (1987) The effect of color and imagery as mnemonic strategies on learning and retention of lexical items in German. Doctoral dissertation, Purdue University.

O'Malley, J.M. and Chamot, A.U. (1990) *Learning Strategies in Second Language Acquisition*. Cambridge: Cambridge University Press.

Oxford, R.L. (1989) Use of language learning strategies: A synthesis of studies with implications for strategy training. *System* 17(2), 235–47.

Oxford, R. (1990) *Language Learning Strategies: What Every Teacher Should Know*. Rowley, MA: Newbury House.

Oxford, R. and Crookall, D. (1989) Research on language learning strategies: Methods, findings, and instructional issues. *The Modern Language Journal* 73(iv), 404–19.

Oxford, R.L. and Nyikos, M. (1989). Variables affecting choice of language learning strategies by university students. *Modern Language Journal* 73 (2), 291–300.

Oxford, R. and Burry-Stock, J. (1995) Assessing the use of language learning strategies worldwide with the ESL/EFL version of the strategy inventory for language learning (SILL). *System* 23, 1–23.

Palacios Martínez, I.M. (1995) A study of the learning strategies used by secondary school and university students of English in Spain. *Revista Alicantina de Estudios Ingleses* 8, 177–93.

Parry, K. (1993) The social construction of reading strategies: New directions for research. *Journal for Research in Reading* 16(2), 148–56.

Padron, Y.N. and Waxman, H.C. (1988) The effect of ESL students' perceptions of their cognitive strategies on reading achievement. *TESOL Quarterly* 22(1), 146–50.

Pérez-Vidal C., Torras, M. R. and Celaya, M. L. (2000) Age and EFL written performance by Catalan/Spanish bilinguals. *Spanish Applied Linguistics* 4 (2), 267–90

Philips, V. (1991) A look at learner strategy and ESL proficiency. *CATESOL Journal*, 56–67.

Piaget, J. (1976) *The Grasp of Consciousness*. Cambridge, MA: Harvard University Press.

Politzer, R.L. and McGroarty, M. (1985) An exploratory study of learning behaviors and their relationship to gains in linguistic and communicative competence. *TESOL Quarterly* 19(1),103–23.

Porte, G. (1988) Poor language learners and their strategies for dealing with new vocabulary. *ELT Journal*, 42, 167–72.

Pressley, M. and El-Dinary, P.B. (1993) Introduction to special issue on strategies instruction. *Elementary School Journal* 94, 105–8.

Pressley, M. El-Dinary, P.B. Gaskins, I. Schuder, T., Bergman, J.L., Almasi, J. and Brown, R. (1992) Beyond direct explanation: Transactional instruction of reading comprehension strategies. *Elementary School Journal* 92, 513–55.

Purdie, N. and Oliver, R. (1999) Language learning strategies used by bilingual school-aged children. *System* 27, 375–388.

Rigney, J.W. (1978) Learning strategies: A theoretical perspective. In F. Harold and J. O'Neil (eds) *Learning Strategies*. New York: Academic Press.

Rossi-Le, L. (1989) Perceptual learning style preferences and their relationship to language learning strategies in adult students of English as a second language. Doctoral dissertation, Drake University.

Rubin, J. (1975) What the good language learner can teach us. *TESOL Quarterly* 9, 41–51.

Rubin, J. (1981) Study of cognitive processes in second language learning. *Applied Linguistics* 11, 118–31.

Rubin, J. and Thompson, I. (1982) *How to Be a More Successful Language Learner*. Boston: Heinle & Heinle.

Sanaqui, R. (1995) Adult learners' approaches to learning vocabulary in second languages. The *Modern Language Journal* 79 (1), 15–28.

Stern, H.H. (1975) What can we learn from the good language learner? *Canadian Modern Language Review* 31, 304–18.

Takeuchi, O. (1993) Language learning strategies and their relation to achievement in English as a foreign language. *Language Laboratory* 30,17–34.

Tarone, E. (1981) Some thoughts on the notion of communicative strategy. *TESOL Quarterly* 15, 285–95.

Tragant E. and Muñoz, C. (2000) La motivación y su relación con la edad en un contexto escolar de aprendizaje de lengua extranjera. In C. Muñoz (ed.) *Segundas Lenguas. Adquisición en el aula* (pp. 81–105). Barcelona: Ariel.

Tyacke, M. and Mendelsohn, D. (1986) Student needs: Cognitive as well as communicative. *TESL Canada Journal* 1, 171–83.

Victori, R.M. (1992) Investigating the metacognitive knowledge of students of English as a second language. M.A. Thesis, University of California, Los Angeles.

Victori, M. (1999) An analysis of writing knowledge in EFL composing: A case study of two effective and two less effective writers. *System* 27 (4), 537–55.

Victori, M. and Lockhart, W. (1995) Enhancing metacognition in self-directed language learning. *System* 23 (2), 223–34.

Vann, R.J. and Abraham, R.G. (1990) Strategies of unsuccessful language learners. *TESOL Quarterly* 24 (2), 177–98.

Wakamoto, N. (2000) Language learning strategy and personality variables: Focusing on extroversion and introversion. *International Review of Applied Linguistics* 38, 71–81.

Wenden, A. (1987) Metacognition: An expanded view on the cognitive abilities of L2. *Language Learning* 37 (4), 573–97.

Wenden, A. (1991) *Learner Strategies for Learner Autonomy*. London: Prentice Hall International.

Wenden, A. and Rubin, J. (eds) (1987) *Learner Strategies in Language Learning*. Cambridge: Prentice Hall International.

Willing, K. (1988) *Learning Strategies in Adult Migrant Education*. Adelaide. National Curriculum Resource Centre,.

Witkin, H.A., Goddennough, D. and Oltman, P. (1979) Psychological differentiation: Current status. *Journal of Personality and Social Psychology* 37, 1127–45.

Wong Fillmore, L. (1976) The second time around: Cognitive and social strategies in second language acquisition. PhD thesis, Standford University, CA.

Zimmerman, B.J. and Martinez-Pons, M. (1990) Student differences in self-regulated learning: Relating grade, sex, and giftedness to self-efficacy and strategy use. *Journal of Educational Psychology* 82 (1), 51–9.